Subversion, Power and Hierarchy in Organisations and Society

Subversion, Power and Hierarchy in Organisations and Society: Carnivalesque Leadership explores a leadership strategy that dates back centuries but has become so normalised that it can be invisible as a strategy. Extrapolating Mikhail Bakhtin's ideas on carnival and its potential for communal freedom and subversive challenge to existing hierarchies, this book identifies components of the carnivalesque, considers why and how they have impact and then maps the application of Carnivalesque Leadership to a series of case studies. Exploratory in nature, these diverse case studies focus on the historic evolution of carnivals in Trinidad and Notting Hill, the safety-valve mechanisms ubiquitous in the education sector, the standardisation of control and release within the corporate sector and the dynamic tension between protest, challenge and fun in Pride events. Readers will benefit from an increased awareness of a strategised Carnivalesque Leadership model and a greater understanding of the potential not only for the safety-valve release of pressure in society and in organisations but also for longer-term change through exposure to alternatives to the official norm.

Jo Trevenna completed her PhD in 2001 and has returned to academic research following a twenty-year career in educational leadership. In addition to pursuing her interest in Carnivalesque Leadership, Jo's research interests focus on Diversity, Equity and Inclusion (DEI) in the corporate and education sectors and pastoral provision in schools.

Routledge Studies in Leadership Research

24. Leadership and China
Philosophy, Place and Practice
Edited by Ralph J. Bathurst and Michelle Sitong Chen

25. Leadership and Narcissism in the Organization
Mateusz Grzesiak

26. Public Sector Leadership
A Human-Centred Approach
Petri Virtanen, Marika Tammeaid and Harri Jalonen

27. Toxic Leadership
Research and Cases
Steven Walker and Daryl Watkins

28. Leadership Styles and Job Performance
The Impact of Fake Leadership on Organizational Reliability
Agnieszka Bieńkowska and Katarzyna Tworek

29. Digital Leadership
Evidence from Theory and Practice
Ahmad M. Salih

30. Charismatic Leadership in Organizations
A Critique of Texts
Iga Maria Lehman

31. Subversion, Power and Hierarchy in Organisations and Society
Carnivalesque Leadership
Jo Trevenna

For more information about this series please visit: www.routledge.com/Routledge-Studies-in-Leadership-Research/book-series/RSLR

Subversion, Power and Hierarchy in Organisations and Society

Carnivalesque Leadership

Jo Trevenna

Routledge
Taylor & Francis Group
NEW YORK AND LONDON

First published 2025
by Routledge
605 Third Avenue, New York, NY 10158

and by Routledge
4 Park Square, Milton Park, Abingdon, Oxon, OX14 4RN

Routledge is an imprint of the Taylor & Francis Group, an informa business

Library of Congress Cataloging-in-Publication Data
Names: Trevenna, Jo, author.
Title: Subversion, power and hierarchy in organisations and society : carnivalesque leadership / Jo Trevenna.
Description: New York, NY : Routledge, 2025. | Series: Routledge studies in leadership research | Includes bibliographical references and index.
Identifiers: LCCN 2024027717 | ISBN 9781032576886 (hardback) | ISBN 9781032579283 (paperback) | ISBN 9781003441649 (ebook)
Subjects: LCSH: Leadership. | Power (Social sciences) | Hierarchies. | Carnival—Psychological aspects.
Classification: LCC HD57.7 .T745 2024 | DDC 658.4/092—dc23/eng/20240719
LC record available at https://lccn.loc.gov/2024027717

ISBN: 978-1-032-57688-6 (hbk)
ISBN: 978-1-032-57928-3 (pbk)
ISBN: 978-1-003-44164-9 (ebk)

DOI: 10.4324/9781003441649

Typeset in ITC Galliard Pro
by Apex CoVantage, LLC

Mikhail Bakhtin has been a hero of mine ever since I was first introduced to his work by Dr Clare Walsh at De Montfort University, Bedford. I had returned to full-time study in my mid-twenties having left school at 16 (people like me didn't really go to university at that time – but, thankfully, change happens). Research for this book has not only cemented Bakhtin's heroic status for me but also built my appreciation of hero activists who employed Carnivalesque Leadership, notably Claudia Jones, Rhaune Laslett, Reverend Troy Perry, Marsha P. Johnson and Sylvia Rivera (amongst many others).

I am eternally thankful to three hero women in my life. To my mother, Jackie Trevenna, and my sister, Julie Taylor, for supporting my forays into all sorts of things including academia and for their endless cheerleading. They are my biggest fans and I am theirs. I am blessed.

And to Faye, who, first, became my civil partner and, second, became my wife. Because change happens. There is no one with whom I would rather experience carnivalesque fun, laughter, collective joy, safety-valve release and take on the subversive challenge of life.

Contents

Acknowledgements

I am indebted to the pioneering work of scholars and translators who enabled wider global access to the work of Mikhail Mikhailovich Bakhtin in the 1980s. Hélène Iswolsky, Caryl Emerson, Michael Holquist and Katerina Clark all played a significant role in translating and offering academic interpretations and explorations of Bakhtin's work and thereby opened up new philosophical explorations of language, literature and culture.

Introduction

The theory of carnival is not the property of one person, but the version of the carnivalesque considered here is associated most with the Russian philosopher and critical thinker Mikhail Mikhailovich Bakhtin. This book extrapolates the carnivalesque from Bakhtin's work and, in doing so, not only holds it in dialogic incompleteness with the dazzling theoretical scope of Bakhtin's work but also holds it in dialogic tension with the work of the translators, editors, critics, academics, archivists and supporters who brought and continue to bring his ideas to the fore. Bakhtin's work was very nearly lost to a wider audience, not only globally but within Russia itself. As a non-Russian speaker and reader, I am totally indebted to and reliant upon and partly determined by the work of numerous translators and editors. My reliance on translators is 100%. Todorov highlights how this limitation creates academic and philosophical vulnerability, claiming that "Bakhtin has been translated by individuals who did not know or did not understand this system of thought" and goes on to identify key issues with what he sees as misleading equivalences of key concepts (xii). This book does not seek to contribute to the continuing interrogation of translator nuances or the debates over authorship or to clarify previously uncertain details of Bakhtin's life. However, in seeking to provide an understanding of origins and possibility, this introduction does offer summaries of Bakhtin's sometimes debatable biographical contexts, his main philosophical explorations and his impact on disciplines from literary criticism and language studies to religious studies, psychoanalysis and sociology. In Bakhtin's polyphonic and unfinalised dialogic framework, such a classification of distinct disciplines is, in itself, troubled. My overarching argument in this book is that Bakhtin's ideas on carnival offer insights into power and leadership that cut across multiple disciplines and sectors and expose the normalisation of power structures that contain and control (via short-term safety-valve release) potentially revolutionary tensions within societies and organisations but also offer a means to channel potential for change over a longer period of time. Bakhtin's "carnivalization of authority" (Clark and Holquist 5)

DOI: 10.4324/9781003441649-1

is held in dialogue with his vision of language rooted in context and his occasionally utopian idealisation of folk culture. Therefore, this introduction explores the background to Bakhtin's ideas before the extrapolation of carnivalesque components in Chapter 1, a consideration of the evidence for the specific impact of these identified and extrapolated components in Chapter 2 before the exploratory application of a Carnivalesque Leadership framework to the case studies in the four chapters that follow.

This text explores, extrapolates and applies only a fraction of Bakhtin's ideas and in no way represents the scale of his oeuvre. The exploratory nature of the approach outlined here means that the scope is broad and exhaustive literature reviews are signposted rather than offered. Moreover, it does not focus on the significance of Bakhtin as a major thinker of the twentieth century. This worthy status has been argued by many including Holquist, Clark, Pomorska, Todorov and Eagleton.[1] Highlighting Bakhtin's uniqueness, Emerson argues that the "contours of his philosophy coincide with no major twentieth-century movement" (4) and that he is not "simply" a theorist of literature but "tended, rather, to invoke literature as illustration of his principles for strategies for living and thinking" (6).

To begin to understand the application of Bakhtin's ideas and philosophy to the idea of Carnivalesque Leadership, it is useful to know the biographical and intellectual contexts that helped form the ideas that are the basis for this book. In doing so, I am mainly reliant on secondary sources, predominantly written by Emerson, Clark & Holquist and Hirschkop. Bakhtin's ideas are non-conformist and were produced in a time of existential threat given that literary accomplishment and criticism in Russia "mattered. You could get arrested and killed for it" (Emerson 10). Bakhtin's life span included the Russian Revolution of 1917, which saw the removal of Tsar Nicholas II; the First and Second World Wars; the rise of Lenin, Stalin and Khruschev; the formation of the Soviet Union; and the start of the Cold War. There are some gaps, and there is some haziness in the details of Bakhtin's life. There are disagreements over the meaning of his words and his works and even disagreements over potential authorship and ownership of texts. This book does not seek to resolve these tensions, and it is not a biography or offer deep analysis of the scope of his philosophy. Instead, it aims to pull through the main themes and ideas associated with Bakhtin before opening up potential new applications and establishing new dialogues and conversations around the application to leadership.

Bakhtin's Life and Historical/Philosophical Context

Born on November 16, 1895 in Oryol, 220 miles southwest of Moscow, Mikhail Mikhailovich Bakhtin was one of five children born to Mikhail Nikolaevich and Varvara Zakharovna Bakhtina. Some argue that the Bakhtin family had noble heritage dating back to the fourteenth century, including Clark and Holquist and Bakhtin himself during an interview with Viktor Duvakin in 1973,[2] but it has also been argued that this is not the case (Hirschkop 9) and that the family was "only" from the financially well-off middle class. Bakhtin's father, Mikhail Nikolaevich, worked for the Oryol Commercial Bank (which had been founded by Bakhtin's grandfather). The family moved to Vilnius in Lithuania in 1905 for Mikhail Nikolaevich's job. Here, Mikhail and his elder brother, Nikolai, entered school and received a classical education. Work then prompted the family to move to Odessa, initially without Nikolai who stayed in Vilnius to complete the initial stage of his schooling. When Nikolai eventually rejoined the family in Odessa, he entered Novorossiskii University. There is some fuzziness around whether or not Mikhail Bakhtin "officially" entered the same universities as his brother, firstly in Odessa and then in Petrograd or whether he just joined some classes.[3] We know for certain that Bakhtin did move to Petrograd in 1916 and attended classes at Petrograd University. Renamed from Saint Petersburg Imperial University at the start of the First World War, Petrograd University proved significant to both Nikolai and Mikhail Bakhtin, particularly through the influence of Professor of Classical Philology, Faddei F. Zelinsky. With a reputation for being a remarkable teacher, Zelinsky's ideas on prose, dialogue, official and unofficial culture and humour are themes developed throughout Mikhail Bakhtin's own work whilst Zelinsky's passion for the importance of ancient Greek and modern Greek folklore is evident in Nikolai Bakhtin's later insistence that the undergraduates he taught at Birmingham University should learn modern Greek. Zelinsky's impact on Mikhail Bakhtin can therefore be traced in this book's discussion of a Carnivalesque Leadership framework that incudes "dialogue," "official and unofficial culture" and "humour."

Nikolai joined the anti-Bolshevik, Tsarist counter-revolutionary White Guard. This decision resulted in Nikolai leaving Russia for good to escape potential retribution following the fall of Nicholas II. Nikolai's career continued briefly in the military, with a stint in the French Foreign Legion, before he settled first in Paris to study at the Sorbonne and the École des Langues Orientales and then moving to England. He secured a PhD from Cambridge with a thesis entitled "Thessaly in the 13th Century BC and the Origin of the Centaur-Lapithai Myth" in 1934 before working as a faculty member at the Southampton University and then Birmingham University. Developing a friendship with the philosopher Ludwig Wittgenstein, Nikolai anglicised his name to Bachtin, married Constance Pantling and settled in Birmingham until his death in 1950. There is no evidence that there was any direct communication between Nikolai and Mikhail after 1918.

Following the departure of his brother, Mikhail Bakhtin sought other sources of intellectual stimulation. In 1916, he had joined the Petersburg

Religious-Philosophical Society, which facilitated challenging debate on religion and the role of the church. Indeed, the church as a source of authority, official culture and calendared festivities remained an area of critical interest for Bakhtin throughout his life. An understanding of the long history of religious festivals is evident in Bakhtin's contextualising work that informs this book's focus on Carnivalesque Leadership. Bakhtin's relationship with religion, the philosophy of religion and his own faith has been interpreted differently by Bakhtin scholars. Typifying the multiplicity and unfinalisability of critical interpretations of Bakhtin's work, Bagshaw summarises potential oppositional polemic to consider interpretations that have positioned Bakhtin either as a "covert theologian" or as an overt analyser of "religious metaphor, language and religious images" and the "extent to which Bakhtin's ideas have potential to contribute to the study of religion" (18).

In 1918, Bakhtin moved to Nevel, a small town 300 miles south of Petrograd. Whether he had graduated from Petrograd University prior to this move is uncertain. Earlier biographical accounts suggest that he did, but Hirschkop's more recent scholarship throws doubt on Bakhtin's university registration status. Regardless of his official university credentials, Bakhtin was seemingly flourishing intellectually. In Nevel, Bakhtin formed part of a small group of intellectuals who regularly gathered for private discussion and to take part in public debate. The group included Matvei Isaevich Kagan, Pavel Nikolaevich Medvedev, Lev Vasilievich Pumpianskii, Ivan Ivanovich Sollertinskii, Valentin Nikolaevich Voloshinov and Maria Veniaminovna Yudina. Several of the group then moved to Vitebsk and Bakhtin joined them in 1920. Close personal and intellectual relationships were formed during this time which lasted for many years. Whilst the term "Bakhtin Circle" has frequently been used by others as shorthand for the intellectual group, I follow Hirschkop here in choosing not to apply the term in this text as it could suggest an unhelpful singularity and inaccurate leadership model (12). Since the early 1970s, there has even been debate as to whether works published under the names of V. N. Voloshinov and P. Medvedev were potentially written by Bakhtin himself (Clark and Holquist; Todorov; Emerson; Morris). For example, Morris highlights the unresolved status of authorship and makes reference to texts assigned to Voloshinov or Medvedev by adding Bakhtin's name thereafter, but Hirschkop concludes the likelihood that Voloshinov and Medvedev were, indeed, the authors of these texts. The disputed authorship debate does not impact on the arguments of this book, but it does, wonderfully, draw attention to the plurality of textual ownership and scope for unfinalisability which is a Bakhtinian preoccupation that will be referred to at points in this text.

When Bakhtin and associates relocated to Vitebsk, it was already established as an intellectual community centred on its most famous son, the artist Marc Chagall. Upon arrival, Bakhtin became involved in public debates and lectures.[4] Most significantly, Vitebsk was where Bakhtin met his future wife, Elena Aleksandrovna Okolovich. Living in the same building as Bakhtin, Elena had previously received a marriage proposal from Chagall himself. She had finished her standard education and was working at the local library. Bakhtin and Elena married in 1921. Whilst his personal life improved, Bakhtin's health deteriorated. He was diagnosed with the bone infection osteomyelitis in his right leg, and it spread to his left leg and hip joint and to his right hand and he was infected with typhoid which further inflamed his right leg.

Despite these serious health issues, he published a short essay "Art and Answerability" in a Nevel newsletter (The Day of Art) in 1919. This essay reflects his interests in German philosopher, Immanuel Kant (1724–1804), and the Neo-Kantian movement that had emerged from Marburg, Germany, in the late nineteenth century and early twentieth century. Significantly, the work of Neo-Kantian philosophers in Russia drew attention of the authorities. Hermann Cohen, for example, was of critical interest to Lenin because of "claiming a militant idealism in which the realm of concepts, logic, is all and the external world is nothing" (Clark and Holquist 58). Cohen sought to dismantle the Kantian dualistic model of internal thought and external experience and the idea that the "world is not given, but conceived" (Cohen cited in Clark and Holquist 59). One of the central tenets of a Neo-Kantian approach is that the process of assimilation between the internal and the external is an unfinalised dialogue. Bakhtin's engagement with, and development of, this idea can subsequently be traced in his lifetime's work on dialogism, open-endedness, polyphony and the unfinalised. Intellectually subversive, the Neo-Kantian influence on Bakhtin and his friends, most notably Matvei Kagan who had studied under Cohen in Germany, may have been a factor in the Soviet authorities' subsequent interest in, distrust of, Bakhtin.

Following the publication of "Art and Answerability" in 1919, Bakhtin produced philosophical essays between 1920 and 1924, which culminated in his delivery of a series of lectures between 1924 and 1925 on Neo-Kantian philosophy. By this point, Bakhtin was living in Leningrad, where most of his friends were already living. Now married, Bakhtin was increasingly prolific as a writer but suffered from further declining health which meant that he received a small state pension which eased some of his financial concerns and reduced the need to work to support his private studies. However, the pension was reduced first in 1925 and again in 1929. With no institutional affiliation, Bakhtin was largely unknown amongst Leningrad's intelligentsia and his poor health was a barrier to him becoming established in the Leningrad community. There is some evidence that he contributed to lectures to librarians about new books due at their libraries and he may have served on the staff in 1927 at the Leningrad State Publishing House and Leningrad

Industrial Bureau. He did undertake private lecturing and lessons during the mid to late 1920s. Despite this precarious financial position, Bakhtin and his wife were able to move into an apartment in 1924 which provided a conducive space for Bakhtin's completion of his book, *Problems of Dostoevsky's Creative Works*, which was published in 1929. When he began receiving royalties from this book, Bakhtin secured an apartment for himself and his wife.

With the start of the Soviet state's first "Five Year Plan" in 1928, Russian intellectuals were increasingly under threat if they were seen to offer any threat to dominant Soviet ideology. Bakhtin was arrested in 1928. The specific charges for his arrest are open to debate.[5] After his arrest, Bakhtin's health deteriorated further and he developed paranephritis of his kidneys. This resulted in his transfer out of prison to Uritsky Hospital in July 1929.

Bakhtin had originally been sentenced to five years in the Gulag Solovki labour camp on the remote Solovetsky Islands on the White Sea. This inhospitable venue would have posed an even greater threat to Bakhtin's already vulnerable health. In September 1929, Bakhtin submitted a request for his case to be reviewed and his wife, Elena Aleksandrovna Bakhtina, actively sought support via their friends and acquaintances. Bakhtin's sentence was commuted to exile in Kazakhstan. A perceived influence in this potentially life-saving agreement was Anatoly Lunacharsky's review of Bakhtin's recently published book on Dostoevsky. Lunacharsky was a prominent Bolshevik who later became Commissar of Enlightenment. His positive review of Bakhtin's book was, according to Emerson, "instrumental" in saving his life (78).[6] Whilst Bakhtin himself disagreed with some of the Lunacharsky review of his book, it is widely acknowledged that this positive review supported Bakhtin's status.

Bakhtin was finally released from Uritsky Hospital to recuperate at home at the end of 1929. Having secured the agreement to self-manage the journey to his place of exile, the couple left for Kustanai in Kazakhstan in the new year of 1930. A weekly report to security police was the only requirement of exile for Bakhtin. During this time, Bakhtin's wife, Elena Aleksandrovna, undertook a variety of jobs including bookkeeper and cashier. Unable to teach because of the charge of "corrupting the young," Bakhtin himself found work in a bureaucratic role for District Consumers' Corporation (Clark and Holquist 254). Bakhtin did give lectures to some of the workers and even started to teach courses in bookkeeping. In August 1934, Bakhtin's exile officially ended but the couple stayed in Kazakhstan given the difficulty of movement. Bakhtin remained in touch with his intellectual friends throughout the exile and took the opportunity to undertake a visit to Leningrad and Moscow to see them. One of these old friends, Medvedev, recommended Bakhtin for a teaching post at the Mordovia Pedagogical Institute in Saransk and he took up post in 1936. This did not last long, however, as Bakhtin felt the threat of being caught up in another purge and resigned his post the same year. Bakhtin's record with the authorities meant he was not allowed to live within 100 kilometres of Moscow. He and Elena Aleksandrovna moved to the town of Savelovo. The worsening condition of his right leg resulted in its amputation in February 1938, and Bakhtin stayed in hospital to recover for two months.

Despite the challenges created by this life-changing illness, Bakhtin's intellectual profile increased during this period as he participated in conferences and undertook lectures and worked on books and essays. Significantly, Bakhtin wrote his doctoral dissertation for the Gorky Institute on "Rabelais in the History of Realism" which was submitted in 1940, and later adapted into the text published in 1965 now known as *Rabelais and His World*. However, the outbreak of the Second World War halted progress with the doctoral submission process. The impact of the Second World War on local schools' staffing meant that Bakhtin, like other former exiles unable to serve in the forces, was recruited to teach. Once fully employed, he returned to teach at the Pedagogical Institute in Saransk, two hundred miles south-east of Moscow. He was promoted to the post of chairman of the Department of General Literature and would later be awarded a commendation for long service in 1947 by the Supreme Soviet of Mordovia which resulted in a larger pension (Clark and Holquist 322).

Bakhtin was finally given the opportunity to defend his Rabelais thesis in November 1946. The timing was significant given that the recently ended war had seen a regression from the relative intellectual liberalism experienced during the hostilities. This included a general backlash towards the celebration of traditional folk forms, and this impacted on the negative institutional response to Bakhtin's thesis. The defence of the thesis proved a long and drawn-out process and was eventually referred to the Higher Attestation Committee for review. The reasons for the Gorky Institute's hesitation and delay are not fully known. He was eventually certified in 1951 at the degree level of *kandidat* rather than *doktor nauk* (Emerson 92). There was a stipulation from the Higher Accrediting Commission to remove some of the "crudely physiological" and "ideologically depraved" sections of the text prior to being accepted into public libraries. Published in 1965 under the title of *The Creative Art of François Rabelais and Folk Culture of the Middle Ages and the Renaissance*, Bakhtin's book represents a "victory of independent scholarship over the cowed (and cowardly) Stalinist-bred bureaucracy" (Emerson 93). The text that most informed this book's discussion of the subversion of, and challenge to, power and hierarchy is therefore a physical manifestation of such a challenge.

A fleeting image of Bakhtin's work as a teacher and academic is provided in a report following a two-week government inspection of Bakhtin's Faculty of Foreign Literature at the teachers' college at

Saransk, which describes his “masterful lecturing style” and “lively and emotional delivery” (Emerson 24). The report was, however, critical of a perceived insufficient control of the curriculum and informal management style which, appropriately summed up by Emerson, suggested that Bakhtin “had no talent for hierarchy and no special interest in exercising authority” (24). The Saransk teacher college became the Mordovia State University in 1957. Whilst his employment hampered his writing output, Bakhtin was the best well known he had been in his adult life and was a kind of celebrity in Saransk (Clark and Holquist 328). The death of Stalin in 1953 and Nikita Khruschev’s promotion to First Secretary of the Communist Party of the Soviet Union saw the rehabilitation of previously exiled and blacklisted academics. As a result, Bakhtin and his wife enjoyed more financial and social freedom and his work continued to gain wider recognition.

Bakhtin became increasingly famous in the last years of his life. Graduate students at Moscow’s Gorky Institute of World Literature discovered Bakhtin’s 1929 book on Dostoevsky. One of these students, Vadim Valerianovich Kozhinov, realised Bakhtin’s association with the institute and accessed Bakhtin’s dissertation on Rabelais. Upon discovering that Bakhtin was still alive, Kozhinov wrote to him and eventually visited Bakhtin and his wife along with other interested graduate students who became “pilgrims” (Duvakin Interviews 196). Kozhinov encouraged Bakhtin to rework the Dostoevsky book and his thesis on Rabelais for publication.[7] After some frustration with uninterested publishers, Bakhtin secured publication for the revised Dostoevsky book in 1963 and the Rabelais book in 1965. Katerina Clark and Michael Holquist’s biography of Bakhtin sums up how the first publication and second edition of the Dostoevsky book represent key points in his life and work: “The first edition saved Bakhtin from physical death in Solovski; the second saved him from the literary death of neglect” (Clark and Holquist 238).

Declining health impacted on the lives of both Bakhtin and Elena Aleksandrovna. Bakhtin’s left leg was now severely compromised, and Elena’s heath was also deteriorating and she increasingly spent time in hospital in Moscow. The couple needed care and were accommodated at the Kremlin hospital before moving to an old people’s home in Grivno, 35 miles south of Moscow in 1970. Here, they had an apartment which enabled them to remain together. Elena was hospitalised in November 1971 for a heart condition and died on December 13.

Following the death of Elena, Bakhtin moved to the House of Creativity in Peredelkino, a hotel that accommodated writers without charge for “creative stays” (Clark and Holquist 338). Bakhtin was supported in an application for the right to live in Moscow, which was approved to enable his relocation in July 1972. He bought a flat and lived with the support of a housekeeper and frequent visits from nurses. Bakhtin regularly received visits from friends and admirers of his work including Kozhinov who continued to support Bakhtin's publications which were needed to provide the financial support for his medical care and general living costs. Soon, however, emphysema alongside his osteomyelitis rendered Bakhtin increasingly in pain and unable to work. Bakhtin died at 2 a.m. on March 7, 1975. His final words, heard by his night nurse, were "I go to thee" (Clark and Holquist 343). Speculation over whether this was aimed at his beloved wife Elena or a religious expression of going to God cannot be clarified. As Clark and Holquist beautifully sum up "he was doing as he expired exactly what he had done throughout his long life, going out to meet the other" (Clark and Holquist 343). Bakhtin was buried in Vvedenskoe cemetery in Moscow beside his wife's grave.

This book is not a biography of Bakhtin and there is a lack of academic depth and challenge within this introduction, but an overview of his context makes his output even more remarkable and helps to frame our understanding of his philosophy not only of literature, culture and language but of human dynamics. When prompted to categorise in 1973, Bakhtin describes himself as "a philosopher. A thinker" (*Bakhtin – The Duvakin Interviews* 41). He left us with a plethora of ideas. His work crosses over academic silos of literary criticism, language theory, cultural theory and, of course, philosophy. This multiplicity is part of the reason for the fast embracing of Bakhtin's work in the West following the publication of key translations. The works cited at the end of this introduction reveal that Bakhtin had more hits in 1984 than breakthrough artist, Madonna.

Through the rapid growth of interest in his work from the 1970s through to the Bakhtin academic boom of the 1980s and 1990s, it has been argued by several including Rzhevsky that this has led to an oversimplistic appropriation of his work, risking turning Bakhtin's ideas into "banalities" (Emerson 65). I am very aware of this danger and of potentially adding to it, given that I am extrapolating Bakhtinian ideas and relating them to a very different set of contexts in an application of leadership theory that was not Bakhtin's focus.

Whilst Bakhtin's exploration of festivals and carnivals is outlined in greater detail in Chapter 1, throughout this book I shall also be engaging with other key Bakhtinian principles. Following is a brief summary of these main themes which in no way is exhaustive or finalised and is incredibly problematic given Bakhtin's subtleties of thought and it is offered only as a means to enrich later discussion.

Dialogism is a thread that runs throughout Bakhtin's philosophy. We can trace Bakhtin's dialogic theories back to an early interest in Ancient Greek philosophy and an engagement with Socrates that remained evident throughout his life. Building on the Socratic dialogue principle that searches for meaning by drawing out and juxtaposing different ideas and perspectives in a dynamic process of exchange, Bakhtin's dialogism is dynamic, multiple and unfinalised.[8] In *Problems of Dostoevsky's Poetics*, Bakhtin states, "Truth is not born nor is it to be found inside the head of an individual person, it is born *between people* collectively searching for the truth" (110). This dynamic model has great potential for exploring leadership as a dynamic relational process offering a codependent counterbalance to more established critical models that view leadership as monological acts of independent units.[9] For Bakhtin, "Life by its very nature is dialogic" (293) which includes not only the relationship between the self and other but also the search for meaning, culture and the very language that forms understanding and meaning.

Relating dialogism to language and literature in his essay "Discourse in the Novel," Bakhtin argues that every word exists in "living interaction" and is "dialogically agitated" (*The Dialogic Imagination* 276). All discourse is in dialogue with prior, concurrent and future discourses. For Bakhtin, this "polyphony" is most readily identified in the novel genre. The interaction of a word is with other words related to the same object which may embody different value judgements, leaving traces in all semantic layers. Bakhtin explains that a single overarching national language is stratified into a myriad of other "languages" such as social dialects, professional jargons, generational languages, languages of authorities and pronunciations within a language. This can take the form of "double-voiced" discourse and parody that has multiple meanings. Dialogism is not just the written word but includes everyday dialogue in conversation with each word "in living conversation" being "directly, blatantly, orientated toward a future answer-word: it provokes an answer" (*The Dialogic Imagination* 280). For Bakhtin:

> nothing conclusive has yet taken place in the world, the ultimate word of the world and about the world has not yet been spoken, the world is open and free, everything is still in the future and will always be in the future
>
> (*Problems of Dostoevsky's Poetics* 166).

In his last article, "Speech Genres," published in 1973 (and cited beautifully by Clark and Holquist at the end of their biography of Bakhtin as forever unfinalised), Bakhtin infinitely spreads the scope of dialogism:

> There is neither a first word nor a last word. The contexts of dialogue are without limit. They extend into the deepest past and the most distant future. Even meanings born in dialogues of the remotest past will never be finally grasped once and for all, for they will always be renewed in later

> dialogue. At any present moment of the dialogue there are great masses of forgotten meanings, but these will be recalled again at a given moment in the dialogue's later cause when it will be given new life. For nothing is absolutely dead: every meaning will someday have its homecoming festival.
>
> (Bakhtin cited in Clark and Holquist 348)

Dialogism extends to polyphony, heteroglossia and unfinalisability in stark contrast to authoritarian official monologism. For me, this is one of the main pulls of Bakhtin's work and the attraction of exploring the application of some of his ideas to the realm of leadership. As Emerson captures: "In an unfinalized world, everything (even a bad thing) can change (even if only a little) – and in the process, it gives birth to something new . . . under the hopeful rubric of 'unfinalizability' that carnival enters" (37).

Bakhtin's philosophy was frequently rooted in literature (the work of Dostoevsky and Rabelais being the most significant examples) or literature used as a means to explore his philosophies. During the 1970s, 1980s and 1990s much of the critical work around Bakhtin's philosophy was further developed and applied his ideas to a wider range of literary texts. My own introduction to Bakhtin's work was as a mature student (when I returned to full-time study having left school aged 16) on my English literature course thanks to Dr Clare Walsh. Bakhtin was not core theory, but there was a growing academic presence at this mid-1990s point. Dr Walsh's focus was double-voiced discourse in the novel genre, but she also outlined the scope of his thinking, and it is that very breadth and depth of Bakhtin's work and appeal that means his work has been extrapolated and appropriated to multiple other disciplines.

Beyond his impact on the study of language, literature and philosophy, which are the most obvious fields of study for Bakhtin's work, his ideas have proved fruitful within many other fields of study. In social and human sciences, the appropriation and extrapolation of Bakhtin's work tend to come in the discussion of the dialogic relationship between people and groups, his exploration of the relationship between the official and unofficial in culture and society and his consideration of power dynamics within language.[10] In the areas of psychology and psychotherapy, Bakhtin's influence can be seen in some discussions of the relational dialogic of the self and psyche, conscious and unconscious, self and other and the fundamental role of language.[11] Potentially extending his work on the dialogic and unfinalisability of language, Bakhtin can be seen to have offered preliminary insights resonant with post-structuralism, postmodernism and post-colonialism.[12]

Academic dialogue with and about Bakhtin's ideas will continue to expand. This book is both expansive (in its potential application to leadership strategy) and reductive in its extrapolation, narrowing and reapplication through a focus on identified constituent components of the carnivalesque. This book does not profess to be anything other than a starting point for exploration and consideration and, in doing so, is unfinalised.

Notes

1 See Pomorska's foreword to *Rabelais and His World* for an appreciation of growing awareness of Bakhtin's importance to scholarship.
2 Duvakin taped six interviews with Bakhtin in 1973, which offer insights into his reminiscences about his friends and other notable people who influenced his life.
3 Hirschkop offers a balanced review of Bakhtin's biographical uncertainties.
4 See Hirschkop; Clark and Holquist for more detailed exploration of this period in Bakhtin's life.
5 See Hirschkop for an overview of the potential reasons for Bakhtin's arrest.
6 Lunacharsky's importance in the formation of early arts policies under the Bolshevik state is considered by Holter, who identifies his "defense of writers" (263).
7 Bakhtin pays tribute to the support of Kozhinov in the fifth of the six interviews in *Mikhail Bakhtin – The Duvakin Interviews, 1973.*
8 Zappen offers a detailed examination of Bakhtin's relationship to the Socratic dialogue.
9 Hersted and Gergen offer an exploration of dialogic leadership.
10 Work exploring Bakhtin's impact on the human and social sciences includes Mayerfeld Bell and Gardiner; Nielsen. This list is not exhaustive.
11 Work exploring Bakhtin's impact on psychology includes Salgado and Clegg; Shotter and Billig; Pollard. Again, this list is not exhaustive.
12 Hirschkop offers a lively discussion of 'appropriate appropriation' of Bakhtin's work in relation to feminist criticism and post-colonial studies.

Works Cited

Bagshaw, Hilary. *Religion in the Thought of Mikhail Bakhtin: Reason and Faith.* Routledge, 2016.

Bakhtin, Mikhail. *The Dialogic Imagination – Four Essays.* Translated by Caryl Emerson and Michael Holquist. Edited by Michael Holquist. The University of Texas Press, 1981.

Bakhtin, Mikhail. *Problems of Dostoevsky's Poetics.* Edited and Translated by Caryl Emerson. University of Minnesota Press, 1984a.

Bakhtin, Mikhail. *Rabelais and His World.* Translated by Hélène Iswolsky. Indiana University Press, 1984b.

Bakhtin, Mikhail. *The Bakhtin Reader: Selected Writings of Bakhtin, Medvedev and Voloshinov.* Edited by Pam Morris. Edward Arnold, 1994.

Bakhtin, Mikhail. *Mikhail Bakhtin – The Duvakin Interviews, 1973.* Translated by Margarita Marinova. Edited by Slav N. Gratchev and Margarita Marinova. Bucknell University Press, 2019.

Clark, Katerina, and Michael Holquist. *Mikhail Bakhtin.* Harvard University Press, 1984.

Eagleton, Terry. *Humour.* Yale University Press, 2019.

Emerson, Caryl. *The First Hundred Years of Mikhail Bakhtin.* Princeton University Press, 1997.

Grathev, Slav N., and Margarita Marinova, editors. *Mikhail Bakhtin – The Duvakin Interviews, 1973.* Buckner University Press, 2019.

Hersted, Lone, and Kenneth Gergen. "Developing Leadership as Dialogic Practice." *Leadership-as-Practice.* Edited by Joseph A. Raelin. Routledge, 2016.

Hirschkop, Ken. *The Cambridge Introduction to Mikhail Bakhtin.* Cambridge University Press, 2021.

Holter, Howard R. "The Legacy of Lunacharsky and Artistic Freedom in the USSR." *Slavic Review*, vol. 29, no. 2, 1970, pp. 262–82. *JSTOR*. Accessed Apr. 29, 2024.

Mayerfeld Bell, Michael, and Michael Gardiner, editors. *Bakhtin and the Human Sciences – No Last Words.* Sage, 1998.

Nielsen, Greg Marc. *The Norms of Answerability: Social Theory Between Bakhtin and Habermas.* State University of New York, 2002.

Pollard, Rachel. *Dialogue and Desire – Mikhail Bakhtin and the Linguistic Turn in Psychotherapy.* Routledge, 2008.

Richter, David H. "Bakhtin in Life and in Art." *Style*, vol. 20, no. 3, 1986, pp. 411–9. *JSTOR*. Accessed Apr. 28, 2024.

Rzhevsky, Nicholas. "Kozhinov on Bakhtin." *New Literary History*, vol. 25, no. 2, 1994, pp. 429–44. *JSTOR*, Accessed Apr. 28, 2024.

Salgado, J., and J. W. Clegg. "Dialogism and the Psyche: Bakhtin and Contemporary Psychology." *Culture & Psychology*, vol. 17, no. 4, 2011, pp. 421–40. *Research Gate*. Accessed Apr. 28, 2024.

Shotter, John, and Michael Billig. "A Bakhtinian Psychology: From Out of the Heads of Individuals and into the Dialogues between Them." *Bakhtin and the Human Sciences: No Last Words.* Edited by Michael Mayerfeld Bell and Michael Gardiner. Sage, 1998, pp. 13–29.

Todorov, Tzvetan. *Mikhail Bakhtin – The Dialogic Principle.* Translated by Wlad Godzich. Manchester University Press, 1984.

Zappen, James P. *The Rebirth of Dialogue: Bakhtin, Socrates, and the Rhetorical Tradition.* State University of New York Press, 2004.

1 Bakhtin's Carnivalesque

Mikhail Bakhtin's theorisation of carnival and its impact on power structures, human relations and social fabric is one of the most significant strands of his wide-ranging work. Bakhtin uses François Rabelais' novels as a springboard for exploring the role of carnival in society and its representation in literature. As outlined in the introduction, Bakhtin's initial text on Rabelais began as a proposed doctoral thesis but the Gorky Institute's protracted response to the thesis in the 1940s was neither smooth nor overly enthusiastic. It is not known if this was a direct response to the perceived quality of the thesis or, rather more likely, reflected institutional discomfort caused by the thesis' subversive overtones given that Bakhtin positions carnivalesque laughter, food, bodily functions and clowning as mechanisms that support the subversion of hierarchies and represent the symbolic momentary destruction of authority and official culture which thereby enables renewal. Such a subversive model raises subversive ideas which can be considerably problematic for those in charge seeking to retain total control at all times. For Bakhtin, carnival "celebrated temporary liberation from the prevailing truth and from established order; it marked the suspension of all hierarchical rank, privileges, norms and prohibitions" (*Rabelais and His World* 10). Such discussion of clearly subversive acts was dangerous and challenging at a time of increasing political, artistic, intellectual and physical control.[1]

Bakhtin was not the first or last theorist who considered the role of carnival or components of carnival in society and culture and/or its representation in literature. In her Foreword to the 1984 translation of *Rabelais and His World*, Krystyna Pomorska highlights engagement with carnival prior to Bakhtin but argues that this focused mainly on the role of humour and concluded that none attained Bakhtin's "depth and exactitude" (xi).[2] Whilst acknowledging the work of other philosophers and critics engaging with themes set out below, my focus in this book remains on Bakhtin's work to provide the structure and philosophical scope to inform the subsequent exploration of Carnivalesque Leadership. Bakhtin's ideas are very much rooted in European scholarship with Ancient Greek thought

DOI: 10.4324/9781003441649-2

and Ancient Roman practice, medieval, renaissance, Enlightenment and post-Enlightenment European thinkers providing the dialogic context for his philosophy. This chapter considers Bakhtin's theorisation of carnival through its ancient European origins to medieval, renaissance and Romantic manifestations before exploring the potential offered by a Carnivalesque Leadership strategy and its constituent parts. However, this book also makes some reference to more ancient links to carnivalesque components evident in the earliest civilisations of Mesopotamia and Egypt. The discussion below is not exhaustive but seeks to contextualise carnival theory before starting to overlay and map extrapolated carnivalesque components on different sectors of society and on different types of organisations in an overt consideration of usually normalised Carnivalesque Leadership strategies.

Carnivalesque Beginnings

Bakhtin traces roots of carnival to the ancient tradition of Roman Saturnalia with its "freedom of laughter" (*Rabelais and His World* Bakhtin 70) and local folklore. He argues that the festivals of medieval and Renaissance Europe were "in part a direct living continuation of Roman saturnalia" (*Problems of Dostoevsky's Poetics* 129). Honouring the god Saturn, the Roman Saturnalia was originally a single day on December 17 but, over the centuries, the festival grew to an extended period from December 17 to 23. During Saturnalia, social norms were relaxed and festivities, including those normally prohibited, were prioritised. During this short period of time, masters invited slaves to feasts (sometimes serving the servants themselves in a full reversal of hierarchical power structures), dress codes were relaxed, gifts were given, feasting was dominant and much alcohol was consumed. This revelry is captured by first-century CE Roman poet, Publius Papinius Statius, who attended a Saturnalian party hosted by Emperor Domitian: "Who can sing of the spectacle, the unrestrained mirth, the banqueting, the unbought feast, the lavish streams of wine? Ah! now I faint, and drunken with thy liquor drag myself at last to sleep" (Statius cited by Welch 144).

Roman Saturnalias offered "an escape from the usual official way" (*Rabelais and His World* 8) and "complete liberation from the seriousness of life" (247). Festivities included the "crowning and uncrowning of a clown" (138) which temporarily subverted existing power structures and differences between superiors and inferiors disappeared for a short time (246). The figure of Saturnalicius princeps (Ruler of the Saturnalia), also known as the Lord of Misrule, is a key figure in these procedures. This role was filled by a member of the lower orders of society who was temporarily promoted to a position of mocking authority. The Lord of Misrule would make mischief and lead insults and games. This appointment of the Lord of Misrule and awarding of chaotic power to someone from the lower strata of society thus represented a sanctioned temporary subversion of norms. Less chaotic Saturnalian activities included lighting candles, giving gifts and (at least initially less chaotic) communal feasting and drinking.

Key aspects of Saturnalia are evident in traditions of Christmas and other calendared religious festivals. In *Rabelais and His World*, Bakhtin highlights calendared festivities including the "feast of fools" (observed on January 1 involving temporary subversion of hierarchy through the parodic anointing of fake clergy), "feast of the ass" (a medieval Christian festival with a focus on the donkey observed on January 14) and "Easter laughter" which is the *risus paschalis* in Easter church liturgy involving jokes and laughter encouraged from the pulpit. Here, the priest's amusing stories and jokes created laughter "as a joyous regeneration" (78).

One of the richest times of the year for sanctioned carnivalesque release centres on the buildup to Lenten sacrifice from Ash Wednesday through to Easter Sunday. The last day before lent is known by different names and has varieties of tradition including Mardi Gras (literal translation from the French into English is "fat Tuesday"), Shrove Tuesday (the name derived from "shrive" which means to be absolved from guilt) and, from the German tradition, Fastnacht (night fast), Karneval (sharing the French/Italian/English Latin root *carne levare* which roughly translates as "removing meat") and Fasching (relating to the last serving of alcohol before Lent).

Bakhtin broadens out his references to the religious festivals to include Corpus Christi in June and performance days of miracle plays and mystery plays. The timing of feasts contributed to their character such as the autumn feasts of Saint Martin on November 11 and Saint Michael on September 29 (both saints of winemaking) which had a "bacchanalian" overtone (80) and the feast of Saint Lazarus in Marseilles with its processions featuring animals, masquerades and dancing (80). Bakhtin also refers to "non-religious" national festivities such as the bullfight which expressed carnivalistic character and festivals of harvesting grapes (*Problems of Dostoevsky's Poetics* 129). Bakhtin's comment that feast is "linked to moments of crisis, of breaking points in the cycle of nature or in the life of society" (*Rabelais and His World* 9) reiterates the link with seasonal cycles and ecclesiastical calendars peppered with symbolism of moments of crisis and past breaking points but also suggests a potential for feast as an untethered response to new moments of crisis and breaking points leading to renewal.[3]

Global calendared carnivals will feature throughout this book but are of particular focus in Chapter 3, which charts the development of Trinidad and Notting Hill carnivals. However, the dynamics and potential of carnivalesque are not limited to calendared carnival but, instead, is omnipresent. Bakhtin highlights how carnival was not "just calendar and momentary: the medieval world participated in two lives: the official and the carnival life" (*Rabelais and His World* 96). Here, Bakhtin broadens the potential scope of the carnivalesque. For Bakhtin,

> Carnivalization is not an external and immobile schema which is imposed upon ready-made content; it is, rather, an extraordinarily flexible form of artistic visualization, a peculiar sort if heuristic principle making possible the discovery of new and as yet unseen things.
>
> (*Problems of Dostoevsky's Poetics* 166)

Indeed, Bakhtin's carnivalesque is not limited to simply the repetition of certain festivities and traditions which enable a temporary liberation from normal structures and responsibilities.

Bakhtin has drawn criticism for his idealisation of carnival and its potential as a "utopian fantasy" (Emerson 164).[4] Such charges may be validated when encountering sweeping statements such as "in carnival time life is subject only to its laws. That is, the laws of its own freedom" (*Rabelais and His World* 7). Bakhtin does not focus on the darker side of carnival either ancient or medieval. For example, the Lord of Misrule at the end of their parodic carnival rule would traditionally risk death either by their own hand or by the hand of another.[5] The potential glossing over or ignoring of dire consequences of some key components of carnival does not render an awareness of Carnivalesque Leadership impact unhelpful. If anything, the normalisation of the consequences of involvement in sanctioned subversion is fully aligned with the normalisation of the Carnivalesque Leadership model which this book seeks to expose and explore. Bakhtin's exploration of carnival establishes a specific philosophical standpoint and, in so doing, does not always detail the life-and-death reality consequences for those involved during a philosophical discussion of the symbolism of life, death and renewal. In the case studies of this book, the potentially dire consequences of carnivalesque freedoms are acknowledged when considering the practical application and recognition of the carnivalesque as a leadership strategy.

Carnivalesque Leadership

Bakhtin's exploration of the elements that build carnival is a useful starting point for understanding the power of Carnivalesque Leadership to both maintain the status quo short term and offer a means for transformation and renewal long term. In both *Rabelais and His World* and *The Problems of Dostoevsky's Poetics*, Bakhtin foregrounds components that combine to create carnival. This is not to suggest that these components operate in distinct silos in Bakhtin's work but, rather, they exist alongside each other. These constituent parts are identified as:

- feast and the communal consumption of food and drink.
- grotesque and the body.
- collectivity and dissolution of the individual.
- laughter and parody.
- mask.

Feast and Communal Consumption of Food and Drink

Bakhtin identifies feast as enabling "temporary suspension of the entire official system with all its prohibitions and hierarchical barriers. For a short time life came out of its usual, legalized and consecrated furrows and entered the sphere of utopian freedom" (*Rabelais and His World* 89). Seasonal feasts reflect change which expresses "the people's hopes of a happier future, of a more just social and economic order, of a new truth" (81). This potential for change is at the centre of Carnivalesque Leadership, with feast and the communal consumption of food and drink as a key constituent.

Bakhtin differentiates "official" feast and "marketplace" feast. Official feasts "sanctioned the existing pattern of things and reinforced it" (*Rabelais and His World* 9). Official feasts, with their preoccupation with rank and hierarchy, offer a "consecration of inequality" (10). In contrast, the marketplace festival world of carnival is one in which "all were considered equal" (10), and Bakhtin claims carnival and marketplace unofficial festivals are a "utopian realm of community, freedom, equality, and abundance" (9). Bakhtin argues that in the world of carnival "all hierarchies are canceled. All castes and ages are equal" (251). Such subversive challenges to existing hierarchy and power structures can be seen in folk festivals which include the Saturnalian reversal of hierarchy featuring a jester being proclaimed king, clownish types elected and even a "mock pontiff" chosen for the day (81). The parodic promotion of a lowly soul to a symbolic position of authority "mimicked serious rituals" including "the election of a king and queen to preside at a banquet" (5). The promotion of mock figures of authority represents both a short-term mocking or parody function and a longer-term potential for subversion given that the process foregrounds the potentially arbitrary and forever temporary assignment of power and authority to those currently in control.

Bakhtin asserts that the "true nature of human festivity" (9) is indestructible and evident in the marketplace feast. This duality leads Bakhtin to consider medieval feasts as having "two faces of Janus": the official ecclesiastical face which looked to the past and sanctioned the existing order and the face of the "people of the marketplace" which looked to the future and laughed (81). In this categorisation, official feasts "sanctioned the existing pattern of things and reinforced it" following temporary subversion and suspension, whereas marketplace festivals offer a "second life" (9) of carnival to "liberate human consciousness and permit a new outlook" (274). Carnival folk culture, Bakhtin argues, "opposed the official and serious tone of ecclesiastical and feudal culture" (4). This distinction between feast either reinforcing hierarchy or enabling renewal and change is fundamental to the different potentials offered by Carnivalesque Leadership explored throughout this book. Carnivalesque Leadership maintains the "two faces of Janus" in offering both the opportunity for the reinforcement of existing hierarchies and the opportunity for permitting new outlooks.

Communal consumption of food and drink is, of course, central to the feast. Bakhtin devotes a whole chapter of *Rabelais and His World* to "banquet imagery" (279) which he sees as a dominant trope of Rabelais' art. From highlighting cattle slaughtering for upcoming feasts and feasts on a ship to the identification of the "carnivalesque war of sausages" (280), Bakhtin not only draws out the prevalence of food and drink but also lifts his discussion out of Rabelais' texts as he considers how "Man's encounter with the world in the act of eating is joyful, triumphant; he triumphs over the world, devours it without being devoured himself. The limits between man and the world are erased, to man's advantage" (281).

Grotesque and the Body

I, for one, do not need Bakhtin to tell me that excessively "joyful" and "triumphant" eating can lead to a grotesque body. Bakhtin identifies the character of Sancho in Cervantes' *Don Quixote* as conveying a "powerful carnivalesque spirit" (22) through his fat belly, appetite and thirst.[6] The grotesque realism of Cervantes' portrayal of Sancho firmly roots the character within the carnivalesque. Combining metaphorical challenge to authority and physical ridicule, at the heart and bottom of the carnivalesque is the grotesque and, specifically, the grotesque body. Essentially, by reducing abstract concepts of nobility and authority to base physical anatomy, the grotesque offers critique of the absurdity of hierarchy and monologic authority and thereby opens them up to ridicule and challenge. More poetically, Bakhtin uses the grotesque as a metaphor for changing perceptions: "Time has transformed old truth and authority into a Mardi Gras dummy, a comic monster that the laughing crowd rends to pieces in the marketplace" (213). This application of the grotesque is manifested clearly during festival and carnival parades (again as we shall consider in more detail in Chapter 3) and highlights the philosophical extension of the grotesque body's symbolism as captured in Rabelais' writing and extrapolated in this book.

The grotesque body exaggerates the life cycle and therefore foregrounds the potential for renewal. Bakhtin identifies "three main acts in the life of the grotesque body: sexual intercourse, death throes (in their comic presentation – hanging tongue, expressionless popping eyes, suffocation, death rattle), and the act of birth" (353). Bakhtin's focus on the body is often narrowed to what he considers the "lower body stratum" comprising genitalia, buttocks, bodily organs and excrement. The lower body stratum is the basest use of the grotesque as a means to give physical challenge and ridicule to abstract authority. Eagleton offers a brutal summary of this idea, stating "Seeing everything as shit may represent a blessed emancipation from the rigours of hierarchy" (17).

Contextualising Rabelais within the "Gallic tradition" rather than an "idealizing tradition," Bakhtin identifies how popular comic medieval tradition associates women with material bodily lower stratum as the incarnation that "degrades and regenerates simultaneously" (240). The reduction of the female to biological function is, of course, incredibly problematic in terms of both the tradition discussed and Bakhtin's non-engagement with such reductionism.[7]

The female body is a focus when linking the grotesque body's relationship with the world and the collective. Bakhtin argues that the grotesque body is not:

> separated from the rest of the world. It is not a closed, completed unit; it is unfinished, outgrows itself, transgresses its own limits. . . . The body discloses its essence as a principle of growth which exceeds its own limits only in copulation, pregnancy, childbirth, the throes of death, eating, drinking, or defecating.
>
> (26)

Here, then, Bakhtin draws the grotesque body into his nexus of the unfinalised and connects it with the dissolution of the individual in the collective.

Collectivity and Dissolution of the Individual

The carnivalesque loss of the individual into the collective is associated, in part, with forms of consumption. Bakhtin himself, it seems, was not a man drawn to alcohol or narcotics although his predilection for copious amounts of hot tea and smoking cigarette after cigarette was well known. Bakhtin's work has been accused of naivety as it downplays the role of alcohol and narcotics in encouraging subversion, accelerating a sense of collectivity and the dissolution of individuality. Roth, for example, argues that "Bakhtin's vision of carnival and carnivalesque was more of a quaint narrative than a coherent program" (16) and cites the downplaying of the role of alcohol and drugs in the "intoxication" of carnival experience. Whilst Bakhtin does not dwell on the role that alcohol played in ancient, medieval and renaissance festivities, he does make reference to the "bacchanalian" overtone (*Rabelais and His World* 80). Such a downplaying of external stimuli reinforces the intoxicating role of the carnival "in itself" as enough of a stimuli for subversion and symbolism. Whilst Bakhtin makes minimal acknowledgement of alcohol, other philosophers have less soberly foregrounded the role of alcohol and drugs in carnival intoxication. For example, in *The Birth of Tragedy*, Nietzsche discusses Dionysiac intoxication and the dissolution of the self into the collective, giving examples from the German Middle Ages with "singing and dancing crowds" embodying Dionysian collapse of the *principium individuationis* into "complete self-forgetfulness" (4). The philosophical links between Nietzsche and Bakhtin have been a point of interest for many Bakhtin scholars.[8] Given that Dionysus is the Greek god of drunken revelry, sexual ecstasy, death and destruction, the associations with Bakhtin's work are clear despite not being foregrounded by Bakhtin himself who, as Renate Lachmann points out, only "in passing points out Dionysian traces in the carnival" (127).[9]

Bakhtin's consideration of feasting offers a means for the individual to transgress individual limitations without a bacchanalian/Dionysiac focus on alcohol. Here, Bakhtin is foregrounding how the individual is transgressed and "exceeds its own limits" (26) in a relationship with the world and also represents a loss of the self into the collective through consumption. Bakhtin's descriptions of the way in which food consumption and the grotesque body erase the separation between "individual" and "world" connects with his multifaceted view of meaning as relational.

The collectivity of carnival and the dissolution of the individual are one of the recurrent aspects of Carnivalesque Leadership explored in this book and one of the reasons for its effectiveness as a leadership strategy. The role of festivals and carnivals in bringing communities together leads at various points in this book to an exploration of belonging. This can prove as "Janus-faced" as other dynamics of the carnivalesque as such events perform "two distinct yet concurrent functions: aiding in the creation of a communal sense of placement and belonging while also distracting from the ongoing marginalization of the socio-economically disadvantaged" (Salarvand 34). This collectivity starts with basic logistics; there is no distinction between spectators and participants in carnival: "carnival is not a spectacle seen by the people; they live in it" (*Rabelais and His World* 7). At another, less operational layer, the "individual feels that he is an indissoluble part of the collectivity, a member of the people's mass body. In this whole the individual body ceases to a certain extent to be itself" (255).[10] Extending this collectivity beyond limits of time and space, Bakhtin's infinite layer is then identified when he argues that "[t]he body of the people on carnival square is first of all aware of its unity in time; it is conscious of its uninterrupted continuity within time, of its relative historic immortality"(255). Loss of individual boundaries into the collective resonates with Bakhtin's presentation of:

> folk-carnival "debates" between life and death, darkness and light, winter and summer, etc., permeated with the pathos of change and the joyful relativity of all things, debates which did not permit thought to stop and congeal in one-sided seriousness or in a stupid fetish for definition or singleness of meaning.
>
> (*Problems of Dostoevsky's Poetics* 132)

Bakhtin's philosophical explorations around the dialogue and debate between such binary oppositions are thus linked to his understanding of dialogic unfinalisability and a rejection of the monological. Again using literature as a mechanism for modelling his philosophy, Bakhtin's discussion of dialogue in Dostoevsky's novels is interwoven with carnivalesque subversion linked to the relation status of meaning:

> The dialogue means of seeking truth is counterposed to *official* monologism. . . . Truth is not born nor is it to be found inside the head of an individual person, it is born *between people* collectively searching for truth, in the process of their dialogue interaction.
>
> (110)

Bakhtin foregrounds commonality between the dialogic and the carnivalesque based on refuting authoritarian monologism, recognising the relational status of meaning (social, philosophical and linguistic) and laughing which undermines singular presentations of truth. In doing so, Bakhtin weaves together key themes of rejecting monologism, the relational status of meaning and laughter in the carnivalesque.

Laughter and Parody

Laughter's role in carnival and festival is multifaceted. Bakhtin links Socratic dialogue and Hippocrates' theories of laughter in his discussion of Ancient Greek culture centred on Menippean satire in *Problems of Dostoevsky's Poetics*.[11] He explores how Socratic dialogue "grows out of a folk-carnivalistic base and is thoroughly saturated with a carnival sense of the world" (109). Carnivalesque liberation involves laughter as playful but with serious potential. Highlighting its corrective potential, Bakhtin argues, "Antique tragedy did not fear laughter and parody and even demanded it as a corrective and a complement" (*Rabelais and His World* 121). Such correction is not a new form of monologism but, instead, is based on the integration of laughter, carnival and dialogism influencing Socrates' philosophy, with Bakhtin stating that "carnival forms of antiquity . . . fertilized the Socratic dialogue and freed it from one-sided rhetorical seriousness" (121) and that the "carnivalistic base of the Socratic dialogue . . . is beyond any doubt" (*Problems of Dostoevsky's Poetics* 132). Here, laughter and humour represent challenge to one-sided, monolithic seriousness.

Laughter is so central to carnival that Bakhtin highlights "small scattered islands of time strictly limited by the dates of feasts, when the world was permitted to emerge from the official routine but exclusively under the camouflage of laughter. Barriers were raised, provided there was nothing but laughter" (*Rabelais and His World* 90). The importance of laughter in both "official" and "unofficial" feasts is interwoven with Bakhtin's perspectives on carnivalesque potential for challenging singular authority. At the opening of the first chapter of *Rabelais and His World*, Bakhtin states that the "history of the understanding, influence, and interpretation of Rabelais is closely linked with the history of laughter itself" (59). The role of laughter in Carnivalesque Leadership is evident in every case study and every strategic overview in every chapter of this book. The potentially liberating ***and*** controlling effects of laughter and its potential to build cohesion ***and*** increase division, to build relationships ***and*** to shatter them is fundamental to human interaction.[12] Since the Ancient Greeks, many philosophers and writers have considered the role of laughter in social relations and as a personal relief mechanism which is explored in greater depth in Chapter 2.

Within Bakhtin's discussion of carnivalesque laughter is a tight focus on parody. Bakhtin argues that medieval parody was not concerned with the negative but, rather, everything was comic. The humorous parodic version becomes the world's "second truth," the "second revelation of the world in play and laughter" (84). Again, we can see how Bakhtin interweaves his theories of laughter and parody with his philosophy of language and meaning as dialogic as captured in his statement in "From the Prehistory of Novelistic Discourse" published in *The Dialogic Imagination* that "every parody is an intentional dialogized hybrid" (76). This dialogised hybrid of parody enables challenge to monological seriousness and represents the "victory of laughter over fear" (*Rabelais and His World* 90). Whilst laughter has the power to challenge authority, Bakhtin refutes the suggestion that this is to simply make light of a situation: "I do not in the least mean to imply that medieval laughter is cheerful, carefree, and joyous laughter" continuing that "Laughter is a weapon, like fists and sticks" (Bakhtin cited by Emerson 96). From a practical carnival perspective, one of the most obvious means of parodically mimicking and mocking those in power and therefore using laughter "as a weapon" is through the use of parade masks.

Mask

At its most basic level, a mask enables an individual to lose themselves and/or engage with an alternative identity and/or identities. Bakhtin identifies the theme of the mask as the "most complex theme of folk culture" which is "connected with the joy of change and reincarnation" (*Rabelais and His World* 39). Simply by donning a mask, we are reincarnated and changed. Negating uniformity and similarity, the mask, for Bakhtin, "rejects conformity" (39) and, instead, "is related to transition, metamorphoses" and contains "the playful element of life" (40). Bakhtin's thoughts on the transformative role of mask can also be traced to the earlier *Problems of Dostoevsky's Poetics* in which he argues that masquerades developed in the early Renaissance absorb carnivalistic forms (130) and that the mask is one of the most significant forms absorbed and kept alive in masquerade.[13] Chapter 3 considers the role of mask in symbolising grotesque authority and subversive challenge in carnival pageants which facilitate ridicule and retribution aligned to Bakhtin's claim that the mask "reveals the essence of the grotesque" (*Rabelais and His World* 40).

Carnivalesque Leadership

The components of the carnivalesque (feast and communal food and drink, the grotesque, the dissolution of the individual into the collective, laughter and parody, mask) separately or, more powerfully, in combination, offer short-term heady freedom and, potentially, longer-term transformation. Bakhtin himself frequently highlights the temporary potential of carnival stating that "carnivalistic life is life drawn out of its *usual* rut" ("Characteristics of Genre" published in *The Dialogic Imagination* 122). As Clark and Holquist point out, however, "Carnival must not be confused with mere holiday play" (300). The temporary carnival, framed and sanctioned by official calendar, can readily be seen to shore up existing power structures. This book explores how temporarily sanctioned carnivalesque currently operates as an effective safety valve in society and organisations. As such leaders are making decisions to employ these strategies. However, these strategies are so naturalised that they are not usually recognised as leadership strategies. This is not surprising given the ancient origins of carnival. Alongside case studies of officially sanctioned temporary carnivalesque safety valves, this book also explores case studies more aligned to Bakhtin's philosophy that carnival is more than this and is the "primordial order" and "extraordinary life force" (*Problems of Dostoevsky's Poetics* 122).

My extrapolation of Bakhtin's ideas represents the simplification of his philosophy and an application to leadership parlance that was not intended by the Russian philosopher. However, Bakhtin's carnival does overtly focus on power and hierarchy and how it is maintained – a significant area of interest in leadership study. Bakhtin's philosophy explores meaning as relational, the potential for subversion and transformation of hierarchies and the loss of the individual in the collective which, again, have consequences for leadership study. Any leadership structure which relies on hierarchy, whether established and maintained by oppression and coercion or by political strategy or charisma and populist appeal, can be both supported and challenged through the strategic employment of carnivalesque components. Most obvious is the use of "safety-valve" mechanisms to shore up existing hierarchies and power structures. Here, the components of carnival (feast and communal food and drink, the grotesque, the dissolution of the individual into the collective, laughter and parody, mask) can temporarily release tensions that quell rebellion and "settle" those being led back into the "norm." This model of carnival is aligned with Anatoly Lunacharsky's influential reading of Bakhtin. As such and within established leadership theory contexts, short-term safety-valve Carnivalesque Leadership represents a transaction.[14] Carnivalesque components, which offer temporary safety-valve release from the norm, can be offered as part of the transaction for social, organisational and corporate compliance. This transactional potential will be explored in the case studies in this book.

Components of carnivalesque also highlight the arbitrary non-essential nature of power and authority and also foreground the very human bodies of those in power which demystifies superiority and authority. It is difficult to remain overawed by the "great men" of history, as categorised and lionised by Scottish philosopher Thomas Carlyle in 1840 as "leaders of men, these great ones; the modellers, patterns, and in a wide sense creators, of whatsoever the general mass of men contrived to do or to attain," or remain in total emotional and psychological submission to a leader when picturing them on the toilet (an early levelling technique recommended to me when a child by my grandmother, Queenie Watts, whenever I was scared of a person in authority).[15] Here, the grotesque body, the "lower body strata" of Bakhtin's carnival, is a base leveller that demystifies the power of some human beings over others and highlights human vulnerabilities and fundamental shared biological status.

Carnivalesque Leadership also challenges traditional perceptions of leadership authority by prioritising the dialogical status of meaning and revealing the limits of the monological. As such, leadership based on singular authority is exposed as fragile, flawed and vulnerable. A basic level of the dialogic focusing on communication dialogue is promoted in recent explorations of dialogic leadership theory as positioned within leadership approaches.[16] Where and when appropriate, Carnivalesque Leadership's relevance to other defined leadership strategies will be highlighted throughout this book. Before exploring how Carnivalesque Leadership is already applied in relation to specific case studies, the reasons why Carnivalesque Leadership is so effective will be outlined in Chapter 2.

Notes

1 Bakhtin's contexts have prompted contrasting arguments about his potential allegiances and critiques. Clark and Holquist highlight that this work, which was written in the Soviet Union in the late 1930s and early 1940s, "cannot fail" to comment on its times and it "represents Bakhtin's most comprehensive critique to date of Stalinist culture" (305). They argue that "the impulses in carnival and in Stalinism were diametrically opposed" (309). See Miller for an overview of what he sees as overtly political readings of Bakhtin's carnivalesque claiming that "scholars who place the most emphasis on carnival represent leftist or now-Marxist readings of Bakhtin, while those involved in the current drive to devalue carnival's place within the Bakhtin canon are avowedly conservative critics" (258). Miller and Platter further explore the diversity of critical engagement with Bakhtin's work identifying different readings of Bakhtin as "classicist," Bakhtin as "apostle of carnival laughter," Bakhtin as an "advocate of an active and interpersonal ethics" and Bakhtin as a "literary theorist" (117–118).

2 Pomorska highlights Russian critics' engagement with this phenomena, citing Belinsky, Chizhevsky and Trubetzkoy.

3 Eagleton refers to the "strictly episodic" nature of Bakhtin's carnival rendering its victories as "flimsy" (33).

4 Amongst the many, Clark and Holquist identify a "strong element of idealization" (310) and Eagleton identifies Bakhtin's potential for "wide-eyed" idealism (32). Morris highlights the criticism levelled at Bakhtin for his "enthusiastic" depiction of carnival which ignores that the marginalised were frequently targets for ritual punishment and Emerson highlights that "real-life carnival rituals . . . were not necessarily cheerful or carefree" (164).

5 Anthropologist James G. Frazer explores the bloody Saturnalian tradition of putting the Lord of Misrule/King of Saturnalia to death at the end of his mock reign (429). Frazer's discussion of the Roman Saturnalian tradition firmly centres it as a means to "vent" pent-up darker passions in specific periods of licence (427).

6 Cervantes, Boccaccio, Shakespeare and Grimmelshausen are referred to by Bakhtin in his discussion of the "carnivalization of literature" (*Problems of Dostoevsky's Poetics*, 157). Discussing a "tight matrix of death with laughter, with food, with drink, with sexual indecencies," Bakhtin also refers to Shakespeare's Falstaff and the gravediggers in *Hamlet* ("Forms of Time and Chronotype in the Novel" in *The Dialogic Imagination* 198–9).

7 Bakhtin's work has engaged feminist critics, particularly focusing on (inter)textual difference and dialogue with otherness. See Bauer and McKinstry; Eigler for sample overviews of different approaches.

8 See Mazour-Matusevich; Clark and Holquist for examples.

9 Lachmann et al. contrast Bakhtin's limited exploration of the Dionysian energy of carnival with the work of Florens Christian Rang and Hans Peter Duerr.

10 Groys argues that Bakhtin insists on the totality of carnival, which destroys and absorbs each individual's body and links this to the Russian tradition of "belonging to the folk (narodnost)" (3).

11 See Halliwell for a comprehensive exploration of Ancient Greek attitudes to laughter.

12 For an engaging romp through philosophical and literary attitudes to humour and laughter, see Eagleton. Here, Eagleton considers laughter as a mechanism for release and ego-edifying superiority. Eagleton explores the physical action of laughter, including the diversity of noises and their relative associations designated under the umbrella of laughter. Chapter 2 explores the role of laughter in the overall impact of carnivalesque leadership.

13 See Massie for an exploration of Bakhtin's theorisation of the role of mask and masquerade in the dissolution of the individual into the collective.

14 See Burns' definition of transactional leadership in which there is an exchange of one thing for another.

15 In his series of lectures "On Heroes, Hero-Worship, and the Heroic in History," Carlyle establishes the "otherness" of great leaders and in doing so promoted a mystifying legacy of unattainability that still permeates perceptions of leadership today as an almost God-given set of talents and skills that most people cannot attain.

16 See Isaacs who argues that business organisations benefit from maintaining a dynamic approach to communication which positions dialogue as "a conversation with a center, not sides" (19) and to reach new understanding rather than "merely" reach agreement.

Works Cited

Bakhtin, Mikhail. *The Dialogic Imagination – Four Essays.* Translated by Caryl Emerson and Michael Holquist. Edited by Michael Holquist. The University of Texas Press, 1981.

Bakhtin, Mikhail. *Problems of Dostoevsky's Poetics.* Edited and Translated by Caryl Emerson. University of Minnesota Press, 1984.

Bakhtin, Mikhail. *Rabelais and His World.* Translated by Hélène Iswolsky. Indiana University Press, 1984.

Bauer, Dale M., and S. Jaret McKinstry, editors. *Feminism, Bakhtin and the Dialogic.* State University of New York Press, 1991

Burns, James MacGregor. *Leadership.* Harper, 2010.

Carlyle, Thomas. "On Heroes, Hero-worship, and the Heroic in History". *gutenberg.org.* Accessed May 1, 2024.

Clark, Katerina, and Michael Holquist. *Mikhail Bakhtin.* Harvard University Press, 1984.

Eagleton, Terry. *Humour.* Yale University Press, 2019.

Eigler, Friederike. "Feminist Criticism and Bakhtin's Dialogic Principle: Making the Transition from Theory to Textual Analysis." *Women in German Yearbook*, vol. 11, 1995, pp. 189–203. *JSTOR*. Accessed May 1, 2024.

Emerson, Caryl. *The First Hundred Years of Mikhail Bakhtin.* Princeton University Press, 1997.

Frazer, James George. *The Golden Bough – A Study of Magic and Religion.* Amazon Print, 2020.

Gorman, David. "Bakhtin and His Circle: A Checklist of English Translations." *Style* 27, no. 4, 1993, pp. 515–20. *JSTOR*. Accessed Aug. 1, 2023.

Groys, Boris. "Between Stalin and Dionysus: Bakhtin's Theory of the Carnival." *Dialogic Pedagogy: An International Online Journal*, 5. Accessed May 1, 2024.

Halliwell, Stephen. *Greek Laughter – A Study of Cultural Psychology from Homer to Early Christianity.* Cambridge University Press, 2008.
Holter, Howard R. "The Legacy of Lunacharsky and Artistic Freedom in the USSR." *Slavic Review*, vol. 29, no. 2, 1970, pp. 262–82.
Isaacs, William. *Dialogue and the Art of Thinking Together.* Doubleday, 1999.
Lachmann, Renate, et al. "Bakhtin and Carnival: Culture as Counter-Culture." *Cultural Critique*, no. 11, 1988, pp. 115–52. *JSTOR*. Accessed Jul. 4, 2023.
Massie, Pascal. "Masks and the Space of Play." *Research in Phenomenology*, vol. 48, no. 1, 2018, pp. 119–46. *JSTOR*. Accessed May 1, 2024.
Mazour-Matusevich, Yelena. "Nietzsche's Influence on Bakhtin's Aesthetics of Grotesque Realism." *Comparative Literature and Culture*, vol. 11, 2009. *ResearchGate*. Accessed May 1, 2024.
Miller, Paul Allen. "The Bodily Grotesque in Roman Satire: Images of Sterility." *Arethusa*, vol. 31, no. 3, 1998, pp. 257–83. *JSTOR*. Accessed Jul. 25, 2024.
Miller, Paul Allen, and Charles Platter. "Introduction." *Arethusa*, vol. 26, no. 2, 1993, pp. 117–21. *JSTOR*. Accessed Apr. 30, 2024.
Morris, Pam, editor. *The Bakhtin Reader: Selected Writings of Bakhtin, Medvedev and Voloshinov.* Arnold, 1994.
Nietzsche, Friedrich. *The Birth of Tragedy.* Dover Publications, 1995.
Roth, Marty. "Carnival, Creativity, and the Sublimation of Drunkenness." *Mosaic: An Interdisciplinary Critical Journal*, vol. 30, no. 2, 1997, pp. 1–18. *JSTOR*. Accessed May 3, 2023.
Salarvand, Helya. "(Re)Locating Pride: Borders, Space, and Policing at Los Angeles Pride". *Aleph, UCLA Undergraduate Research Journal for the Humanities and Social Sciences*, vol. 19, 2022.
Todorov, Tzvetan. *Mikhail Bakhtin – The Dialogical Principle.* Translated by Wlad Godzich. University of Minnesota, 1984.
Welch, Katherine E. *The Roman Amphitheatre: From Its Origins to the Colosseum.* Cambridge University Press, 2007.

2 How and Why Is Carnivalesque Leadership Effective?

Leaders have regularly employed Carnivalesque Leadership strategy for centuries, yet the components of this strategy can seem so common that they have become normalised and naturalised and therefore may not seem strategic. By recognising and employing component aspects of Carnivalesque Leadership, leaders enable temporary, sanctioned subversion to release built up tensions and dissipate potential threats which can reinforce existing power hierarchies. However, this is not a one-dimensional model that only offers temporary safety-valve release in order to shore up existing power structures. Instead, Carnivalesque Leadership, by offering a sanctioned, subversive break from the norm, exposes alternative modes and models of being that can bring about long-term change.

This chapter explores some of the reasons *how* and *why* Carnivalesque Leadership is so effective. These effects can be grouped together as:

- releasing group and individual tension.
- promoting chemical messenger release and reducing stress.
- providing existential comfort, wellbeing and sense of belonging through collectivity.
- subverting existing power dynamics that offers potential for change.

These effects are generated through and across the different Carnivalesque Leadership components of laughter and parody, mask, the dissolution of the individual into the collective and feasting with communal consumption of food and drink. These components can have other significant consequences involving dancing, singing and, of course, fun.

This consideration of why and how Carnivalesque Leadership has proved so effective over the centuries starts with an exploration of how laughter releases the tensions that build up within individuals, groups, societies or organisations. Eagleton offers a useful analogy when he argues that humour "does for adults what play does for children, namely liberates them from the despotism of the reality principle and allows the pleasure principle some

DOI: 10.4324/9781003441649-3

scrupulously regulated free play" (19).[1] Carnival, of course, extends the potential for play and exceeds the limitations of laughter in and of itself through temporary liberation and subversion of the norm. Although not regularly associated with the serious business of leadership, the facilitation, generation and sanctioning of laughter can instantly change an individual's psychological state, transform group dynamics and build moments of collectivity. Acknowledging the ancient recognition of its power and importance, Bakhtin highlights the "Roman tradition of the freedom of laughter during the Saturnalia and the role of laughter during the triumphal marches and the funeral rites of notables" (*Rabelais and His World* 70). Over the centuries, philosophers and theorists have explored the power of, and behind, laughter and, in doing so, offer insights into its effectiveness as a component of Carnivalesque Leadership. Whilst this book does not profess to offer an exhaustive critique of critical approaches to laughter and humour, an overview is useful when considering why the use of humour and laughter is an impactful Carnivalesque Leadership strategy.

The "healing virtue of laughter" (179) is foregrounded by Bakhtin in *Rabelais and His World* as he summarises Hippocrates' attitudes to its "curative power" (162) on the body and mind. François Rabelais himself completed medical training and wrote about the interrelation of a doctor's "cheerfulness" and good humour and the wellbeing of the patient.[2] Indeed, medical research into the therapeutic benefits of laughter, particularly in relation to mental wellbeing, is ripe with evidence that laughter decreases stress hormones, notably cortisol, and increases levels of dopamine, serotonin and endorphins. Given that work-related stress has significant negative impact on organisations, potentially any leadership activity that reduces the stress and therefore the cortisol experienced by those being led is beneficial to organisations and, thus, can constitute effective leadership.[3] The association between a leader having impact on the endorphins, dopamine, serotonin and oxytocin experienced by those being led has crossed into mainstream leadership strategy parlance with Simon Sinek proving particularly influential with his work in this area.[4] Within academia, there has been a relative lack of adequate research into "potential direct links between leadership behaviours and objective indicators of stress such as cortisol" (Rowold et al. 220). There is more research on the cortisol levels experienced by leaders than a leader's impact on the cortisol levels of those that they lead due to specific leadership strategies.[5] Whilst more research is needed in this area (and I am not expert enough to do this), there is enough evidence available to suggest that a reduction in cortisol and the release of dopamine through humour and laughter offers a chemical messenger release to individuals and groups.

Research exploring leaders' use of humour and how it can impact on those they lead is summarised by Avolio et al. in their gloriously titled article "A Funny Thing Happened on the Way to the Bottom Line: Humor as a Moderator of Leadership Style Effects" which considers potential connections between the use of humour and leadership style.[6] The facilitation of laughter in Carnivalesque Leadership can be seen to have mental and physical benefits for those being led and therefore promote a sense of wellbeing within that specific environment. The release offered by laughter is easily aligned to carnivalesque release. Herbert Spencer describes how "mirth is caused by a gush of agreeable feeling which follows the cessation of unpleasant mental strain" (460) and, in *Jokes and Their Relation to the Unconscious*, Sigmund Freud highlights that jokes can offer a catharsis from repressed tensions and offer a venting release from constraints.[7] In his 1709 "An Essay on the Freedom of Wit and Humour," Lord Shaftesbury (Anthony Ashley-Cooper) highlights the double-edged role of laughter as both a safety-valve release and a means of ridicule, arguing that the

> natural free spirits of ingenious men, if imprisoned or controlled, will find out other ways of motion to relieve themselves in their constraint; and whether it be in burlesque, mimicry, or buffoonery, they will be glad at any rate to vent themselves, and be revenges upon their constrainers.
> (cited in Klein 34)

Indeed, laughter is not simply a benevolent and jolly response to stimuli that releases tensions. Laughter has teeth and it can bite.

Seeking to understand and categorise different forms and meanings of laughter has proven of interest to philosophers and anthropologists. In 1898, Carus sought to link different sounds of laughter to different meanings, claiming:

> The laughter in e, "Hee-hee!", is the hiss and sneer of a trickishly gained victory; the laughter in ey, "Hey-hey!", expresses contempt at a worsted wretch who is now at our mercy; the laugh in oh, "Hohoh!" is a scoff of self-exaltation . . . . The object of our laughter is pooh-poohed by a "Hoo, hoo, hoo!
> (262)

Operating as a "weapon of the weak" (Scott cited by Swinkels and de Koning 8), humour and laughter are often rooted in power dynamics. Laughter and parody, more specifically, can operate in the ridiculing sneer aimed at others perceived to be inferior, particularly those who have been humiliated. Promoting self-satisfaction and boosting individual ego, laughter in response to perceived humiliation of others generates and reinforces interpersonal power differentials.

Ancient Greek philosophers explored the impact of laughter and mockery with Plato's *Philebus* highlighting the roots of comedy in malicious intent and Aristotle highlighting "phronesis" as the awareness of the appropriateness (or not) of the timing and the audience of the targeted humour. In Chapter VI of *Leviathan*, Thomas Hobbes identifies the power differentials in laughter describing how the "grimaces called laughter" are a response to "the apprehension of some deformed thing in another, by comparison whereof they suddenly applaud themselves." Such views of laughter fall under categorisation of laughter within "superiority" theory which renders humour "essentially heartless" (Eagleton 43). Born a century later than Hobbes, Francis Hutcheson draws attention to laughter as a means of correcting behaviours and operating as a social control, stating "Men have been laughed out of faults which a sermon could not reform" (cited in Eagleton 41). However, Hutcheson also rejects simplistic models based on humour and laughter as solely expressing superiority and, instead, his work focuses on humour generated by incongruity.[8]

The deep incongruity of human idealism and human atrocity is central to the work of philosopher, Hannah Arendt, who stimulates controversy in her work on incredulity and the power of laughter to express contempt. Famous for her critique of the 1961 trial of Nazi, Adolf Eichmann, for crimes against humanity, war crimes, crimes against the Jewish People and membership of a criminal organisation, Arendt coined the phrase "the banality of evil" to capture the "laughter-inducing" incredulity of the "normality" of the bureaucrat Eichmann, stating "the horrible can be not only ludicrous but outright funny" (Arendt *Eichmann in Jerusalem* 46). In her essay "On Violence," Arendt considers personal authority which fosters the power to make people obey without coercion or persuasion. Here, she also identifies the potential to challenge such authority without coercion or persuasion by using ridicule, stating "To remain in authority requires respect for the person or the office. The greatest enemy of authority, therefore, is contempt, and the surest way to undermine it is laughter" (144). Here, laughter is positioned as a means to challenge authority with the example associated with Arendt providing a response to the horrific abuse of power. I am not seeking to apply a Carnivalesque Leadership model to the most horrific of situations; however, Arendt's exploration does foreground the release and challenge of laughter.

During temporary carnivalesque subversion, laughter and parodic mimicry can sneeringly be aimed at those in power in a sanctioned subversive act. The carnivalesque model temporarily sanctions contemptuous laughter as well as laughter generated through opportunities for subversive fun. In comic mimicry, parody can offer a powerful weapon against obvious targets for ridicule and attack.[9] Parody plays a significant role in many traditional street carnivals through the use of parodic masks and the donning of costumes associated with figures of authority as discussed in more depth in Chapter 3, which focuses on the carnivals of Trinidad and Notting Hill.

The use of mask in parody offers us a literal and metaphorical example of the carnivalesque combination of the potential freedom from individual identity and the potential for parodic humour and subversion. For centuries, the donning of a mask has enabled individuals to temporarily hide their physical identities; symbolise and enact transformation; promote integration of, and engagement with, otherness; foreground the performativity of existence; shake off limits of the self and offer play and parody associated with character masks.[10] The power dynamics generated by mask is central to Bakhtin's discussion of mask and masquerade. Carnival masks typically exaggerate facial features as considered in Chapter 3 and most obviously embody Bakhtin's focus on medieval and Renaissance European cultures' playful metamorphosis enabled by masks as well as the potential for grotesque parody of authority. Mask wearing enables exploration of identity, the development of character, empathy and understanding of different perspectives and building different relationships. In contemporary culture, mask wearing for adults is most frequently identified with masks featuring images of famous people and figures of authority most readily seen at sporting and community events as both celebratory and parodic. In addition to offering a sardonic, lampooning challenge to authority and enabling the temporary loss of self, the playful adopting of another identity through mask wearing, whether as a child or as an adult, provides immediate release from personal responsibilities, social expectations and perceived norms and, in doing so, offers emotional relief.

Mask wearing is ancient. Anthropologists, including one of the most famous of them all in Western academia, Claude Lévi-Strauss, set early parameters for exploring the role of mask wearing in indigenous culture, with power relations, spiritual transformation and religious significance embodied in the tribal mask.[11] Tonkin specifically highlights anthropological and philosophical approaches to mask wearing which explore how masks "elicit and manage Power" (23).[12] When considering mask as a component of Carnivalesque Leadership, the power dynamics generated is of paramount importance. Mask wearing is not, however, a common feature of any NASDAQ 500 company even if all the other components of Carnivalesque Leadership are evident in such organisations. The question, therefore, is whether mask wearing can have any major role in Carnivalesque Leadership beyond "actual" carnivals, festivals, parties and childish play. There might be a temptation to consider "masking" in line with the contemporary parlance of "masking" in leadership relating to mechanisms used by individuals to conceal personality traits and/or psychological and sociological tendencies. Whilst such an approach may be fruitful in itself, such a metaphorical swerve will not be explored in this book. Instead, the case studies in the following chapters seek to offer more concrete examples of Carnivalesque Leadership in action.

Short-term, sanctioned parody can stimulate malicious laughter and express contempt of the parodic focus. For example, when the appearance, background or behaviour of someone in authority is the focus of parody, this can serve to destabilise the power base and foster subversion beyond the temporarily sanctioned carnivalesque period. However, if a leader clearly (and in good humour) offers themselves up for parody, this can establish social bonds by foregrounding the humble humanity of the target and establishing greater mutual understanding. This controlled and sanctioned parody does not therefore generate contempt but, rather, has the opposite effect by increasing social bonds which, in turn, promotes collectivity and sense of shared community and purpose longer-term. As such, the impact of carnivalesque parody, laughter and humour is not just limited to the period of sanctioned subversion and the impact is therefore nullified. Whilst Shakespeare's Olivia in *Twelfth Night* (his most carnivalesque play) argues, "There is no slander in an allowed fool, though he do nothing but rail" (Act 1, Sc V), there is potential impact from an "allowed fool."

Laughter has the potential to be communal within any context simply because laughter always has the potential to be contagious. We often simply laugh because someone else does.[13] Such communal laughter can contribute to the dissolution of the individual into the collective and can influence group dynamics by expressing and stimulating shared contempt or creating opportunities from social bonds in a team, organisation or social group. Van Roekle argues that ridiculing the same subject matter builds rapport between people from very diverse backgrounds. Common examples of this in the workplace include an office ringleader offering humorous snide comments about the bosses amongst other team members or rebellious teenagers making jokes at the expense of figures of authority within schools.

Contagious shared laughter like other components of Carnivalesque Leadership can therefore promote the dissolution of the individual into the collective. Feasts involving communal eating and drinking are another obvious example. Providing opportunities for social bonding and the simultaneous release of endorphins, communal consumption of food is a common strategy employed by leaders to build relationships and commonality. From cake days, lunch runs, lunches out to full-blown celebratory meals at key points in the year, the sharing of food and drink is not only an opportunity for a group "to express collectively those sentiments which maintain its existence" but it also generates a social occasion "when jokes and gossip are exchanged" (Powdermaker 237).[14] The meaning of shared food has long been considered by anthropologists.[15] Discussing food as a "code," Douglas argues that "the messages it encodes will be found in the pattern of social relations being expressed" (61). Such social relations centred on collective food consumption, with opportunities for laughter and social bonding, mean that the causality of endorphin release is complex, that is: is it food alone, laughter alone or social bonding alone or a combination of these factors that produces endorphins and therefore improves wellbeing?[16] In the discussion of Corporate Carnivalesque in Chapter 5, work patterns and routines, such as drinks out and meals out, are considered as examples of Carnivalesque Leadership including extreme examples from across globe such as the Japanese corporate drinking custom, *nomikai.* Other examples of shared food and drink consumption involve religious significance such the Islamic major feasts of Eid al-Fitr and Eid al-Adha, the Hindu feast of Diwali, Jewish Passover, the Sikh tradition of Vaisakhi and the Christian feast of Christmas. Whilst a discussion of the significance of food and drink consumption in religious festivals is beyond the remit of this book, the impact on communal relationships is clear.

Far removed, at times, from religious sobriety and restraint, Chapter 5 explores case studies that develop the discussion of communal drinking begun in Chapter 1. As already highlighted, intoxication gently discussed by Bakhtin does not rival the disorienting height of intoxication philosophised by Nietzsche when linking the consumption of intoxicating substances to the dissolution of the individual into the collective in *The Birth of Tragedy.* The case studies considered in this book do extend Bakhtin's relatively conservative exploration of carnivalesque stimuli that build social bonds further into the Dionysian revelry.[17]

Intoxication is just one of the Carnivalesque Leadership components that promote the dissolution of the individual into the collectivity. Such shedding of individuality offers relief from the pressures of individual ego and can offer existential relief. Ideas swirling around the loss of the individual within the collective take different forms. At one end of the scale is a general sense of belonging which helps to create purpose and meaning and collective impetus. At the other end of the scale is extreme deindividuation which has the potential to counteract existential isolation and fear. Applying Terror Management Theory (TMT), Xiao et al. identify how group identification alleviates the terror of individual death. Here, the dissolution of the individual into the collective may provide relief in the relative comfort of realising the continuation of the collective. The loss of the individual within the collective is a complex phenomenon in its own right and these complexities are beyond the remit of this book. However, the social group aspects of the carnivalesque will feature significantly in this book. For example, the dissolution of the individual into the corporate collective can drive staffing stability, corporate compliance and significantly contribute to establishing and embedding a shared vision as discussed in Chapter 5. The sharing of food and drink, contagious laughter and parody alignment are all constituent parts of the carnivalesque communal impetus which centres on group participation. Providing examples of Carnivalesque Leadership, the next chapter considers how group participation in carnivals contributes to the creation of a communal sense of place and belonging.[18]

Notes

1 In *Humour*, Eagleton offers a lively discussion of different theoretical approaches to humour and its effects. For example, in his discussion of release theory, he draws on Sandor Ferenczi's position that "remaining serious is a successful repression" (15) as he discusses BBC Radio's *The Goon Show*, Monty Python sketches and Boy Scout japes.

2 See MacLean's exploration of Rabelais' prescription for laughter and Williams for specific analysis of Rabelais' exploration of medicine and humour. Amongst the vast, more recent and clinically sound medical research undertaken on the subject of the medical impact of humour and laughter, see Martin; Dunbar et al; Mehu and Dunbar.

3 See Rowold et al.; Sonnentag and Frese. This list is clearly not exhaustive. Any suggestion that a work leader has the control over an individual workers' total wellbeing is overly simplistic, but there can be some impact. The discussion of Corporate Carnivalesque in Chapter 5 explores this in more depth.

4 Sinek focuses on how leaders can generate endorphins, dopamine, serotonin and oxytocin in their teams. See Sinek's *Leaders Eat Last* for a consideration of the impact of chemical messengers in different leadership scenarios.

5 See Sherman et al.

6 The prevalence of humour as a leadership strategy has been identified as potentially sector specific by Vecchio et al., and their work on the educational section will be considered in the next chapter.

7 Eagleton refers to Freud's views on the pleasurability of the joke coming from the superego relaxation providing the anarchic ego (13). Miller and Platter summarise opposing critical views of Bakhtin's relationship with psychologism and psychoanalysis.

8 See Telfer for a detailed examination of his theoretical challenge to Hobbes and development of own theoretical position on laughter based mainly on incongruity.

9 See D'Errico and Poggi for an explorative categorisation of the parody impact.

10 Pollock offers a summary of anthropological approaches to the meaning of masks and focuses on how "masks achieve their special effect by modifying those limited number of conventionalized signs of identity" (584).

11 In *The Way of Masks*, Lévi-Strauss considers ritual masks and the myths associated with those masks used by Amerindians of the Northwest Coast of Canada, highlighting how the composition and aesthetics create relational meaning between tribes.

12 Tonkin differentiates between what she sees as "mask" as an object and "Mask" as "mask-in-action" when utilised by somebody to create a complex unit – mask+costume+carrier. Tonkin considers power differentials between those who wear masks in indigenous cultures and those who do not, identifying how the mask carrier is said to assume power and exert control (243).

13 See Provine for an exploration of laughter as contagion and its anthropological roots.

14 See Dunbar for sample research into the social bonding prompted by communal eating.
15 See Hayden; Hayden and Villeneuve for archaeological, anthropological and ethnographic explorations of feasting. This is a signpost and not an exhaustive literature review.
16 See Dunbar's summary of the complexity of causality.
17 Critical interest in the dissolution of the self into the collective is broad ranging and extends well beyond Bakhtin's remit. The impetus for collectivity through physical activities will be explored in Chapter 5 whilst the role of music in the dissolution of the individual will be acknowledged in every chapter of this book.
18 See Markwell and Waitt for a discussion of the "place-based" sense of belonging generated by festivals. See also Salarvand for a discussion of how festivals can therefore distract from the marginalisation of the most disadvantaged in communities.

Works Cited

Arendt, Hannah. "On Violence". *Crises of the Republic.* Harcourt, 1972.
Arendt, Hannah. *Eichmann in Jerusalem – A Report on the Banality of Evil.* Penguin, 2022.
Avolio, Bruce J., et al. "A Funny Thing Happened on the Way to the Bottom Line: Humor as a Moderator of Leadership Style Effects." *Academy of Management Journal*, vol. 42, 1999, pp. 219–27.
Bakhtin, Mikhail. *The Dialogic Imagination – Four Essays.* Translated by Caryl Emerson and Michael Holquist. Edited by Michael Holquist. The University of Texas Press, 1981.
Bakhtin, Mikhail. *Problems of Dostoevsky's Poetics.* Edited and Translated by Caryl Emerson. University of Minnesota Press, 1984a.
Bakhtin, Mikhail. *Rabelais and His World.* Translated by Hélène Iswolsky. Indiana University Press, 1984b.
Carus, Paul. "On the Philosophy of Language." *The Monist*, vol. 8, no. 2, 1898, pp. 250–72. *JSTOR*, Accessed May 2, 2024.
D'Errico, Francesca, and Isabella Poggi. " 'The Bitter Laughter'. When Parody Is a Moral and Affective Priming in Political Persuasion." *Front Psychology*, vol. 9, no. 7, 2016, p. 1144. *PubMed.* Accessed May 4, 2024.
Douglas, Mary. "Deciphering a Meal." *Daedalus*, vol. 101, no. 1, 1972, pp. 61–81. *JSTOR.* Accessed Oct. 10, 2023.
Dunbar, R. I. M. "Breaking Bread: The Functions of Social Eating." *Adaptive Human Behavior and Physiology*, vol. 3, no. 3, 2017, pp. 198–211. *PubMed.* Accessed Nov. 6, 2023.
Dunbar, R. I. M., et al. "Social Laughter Is Correlated with an Elevated Pain Threshold." *Proceedings of the Royal Society B: Biological Sciences*, vol. 279, no. 1731, 2012, pp. 1161–7. *PubMed.* Accessed Nov. 6, 2023.
Eagleton, Terry. *Humour.* Yale University Press, 2019.
Freud, Sigmund. *Jokes and Their Relation to the Unconscious.* Translated by James Strachey. Norton & Company Inc, 1960. *Internet Archive.* Accessed Jan. 13, 2024.
Hayden, B. "Fabulous Feasts: A Prolegomenon to the Importance of Feasting." *Feasts: Archaeological and Ethnographic Perspectives on Food, Politics, and Power.* Edited by M. Dietler and B. Hayden. University of Alabama Press, 2010.

Hayden, B. *The Power of Feasts from Prehistory to the Present.* Cambridge University Press, 2014.

Hayden, B., and S. Villeneuve. "A Century of Feasting Studies." *Annual Review of Anthropology*, vol. 40, 2011, pp. 433–49.

Hobbes, Thomas. *Leviathan.* Project Gutenberg, eBook. Accessed Dec. 28, 2023.

Klein, Lawrence K., editor. *Characteristics of Men, Manners, Opinions, Times.* Cambridge University Press, 2000.

Lévi-Strauss, Claude. *The Way of the Masks.* University of Washington Press, 1988.

MacLean, Ian. "Dr. Rabelais's 500 Year Old Prescription: Laughter Really Is the Best Medicine." *BMJ: British Medical Journal*, vol. 308, no. 6932, 1994, pp. 803–4. *JSTOR*. Accessed May 4, 2024.

Markwell, Kevin, and Gordon Waitt. "Festivals, Space and Sexuality: Gay Pride in Australia, Tourism Geographies." *Tourism Geographies*, vol. 11, no. 2, 2009, pp. 143–68.

Martin, Rod A. "Is Laughter the Best Medicine? Humor, Laughter, and Physical Health." *Current Directions in Psychological Science*, vol. 11, no. 6, 2002, pp. 216–20. *JSTOR*. Accessed May 4, 2024.

Mehu, Marc, and Robin I. M. Dunbar. "Naturalistic Observations of Smiling and Laughter in Human Group Interactions." *Behaviour*, vol. 145, no. 12, 2008, pp. 1747–80. *JSTOR*. Accessed Apr. 21, 2024.

Miller, Paul Allen, and Charles Platter. "Introduction." *Arethusa*, vol. 26, no. 2, 1993, pp. 117–21. *JSTOR*. Accessed Apr. 30, 2024.

Nietzsche, Friedrich. *The Birth of Tragedy.* Dover Publications, 1995.

Pollock, Donald. "Masks and the Semiotics of Identity." *The Journal of the Royal Anthropological Institute*, vol. 1, no. 3, 1995, pp. 581–97.

Powdermaker, Hortense. "Feasts in New Ireland; the Social Function of Eating." *American Anthropologist*, vol. 34, no. 2, 1932, pp. 236–47. *JSTOR*. Accessed May 4, 2024.

Provine, Robert R. "Laughter." *American Scientist*, vol. 84, no. 1, 1996, pp. 38–45. *JSTOR*. Accessed May 5, 2024.

Roekel, Eva van. "Uncomfortable Laughter: Reflections on Violence, Humour and Immorality in Argentina." *Etnofoor*, vol. 28, no. 1, 2016, pp. 55–74. *JSTOR*. Accessed May 2, 2024.

Rowold, Jens, et al. "The Effects of Transformational and Instrumental Leadership on Followers' Levels of Cortisol." *German Journal of Human Resource Management/Zeitschrift Für Personalforschung*, vol. 31, no. 3, 2017, pp. 219–37. *JSTOR*. Accessed May 5, 2024.

Salarvand, Helya. "(Re)Locating Pride: Borders, Space, and Policing at Los Angeles Pride." *Aleph, UCLA Undergraduate Research Journal for the Humanities and Social Sciences*, vol. 19, 2022.

Shakespeare, William. *Twelfth Night. shakespeare.mit.edu.* Accessed Jul. 26, 2024.

Sherman, Gary D., et al. "Leadership Is Associated with Lower Levels of Stress." *Proceedings of the National Academy of Sciences of the United States of America*, vol. 109, no. 44, 2012, pp. 7903–7. *PubMed*. Accessed Jan. 13, 2024.

Sinek, Simon. *Leaders Eat Last.* Penguin Random House, 2014.

Sonnentag, Sabine, and Michael Frese. "Stress in Organizations." *Handbook of Psychology, Second Edition.* Edited by Irving B. Weiner. John Wiley & Sons Inc. 2013, pp. 560–92. *ResearchGate*. Accessed Jul. 24, 2024.

Spencer, Herbert. "Physiology of Laughter." *Essays: Scientific, Political, & Speculative.* Wellcome Collection.org. Accessed May 5, 2024.

Swinkels, Michiel, and Anouk de Koning. "Introduction: Humour and Anthropology." *Etnofoor*, vol. 28, no. 1, 2016, pp. 7–10. *JSTOR*. Accessed May 3, 2024.

Telfer, Elizabeth. "Hutcheson's Reflections Upon Laughter." *The Journal of Aesthetics and Art Criticism*, vol. 53, no. 4, 1995, pp. 359–69. *JSTOR*. Accessed May 5, 2024.

Tonkin, Elizabeth. "Masks and Powers." *Man*, vol. 14, no. 2, 1979, pp. 237–48. *JSTOR*. Accessed May 10, 2024.

Vecchio, Robert P., et al. "The Influence of Leader Humor on Relationships between Leader Behavior and Follower Outcomes." *Journal of Managerial Issues*, vol. 21, no. 2, 2009, pp. 171–94. *JSTOR*. Accessed May 10, 2024.

Williams, Alison. "Sick Humour, Healthy Laughter: The Use of Medicine in Rabelais's Jokes." *The Modern Language Review*, vol. 101, no. 3, 2006, pp. 671–81. *JSTOR*. Accessed Nov. 9, 2023.

Xiao, Zilun, et al. "The Effect of Group Identification on Death Anxiety: The Chain Mediation Role of Close Relationships and Self-Esteem." *International Journal of Environmental Research and Public Health*, vol. 19, no. 16, 2022. *ResearchGate*. Accessed May 5, 2024.

Young-Laughlin, Judi, and Charles D. Laughlin. "How Masks Work, or Masks Work How?" *Journal of Ritual Studies*, vol. 2, no. 1, 1988, pp. 59–86. *JSTOR*. Accessed May 3, 2024.

3 Carnivals and Carnivalesque Leadership

It is no surprise that street carnivals, as we best know them today, are characterised by carnivalesque components that increase social bonds and promote the dissolution of the individual into the collective, provide opportunities for laughter, parody, mask wearing, bodily excess and collective food and drink consumption. Dancing, parading and music-making during these events are significant collective experiences that may not preoccupy Mikhail Bakhtin's theorising of carnival, but they are crucial elements of carnival experience today and will be considered in this chapter as joyous manifestations of the carnivalesque. Despite the prevalence of carnivalesque components, carnivals also provide a means of exploring how and why carnivals may *not* always fit the model of Carnivalesque Leadership starting to be constructed in this book.

Carnival calendars, from ancient times through to medieval times through to modern times, share many similarities of tradition and purpose. Globally recognised festivals provide tension-releasing licenced freedoms that are then immediately followed by reinforced normality and control. However, over time it is possible to track how carnivals in, and of, themselves lead/reflect significant social change. This chapter explores how carnivals, with case studies of Trinidad and Notting Hill, London, offer a contemporary safety-valve release from the norm and opportunities for parody, mockery and constitute (at the very least) a temporary subversion of hierarchy. Beyond this, these carnival traditions in, and of, themselves, offer insights into Carnivalesque Leadership and the dynamics of state-sanctioned control of such temporary release. The resulting potential for change is outlined in the history of both Trinidad and Notting Hill carnivals.

Trinidad Carnival[1]

The Trinidad and Tobago carnival is an example of pre-Lenten carnival and is held before Ash Wednesday which, in the Christian calendar, traditionally signals the start of a period of abstinence lasting to Easter Sunday.

DOI: 10.4324/9781003441649-4

The brief summary of the development of the Trinidad carnival that follows highlights its European, African and Indian influences. The selectivity involved in such summarising can be overtly ideological. Hollis Urban Liverpool draws attention to the Eurocentric tendency to singularly locate the origins of Trinidad carnival in the bloodline of European colonisers and rejects this monological approach to, instead, explore French, Spanish, English, "Free Coloureds" and African versions of the Trinidad carnival. In doing so, Liverpool locates traditions of mask wearing evident in modern carnival to medieval Venice, ancient Greece and ancient Egypt as well as the traditions of West African masking (34). Owusu and Ross also highlight the "dominant ideologies" that associate the "origins of carnival with Christianity and European Colonisers in the Americas" (4). Indeed, any arguments (Hollis critiques Carr and Anthony in particular for this) of a "pure" colonial French heritage is undermined given the prevalence of similar celebrations in Brazil and other islands in the Caribbean without such an obvious French Creole connection.[2]

Like many a summary, this one does indeed start by identifying the European influence on the Trinidad carnival rooted in oppression but it does not end there. As Hill points out in his seminal study, Trinidad carnival is "not simply a retention of a European-inspired festival . . . . its ancestry is different" (5).[3] Mardi Gras on the island was certainly first celebrated by elite white French plantocrats who exploited slaves originally taken from West Africa. Under the period of British rule from 1797 to emancipation in 1834, carnival was, argues Hill, "an important institution for whites and free coloreds" (10) with little involvement of the enslaved except as onlookers. These versions of early Trinidad carnivals centred on masquerade balls and street promenading and house to house visits which are aligned with European traditions.[4] Brown argues that "neither the free blacks nor the slaves were allowed to join the celebrations of the whites" (84). However, there is some argument that slaves were involved in the celebrations pre-emancipation. Tsuji cites evidence from a letter written by an English administrator in 1826 who disapproves of "the gaiety of the place" during carnival season when "High and low, rich and poor, learned and unlearned, all found masking suits for the Carnival" (84). Alleyne argues that French settler slave owners showed "leniency" towards slaves during carnival (120). Liverpool uses diary entries from 1831 to 1832 to show that the enslaved were involved in carnival activities prior to emancipation and that assimilation between traditions was well underway (33). Such a model firmly positions carnival as only a temporary, momentary release from normal hierarchies in terms of release from the norm for those at the top of the social hierarchy. Here, in this first stage of carnival in Trinidad, carnivalesque release is temporarily sanctioned by those in power, with only little evidence of subversion of established power hierarchies involving those without power.

The abolition of slavery in 1834, with full freedom only granted to agricultural and domestic workers in 1838 following a transitional period of "apprenticeship," has been identified as a key moment whereby carnival started to transition away from this imported version of French Mardi Gras towards the model of carnival seen in Trinidad and Tobago today.[5] In the process of transition, carnival became more imbued with other traditions and rituals that represented a challenge to existing colonial hierarchies in line with Nurse's assertion that the post-emancipation carnival became "an annual ritual of social protest and resistance by the African population against the hegemony of the European elite" (Nurse cited by Raj 29). Indeed, the development of carnival in Trinidad tracks attempts by those in power to limit carnival itself until their power and control is lost and carnival becomes its own model of freedom and release.

Explored in the work of Cohen, descriptions of this second stage of Trinidad carnival have increasingly recognised the transformation of carnival from European traditions to embracing different musical forms, different dances and different forms of masquerading (Mas') infused with and celebrating African artistic patterns. La Rose offers a detailed exploration of this next stage in the development of the Trinidad carnival with contributing West African traditions and the influence of the Creole festival, Canboulay/Kambule. The language around this festival has evolved with increasing transition from Canboulay to Kambule from the Kikongo meaning of "procession."[6] As such, references hereafter may be to Canboulay if cited from a source or Kambule in general discussion. The language used to identify aspects of Kambule is also rich with significance. In Kwéyòl/Creole, the procession with "burning canes" can often be referred to as *cannes brulées*. La Rose explains that this style of night procession features call and response singing, drumming, dancing, Kalenda stick fighters and the carrying of lighted torches or *flambo* (in Kwéyòl/Creole, "burning torches" = *flambeaux*) and concludes that the "Canboulay Carnival took over and forever transformed the Mardi Gras carnival of the planters and laid the foundations for the Caribbean Carnival that exists today" (4).[7] Elder also firmly locates the rise of Kambule carnival in resistance and emancipation and highlights that it symbolises the cane burning undertaken by freed slaves of African heritage to celebrate their "freedom from slavery." Significantly, the African impetus did not come only from the slaves freed from the plantations, but there was also an influx of already legally free Africans who had arrived in Trinidad between 1783 and 1867 (Fergus; Liverpool). As such, an argument that African-influenced carnival development is rooted only in the "granting" of emancipation by white Europeans is limiting.

The transition away from a French European Mardi Gras model to the forms of street carnival associated with Trinidad and Tobago today is characterised by power struggle, subversion and resistance, with numerous legislative attempts at control from the British colonial government and acts of resistance by Trinidad communities as the culture of carnival continued to evolve. In one such example of control and subversion, in 1846, Governor McLeod banned masks from street parades but this was impossible to police and was rescinded the following year (Hill, *The Trinidad Carnival* 20).

Carnivals during the period between 1860 and 1896 are commonly referred to as Jamette carnival. Taken from the French word *diametre* suggesting being "beneath the diameter of respectability, or the underworld" ("Carnival" – nalis), Jamette carnival is associated with the underclass (Pearse 188) and has since been characterised as attracting those at the margins of society. This period became known for kalinda bands who, according to Brown, traded insults through song and were associated with the potential for violence (87). The Trinidad and Tobago Government Library now refers to Jamette carnival at this time as "a necessary release from the struggle that was their daily lives" ("Carnival" – nalis). By this stage, carnival was attracting a great deal of attention in newspaper editorials with the *Port of Spain Gazette* (March 9, 1870) demanding "an end to the obscene and disgusting buffooner"(*sic*) associated with the Jamette carnival (cited in Rohlehr 6). Here, then, carnival in Trinidad offers only some limited elements of the carnivalesque as categorised in this book as a period of licenced freedoms sanctioned by leaders when hierarchy is subverted, and there are opportunities for the dissolution of the individual into the collective and there is a sanctioned (and joyful) break from the norm to enable safety-valve release. Instead, carnival freedoms are continuously curtailed by those in power. Previously in the late eighteenth and early nineteenth centuries, carnival was associated with those in power, the plantocrats, who sanctioned their own carnivals. In the second half and end of the nineteenth century, now that carnival was developing through the culture of the masses, those in power, the colonial British government, undertook regular attempts to limit carnival freedoms.

Despite such legislative attempts, carnivals continued as a means of subversive expression. Cohen argues that the carnival participants used the event to "criticise and ridicule the ruling classes and their culture and over the years had frequent clashes with the police" (70). The British colonial authorities' continuing attempts to control and restrict carnival during this period is most notoriously and violently exemplified by the Canboulay Riots of 1881 when colonial police, led by Captain Baker, attempted to clamp down on carnival procession at Port of Spain, but revellers resisted and several were killed.[8] Following this uprising, the colonial government passed laws which further restricted Kambule activities. The torchlight processions were declared illegal, the playing of African musical instruments banned and "the old kalinda songs, deemed obscene and exciting to street-fights, went underground" (Elder 102–3). The Peace Preservation Ordinance of 1884, issued by Governor Freeling, states:

> Whereas it is a practice on certain occasions for numerous persons, many of whom are armed with sticks or otherwise, to parade the streets, carrying lighted torches, beating drums, fighting and otherwise disturbing the peace, and it is expedient to enable the Governor to prohibit the same.

Thereafter, the carrying of lighted torches, the "beating of any drum, the blowing of any horn or the use of other noisy instrument," any "dance or procession" and any collection of people "armed with sticks" were banned.[9]

Given the symbolic importance of carrying lit torches in Kambule, such legislation was a heavy-handed effort to kill carnival symbolism. These legislative crackdowns prompted adaption rather than submission, however. For example, the attempted banning of drums in the 1880s led to the use of tamboo-bamboo sticks "which consisted of tuned lengths bamboo that were stamped on the ground to produce a sound like drumming, but not as loud" (Brown 87). Demonstrating "creative resilience" to maintain annual "masquerade against repeated repressive measures" (Hill, *The Trinidad Carnival*; 48), tamboo-bamboo provided "a cohesive force within the grass root sector of the community that had continued to provide cultural continuity" (Charles 36). The tamboo-bamboo was a popular carnival instrument until the steel pan took over. In a letter dated 1965, Reginald Straker reminisces about the transition:

> It all started in 1936 in Tanty Willie's yard about carnival time. The boys gathered as usual to beat bamboo; one of them, Sousie Dean, picked up a dustbin and started beating it, there was an old motor-car in the yard and Arnim began to beat the gas tank. Realizing it was sounding sweet they discarded the bamboo. Rannie Taylor got hold of a paint pan, Killie found a piece of iron and my brother, Mussel Rat, suggested the cutting down of a cement drum to be used as a kettle and so the first steel band was formed in time for carnival day.
>
> (Straker cited by Hill *The Trinidad Carnival*; 48)

The role of music in carnival development in Trinidad is an area of academic study in itself, and this chapter only seeks to offer a basic outline that corresponds to carnivalesque freedoms and attempted restrictions, with the central role of calypso also considered in this chapter. Such authoritarian restrictions were spread wider than "just" the cultural development of carnival as exemplified by the colonial government's later Theatres and Dance Halls Act 1934, which legislated:

(a) no profane, indecent or obscene songs or ballads shall be sung or spoken.
(b) no stage play or song shall be presented or sung which is insulting to any individual or section of the community, whether referred to by name or otherwise.
(c) no acting or representation calculated to hold up to public ridicule or contempt any individual or section of the community shall be presented or performed.
(d) no lewd or suggestive dancing shall be performed.
(e) all performers and dancers shall be decently attired (12).

Adaptions prompted by such legislation contribute to the unique character of Trinidad carnival. The attempted legislative eradication of drums can be seen to have contributed to the increased use of tamboo-bamboo and the development of the steel pan instrument in the 1930s and 1940s so central to carnival today. By the mid-1950s, steel pans had become standardised which facilitated steel bands playing either stationary at fetes or on mobile floats in carnival parades.

Another unique musical characteristic of the Trinidad carnival not only reflects adaption to circumstance and parodic resistance to authority control but has also contributed explicitly to bringing about change: calypso.[10] Songs had long been a focus for the authorities seeking to control the bawdy, licentious aspects of Trinidad carnival. In his report on the Canboulay Riots of 1881, R. G. Hamilton, a colonial representative from London (Guzda 3), for example, identifies the subversive, bodily excess of carnival songs:

> It is common during Carnival for the vilest songs, in which the names of ladies of the island are introduced to be sung in the streets, and the vilest talk to be indulged in while filthy and disgusting scenes are enacted by both sexes, which are beyond description and would be almost beyond belief were it not that they were vouched for by witnesses of unimpeachable credibility.
>
> (Hamilton cited by Rohlehr 3)

Operating both as a means of popular parody and as a vehicle for social commentary, calypso affects and captures change. For example, the lyrics of famous calypsonian, The Mighty Sparrow, in "The Slave" capture the drive for change embodied in calypso:

> We had to chant and sing to express our feelings
> To dat wicked and cruel man

That was the only medicine to get them to listen
And is so calypso began[11]

The origins of calypso are routinely identified in the call-and-response forms that accompanied the Kambule and rooted in African music heritage.[12] The heritage of calypso is seen as potentially more heterogenous than "just" Kambule, with Crowley, for example, identifying the potential East Indian influence, Winer identifying Spanish influence and Rohlehr acknowledging the absorption of European, West Indian, Latin American, North American and Indian music in the development of the form.[13]

The language used in calypso reflected the transition from Spanish colonial rule with French plantocrats owning much of the land to British colonial rule, as encapsulated by the calypsonian Lord Executor who sang:

From abolition to ninety-eight
Calypso was still sung in its crude state
From French to English it was then translated
By Norman Le Blanc who became celebrated
Then it was rendered grammatically
In oration, poetry and history

With its memorable tunes and often biting lyrics, calypso had impact on the general population and those in power. Crowley argues that Sir Patrick Renison, Colonial Secretary of Trinidad, admitted that the government took note of calypsos criticising policies, with command performances of calypsonians actually hosted at Government House ("Towards a Definition of Calypso" 65).

The previous attempted clampdown on "profane, indecent or obscene songs or ballads" and the banishing of presentations and performances that "hold up to public ridicule or contempt any individual or section of the community" in the Theatres and Dance Halls Act 1934 had offered little protection for authorities from the sharp focus of the calypsonians. Rohlehr argues that these laws were passed to protect the class and race in power from being targets of calypso critique and thus "from the scrutiny of an underclass whose carnival style had permanently entered the area of serious political discourse" (9).[14]

Despite attempts to control language and critique, calypso flourished with calypsonians famously holding up "a mirror of the struggle for an egalitarian society" (Rohler in Owusu and Ross 45) with titles such as "Sedition Law" by King Radio, "Money Is King" by Growling Tiger and "Commissioner's Report" and "History of Carnival" by Atilla the Hun. Calypso lyrics critiqued British rule before independence in 1962 and continued to engage with political forces post-independence. The first leader after independence,

Dr Eric Williams, was even celebrated in the song "William the Conqueror" by The Mighty Sparrow.

The Calypso King competition entered the carnival in 1939, with Growling Tiger the first to be crowned. With only a break for World War II, the calypso competition is a central point of carnival. The status of King for a singer of subversive, challenging songs is fully aligned with carnivalesque tradition. The term became gender neutral as Calypso Monarch after Calypso Rose proved victorious in 1978. The social commentary aspect of calypso remains central to the craft with the Calypso Monarch in 2020, Terri Lyons', song "Meghan My Dear" lampooning the British royal family and its relationship with Prince Harry and Meghan Markle.

Calypso is just one of the many outlets for subversion and parody that has become sanctioned and celebrated during the history of Trinidad's carnival. Temporary subversion and safety-valve release has not just simply led to the reinforcing of the status quo but has shown the potential for long-term change through parodic and mocking intent. The role of the masquerade bands in carnival is another complex example of temporary subversion. The playing of stock characters has symbolic potential for both safety-valve release and social critique which can impact change. Mas' bands offer large group involvement featuring masquers wearing costumes based on history, current events, films and carnival traditions. The *negre jardin* is one of the traditional mas' stock characters of the plantocratic era which involved owners parading in costumes of the garden slave. Alleyne relates this specific tradition to Bakhtin's model of the topsy-turvy mockery in carnival and argues that whilst many whites portrayed the *negre jardin* in rags and blackface, the "black slaves inserted themselves into the turning-the-world-upside-down-for-a-day that was Carnival: they dressed in the cast-off clothing of their masters and whitened their faces and hair using flour" (120).[15] In this carnivalesque model presented by Alleyne, which suggests the temporary reversal of hierarchy, the power differentials are so extreme that the plantocrat mockery of the slaves further affirms domination, whereas the slaves dressing up as white authority figures is a mocking act of resistance. Other mas' carnival characters dating back to the nineteenth century include "Jab Jab," from the French patois "Diable Diable" (Devil Devil); Dame Lorraine (a parodic exaggerated presentation of nineteenth century plantocrat female, often played by men); the Midnight Robber; the Burrokeet ("donkey-man" character); fancy clowns; imps; and a series of beasts including bats and dragons.[16] The role-playing of stock characters, complete with costumes and masks, frequently involved gender cross-dressing and had a parodic, subversive intent that both challenges and reinforces stereotypes. Popular mas' characters across the history of Trinidad carnival have also included a version of the European Pierrot clown which first appeared during the plantocrat phase of carnival. This character can then be traced through to "Pierrot grenade" (meaning "Pierrot from Grenada," a "mock" Pierrot) which was the freed slaves' caricature of their former masters' elaborate masquerade which first appeared during the Jamette Carnival era (Kerrigan "Creatures of the Mas'" 5). The parodic development of this character is considered by Hill who highlights that the authorities demanded in 1892 that all "would-be Pierrot masqueraders should first obtain a licence from the police" (The Trinidad Carnival; 30). By taking away the power of the mask for identity anonymity, the authorities therefore signalled the death knell for a popular carnival character and therefore did away with the parodic threat.

The changing prevalence of key stock mas' characters reflects changes in power, authority and hierarchy in Trinidad. Whereas the *negre jardin* was prevalent in the plantocrats' Mardi Gras versions of carnival, the character is now extinct in this format. Significantly, Hill explores how the character of *negre jardin* "was adopted by the ex-slaves for their Canboulay procession, then upgraded into the costume of the King Stickman or Batonnier which was later replaced by the gorgeously arrayed Pierrot" ("Traditional Figures" 16). The clampdown on the popular Pierrot character highlights continuing attempts to control carnival by the British colonial authorities. The parodic, mocking potential of mas' costume traditions is fully aligned with the carnivalesque challenge to hierarchical figures. However, the history of Trinidad carnival provides examples of authoritarian attempts to limit particular mas' characters. As such, despite having so many carnivalesque features, this stage of Trinidad carnival is not aligned to the carnivalesque model informed and extrapolated from Bakhtin that is starting to be explored in this book. The shift to sanctioned, standardised forms of carnival, more aligned to the Carnivalesque Leadership model in which the state sanctions and is complicitly involved in the temporary subversion of power and hierarchy, began to gather pace after the Second World War with "all its disruptions of the old social order" which is when, Kerrigan argues, "revellers from the privileged classes began to stray into a street mas . . . . The era of 'pretty mas' had begun" ("Creatures of the Mas'"). Kerrigan links the "pretty mas revolution which started in the 1950s" with "the increasing commercialisation of Carnival . . . [which] has left these traditional characters stranded." ("Creatures of the Mas'"). Pretty mas' costumes, sometimes referred to as "bikini and beads," now dominate the carnival "where players wear simple bikinis as costumes" and "the participants' bodies replace the costume" (Gugolati 5).[17]

There are mas' characters, particularly the Dame Lorraine character, and the crowning of the carnival King and Queen who are chosen to symbolically rule over the carnival, still evident today, that align with the carnivalesque model explored in this book.[18] The parodic coronation of the carnival king and queen and the crowning of the Calypso Monarch all happens at Dimanche Gras on the night before the traditional carnival parades on Monday and Tuesday before Ash Wednesday. This coronation timing means that the fake royalty is in place ready for "J'Ouvert" at dawn the following morning and the street parades and other festivities that follow. Harking back to the night-time traditions of Kambule, J'Ouvert welcomes the break of day and sees thousands of revellers "in old clothes covered with mud, or as Blue or Red Devils, or drenched in black oil (Oil Men)" (Martin 227). Again reflecting the assimilation and transformation of plantocrat Mardi Gras traditions, "ole mas" characters have played a significant role in J'Ouvert since the nineteenth century. Alleyne-Dettmers offers the example of how, after Trinidad and Tobago gained independence, the 1962 J'Ouvert Parade was inundated with "ole mas" characters as if in recognition of a move to independence. A parodic addition to these characters was "a very distinguished-looking gentleman" who depicted the Governor General of the West Indies Federation. His placard displayed "Lord Hailes Seeing His Last Carnival" (331). Like the rest of carnival, J'Ouvert is rich with pre- and post-emancipation, colonial and post-colonial power symbolism. The 1970 J'Ouvert mas' included masqueraders dressed as African warriors and famous African personalities. The mas' presentation "The Truth about the Blacks: Past and Present" featured placards of protest and costumes to represent black heroes (Alleyne-Dettmers 331). Emerging from a direct challenge to authority through Kambule, J'Ouvert is now an essential aspect of Trinidad and Tobago carnival and involves thousands of local and tourist revellers at sunrise throwing colourful paint, mud, powder and even chocolate at each other. This sanctioned subversion is symbolically resonant and offers fun and laughter which promotes the dissolution of the individual into the collective. Rather than donning a costume for carnival, J'Ouvert participants are dressed in "rags" which, for Alleyne-Dettmers, constitutes a "de-costume" making J'Ouvert an "unmasking 'which operates in' counter-balance to masking in the carnival parade" (334).

Modern Trinidad and Tobago carnival provides other examples of celebrating and commemorating the long tradition of resistance and subversion within the annual carnival structure. For over twenty years, the Friday before carnival sees the performance at Piccadilly Street in East Port of Spain of a re-enactment of the "Canboulay Riots" delivered through the play "Kambule" written by Eintou Pearl Springer. The development of modern Trinidad and Tobago carnival to include such recognition is not without its tensions in terms of both continuing challenges to hierarchical structures and the determination of which traditions become approved and ultimately state-sanctioned. The focus of this chapter is typically on the shift from elite European Mardi Gras traditions to a model of carnival enriched with wider traditions, notably West African traditions. These were not the only non-European influences on the development of modern Trinidad carnival, however.[19] The abolition of slavery in 1834 meant that plantation owners looked elsewhere for labour and, from 1845, East Indian indentured labourers were brought in to replace the slave workers on the plantations and bought with them their own festival traditions.[20] Of these traditions, Hosay celebrations are the most relevant for this discussion. Hosay is the Trinidadian version of the Islamic Muharram observances which commemorate the martyrdom of Prophet Muhammed's grandson Hussein and his brother Hassan which culminate in a procession. Hosay features blazing torches, stick fights, songs, drums and cymbals. Sankeralli argues that Hosay "broke the ethnic barrier separating the Indian and African communities" (204) and explores the Indian presence and influence on the three key components of carnival: steel band, mas' and calypso. In recognising potential cross-overs and similarities from different heritage pathways, concepts of cultural ownership and identity and dominance are inevitably raised. Just as the Kambule was targeted by colonial forces, the Indian community festivals were similarly targeted by the authorities and, on October 30, 1884, the police and military opened fire on the Hosay procession killing at least 16 revellers and injuring over 100.[21] The Hosay Riots of 1884 and the Canboulay Riots of 1881 are both bloody examples of British colonial leaders trying to control potential subversion. Brereton argues that the Trinidad and Tobago government's partial funding for the re-enactment of the Canboulay Riots is in stark contrast with the contemporary lack of funding for a re-enactment of the Hosay riots and reflects an imbalance in Afrocentric and Indocentric national narratives. Such an imbalance in recognising influence can be reflected in academic work, an example being from Brown who, when discussing carnival and calypso heritage and having identified the influx of indentured Indian workers since 1845, does not discuss the impact of Indian culture on national culture given that it "remained outside the synthesis that produced national culture in Trinidad until the twentieth century" (83). Ramcharitar argues that the modern Trinidad and Tobago carnival "is a tradition re-invented for political purposes" (24) and explores tensions between support for the promotion of carnival as national culture and how this promotion has operated as a political mechanism to marginalise Indian communities in Trinidad. For Scher, carnival has become a "tacit state sponsored project" that has denied other ethnic minority, notably Indian and Chinese, involvement in building the carnival traditions (478).

Racial and ethnic dynamics are a moving force in Trinidad's carnival as events reflect political and social change and/or resistance to change. Changes in gender dynamics are also reflected in carnival as evidenced by the switch in calypso monarch title and a debate around the "feminisation" of carnival (de Freitas 6) and greater critical debate centred on the intersections of race and gender evident in the "contested space of liberation and tradition" (Raghunandan 193). The discussion offered in this book does not profess to offer anything like a comprehensive outline of racial and gender power balance and a full account and debate regarding those not being represented in Trinidad and Tobago carnival but, instead, offers these as examples of the process of Carnivalesque Leadership in terms of what and who is being temporarily sanctioned and by whom.

In a carnivalesque model, the spaces provided by carnival offer an opportunity for both safety-valve release through a subversive break from the norm and the potential for longer-term change, partly through increased visibility of different traditions and cultures. However, the carnivalesque is a sanctioned model and there is, therefore, an authority involved in the sanctioning and prioritising of what comprises carnival. Alleyne argues that "From the nineteenth century to the present, the Trinidad Carnival has been a space of cultural innovation and hybridisation, of political satire and protest, and lately of constitution of national identity" (120). However, this hybridisation is still evolving and a Carnivalesque Leadership lens is useful when considering what components are sanctioned and which are not as well as a means to consider its seemingly temporary status.

Today, the Trinidad and Tobago carnival is a major tourist attraction, high spot of the global carnival calendar and a respected heritage site. The rest of this chapter is dedicated to exploring how a Carnivalesque Leadership framework might also be applied to another high spot on the global carnival calendar: Notting Hill, London, which is deeply indebted to the Trinidad carnival. The influential diaspora of carnival traditions through emigration and global exposure has become a site of contest. Indeed, the foregrounding of specific components that comprise the Trinidad and Tobago carnival is relevant given recent attempts by the Trinidad and Tobago government to copyright certain aspects of the carnival. Reflecting concern around its global appropriation which could potentially threaten its heritage and the uniqueness of the carnival itself, the three main components focused upon in copyright pursuit are mas' (costumes associated with masquerade), calypso (developed in Trinidad) and steel pans (invented in Trinidad).[22] The Trinidad and Tobago Copyright Collection Organisation (TTCCO) has also established the "Work of Mas'" under copyright to protect original performers, composers, producers and bandleaders or Mas' projects. The Carnival Institute of Trinidad and Tobago (CITT) was established in 1999 to secure and preserve its traditions.

Registering the unique aspects of the Trinidad and Tobago carnival and the threat of homogenising globalising carnival culture, such organisations also reflect potential commercial benefits and threats. During the 1980s, state involvement in carnival increased as attempts were made to expand the economic potential of the festival (Kerrigan "The Economics of Pretty Mas'"). Today, tourists experiencing the carnival can join a mas' band and take part in carnival parades, hiring costumes and preparing by learning some of the songs. The potential commodification of the Trinidad carnival is considered by Scher, who locates the carnival with economises surrounding heritage tourism. The costumes available for hire by tourists reflect the shift more towards "Pretty Mas'" in carnival. The potential commodification of components of Carnivalesque Leadership is considered more broadly in Chapter 5, which starts to explore "Corporate Carnivalesque."

In 1972, Hill argued that Trinidad carnival is "rooted in its soil" and that it "cannot travel except as a second-hand film image of itself" (119). Whilst it is not an exclusive source of influence, the influence of Trinidadian carnival can be seen globally. The contextualising dynamics of place and context add their own layers to such travelling traditions. Europe's largest street carnival in London's Notting Hill, for example, certainly has roots very firmly in the carnival traditions of the Caribbean island. The development of the Notting Hill Carnival is characterised by power dynamics, opportunity for collectivity and safety-valve release from everyday oppression.

The emigration of Trinidad carnival to London was symbolically and operationally via the HMT Empire Windrush in 1948 as the Windrush generation entered the UK. A shorthand for West Indians who answered the call for help from the British government, the Windrush generation were workers who emigrated to the UK to help rebuild the economy after the end of World War II. Between 1948 and 1973, approximately 550,000 West Indians migrated from the West Indies to the UK (Hewitt and Isaac). The contemporary song "London Is the Place for Me" by calypsonian Lord Kitchener captures an optimism and positivity for this opportunity:

> Well, believe me I am speaking broadmindedly
> I am glad to know my Mother Country
> I have been travelling to countries years ago
> But this is the place I wanted to know
> London that is the place for me

Lord Kitchener wrote the song during the journey to England and performed his calypso on Tilbury docks for the Pathé News cameras.[23]

Despite the positivity and optimism captured in this calypso, the Britain that the newcomers wanted to make home was frequently hostile. Discrimination and racist attitudes were commonplace, partly from the influence of fascist organisations such as the British Union of Fascists and the impact of the overt anti-immigration agenda of the League of Empire Loyalists and the White Defence League. Entrenched racism and bigotry also combined with the difficult post-war conditions which created competition for jobs and economic strife fuelled antagonism. Tensions came to a head in the Notting Hill riots that started over the late summer bank holiday weekend in August 1958. This uprising is recognised by some as the impetus behind the phenomenon that became the Notting Hill Carnival.[24] During the riots, a large group of white "Teddy Boys" attacked black residents leading to counterattacks. The disturbances lasted two weeks.[25]

One of the most significant responses to this tension and disorder provides one of the modern world's greatest examples of Carnivalesque Leadership, complete with its ability to bring about long-term change, challenge authority, build collectivity and provide immediate safety-valve release. This response was led by activist and journalist Claudia Jones who began a tradition that some see as leading to the annual Notting Hill Carnival.[26] Born in Trinidad in 1915, Jones was raised and lived in New York (where she was imprisoned for her involvement with the Communist Party). Her subsequent exile prompted a move to London in 1955. Utilising her experience as a journalist to challenge and transform attitudes, Jones founded the *West Indian Gazette* (WIG) in 1958 on behalf of the editorial committee established by The West Indian Workers and Students Association (Hinds 126). With her activism, experience and force of personality, Jones was uniquely positioned to set up a Caribbean Carnival Committee, sponsored by the WIG, in November 1958 to plan and execute the organisation of an event to celebrate West Indian culture and build a sense of shared community in the face of recent events.[27] Carnival was one of the many strands of Jones' response to the racial tensions in London and typified her belief in "the role of the arts in bringing people together for common aims" (Jones cited in Prescod 151). More specifically, it was carnival in, and of, itself that offered a different kind of opportunity to challenge hierarchies. Corrine Skinner-Carter, a Trinidadian dancer and associate of Jones, describes her as "a great leveller" and identifies that "carnival in itself is a great leveller of people, it's a thing in Trinidad that brings all nations, creeds, colours, everybody together" (Skinner-Carter, cited in Prescod 153). In direct response to the social and racial tensions experienced in areas of London such as Notting Hill, the Caribbean Carnival Committee set about planning a Caribbean-themed carnival. They worked quickly and whilst the British weather was not conducive to Caribbean Carnival it did not prove to be a barrier: it was simply held inside at St Pancras Town Hall on January 30, 1959, with Jones being the leading force behind its organisation and development. The choice to host a carnival, in and of itself, was a carnivalesque act of leadership. Hammond Perry rightly argues that the choice of the Trinidad tradition of carnival which had "historically challenged the machinations of colonial authority in the Caribbean" was politically motivated in accordance with Jones' belief that "a people's art is the genesis of their freedom" (Jones cited in Hammond Perry, 132–3). Named the "Caribbean Carnival," the event at St Pancras Hall was decorated to recreate Port of Spain, Trinidad, with trademark costumes, dancing, steel bands and a beauty contest.[28] The indoor carnival also featured calypsonian, The Mighty

Terror, who had released a calypso titled "No Carnival in Britain" in 1955. For the event, The Mighty Terror even created a new song "Carnival at St Pancras." The BBC broadcast 30 minutes of the event including the crowning of the Carnival Queen, and part of the proceeds was assigned to help build a legal fund for white and black defendants in London.[29]

The racial tensions that had prompted the first indoor Caribbean Carnival in January 1959 continued and, on May 17, 1959, a black man, Kelso Cochrane, was murdered by a group of white men on Southam Street (close to Notting Hill) in a racially motivated attack.[30] Kelso Cochrane's funeral was held at St Michael and All the Angels on Ladbroke Grove on June 6. It was a high-profile event, with hundreds of people joining a procession to accompany the funeral party to Kensal Green Cemetery. Recognition of the significance of both the murder and the public response was shown by newspaper and television news coverage of the funeral. The police investigation into the murder proved controversial in its focus on robbery as a motive rather than race (Berg; Hammond Perry). In response, a group of activists, including Jones, submitted an open letter to the Prime Minister, Harold Macmillan, stating "Hardly the ink has dried on the screaming headlines in the national press about the racist disgrace of Nottingham and Notting Hill Gate of late August, [and yet] another heinous crime has been committed" (cited in Hammond Perry 128). Public demonstrations, rallies and protests promoting inter-racial harmony followed, and organisations including the People's National Movement, the Committee of African Organizations (CAO), the Inter-Racial Friendship Coordinating Council (IRFCC), the West Indian Students' Union, the Coloured People's Progressive Association (CPPA), the British Caribbean Association and the Association for the Advancement of Coloured People (AACP) raised awareness of the specific case of the Cochrane murder and sought to foreground and combat the wider societal issues.[31]

The Caribbean Carnival had started as an attempt to work through racial tensions and bring communities together in celebration of West Indian traditions, and they served to increase visibility. Significantly, the Caribbean Carnival events also offered a temporary release from the norm which, for Prescod, would have appealed "to a socialist revolutionary" (Prescod 160) like Jones with its subversive licence. The indoor Caribbean Carnival followed annually until Jones died on Christmas Day 1964 (her ashes were interred next to Karl Marx's tomb in Highgate Cemetery); thus, bringing this annual Caribbean Carnival to an abrupt stop/pause (dependent if these events are seen as a precursor to Notting Hill Carnival or not).[32]

The next stage in the development of carnival in London set its location firmly in Notting Hill. On August bank holiday 1965, community activist and social worker, Rhaune Laslett, organised an outdoor procession, the

Notting Hill Fair parade, for different ethnic groups living in Notting Hill (Prescod 162) and, thus, set the annual calendar timing and location for Notting Hill Carnival. The first street parade in 1965 was "led by an Englishman who rode in a stagecoach, masquerading as Queen Victoria" (Cohen 67). This parodic dressing up as a mock monarch is, of course, perfectly carnivalesque in its subversive undermining of hierarchy and temporary mockery. Highlighting her spirituality, Cohen relates Laslett's claimed "vision" of different ethnic groups in a joyful procession (67) that inspired the event.

Laslett is regularly credited with starting the Notting Hill Carnival parade as we know it today with its calypso, steel band music, extravagant costumes and joyful procession over the late summer holiday weekend (Pryce; Gutzmore). Like the earlier indoor Caribbean Carnival organised by Claudia Jones, the Notting Hill Fair parades maximised the collectivity of carnival, provided the opportunity for safety-valve release and temporary subversion. Laslett continued to grow the event with local community support until 1970 when increasing community tensions prompted her decision to cancel the event last moment (Cohen 68). However, the carnival had been embedded enough in the local community that it still went ahead without Laslett at the helm.

The social background for this developmental stage of London's carnival is partly provided by Conservative MP, Enoch Powell's "Rivers of Blood" speech of 1968, which notoriously located current and future problems in UK society on immigration from the commonwealth and warned against the proposed Race Relations Bill. Right wing organisations such as the National Front were growing and relationships between the police and some local communities were increasingly frayed. One of the most significant eruptions in this tension came when the police undertook a series of raids of Notting Hill's popular Mangrove Restaurant on All Saints Road (Cohen 69). The restaurant was a hub of intellectual and cultural energy, attracting figures including Bob Marley and Jimi Hendrix, and it had become unofficial headquarters of the organisers of the Notting Hill Carnival. The venue also became frequented by members of the British Black Panthers Movement (BBPM) which was founded by Nigerian playwright and activist, Obi Egbuna, in April 1968 and had its headquarters briefing on Portobello Road, Notting Hill. Altheia Jones-LeCointe was a prominent figure in the BBPM, Barbara Beese was a member and Darcus Howe, founder of the Black Eagles movement, would later join the BBPM (Angelo 2018). The intense police targeting of the Mangrove Restaurant increased local tensions. A protest march on August 9, 1970, was organised by the newly formed Action Committee for the Defence of the Mangrove in alliance with the BBPM with the aims "to protest against police harassment" and to call an "end to the persecution of the

Mangrove Restaurant" as set out in a letter sent to the Home Office, the Prime Minister, the Leader of the Opposition and the High Commissioners for Jamaica, Trinidad, Guyana and Barbados (cited by Howe *From Bobby to Babylon* 52). The march set off from the Mangrove Restaurant to the local police station and was met by a large contingent of police. Howe describes the "pure, unadulterated, unlicensed brutality" (*From Bobby to Babylon* 54) of the police which resulted in the arrest of nine community leaders who would become known as the "Mangrove Nine," including Frank Crichlow, founder of Mangrove Restaurant, plus Beese, Jones-LeCointe and Howe. The nine activists were arrested, charged and put on trial for inciting a riot and other lesser charges. The trial was a landmark in British legal history and a marker in the pursuit of civil rights. The Mangrove Nine were eventually acquitted of the most serious charges of inciting a riot. In the summing up of the trial, the judge, His Honour Edward Clarke QC, said the trial had "regrettably shown evidence of racial hatred on both sides" ("Mangrove Nine Protest"). This statement represents official recognition of racial discrimination by the Metropolitan Police.

Cohen identifies a seismic shift after 1970 when "Carnival became almost exclusively West Indian in its leadership and arts and nearly so in attendance" (68) and a more Trinidadian style in theme, performance and culture. Leadership of the Notting Hill Carnival transferred to Leslie Palmer who is attributed with refining the model to enable the next stage of its development, drawing on traditional Trinidadian masquerades and introducing static sound systems. Under Palmer's leadership, the Notting Hill Carnival increased exponentially and, by 1975, it is estimated that attendance reached half a million people (Gutzmore, 31).[33] The growth of the carnival generated a fresh wave of antagonism and conflict with local councillors, the police, some local residents and an organisation led by George Clarke named "The Golborne 100" and its associated local newsletter "The Golborne." They started a campaign which sought to get Notting Hill Carnival banned or at least moved to the enclosed White City Stadium. A formal request to the Home Secretary urged for the ban to ensure "peace and quiet" on the streets (Dhondy 1563). The counter-response to the first "serious attempts by authorities to challenge the organisation of Carnival" is captured in *Race Today*. Published by the *Race Today* Collective and edited by Darcus Howe, *Race Today* played a significant role in supporting the carnival and both highlighted and challenged oppositional forces which sought to limit its scope.[34] In the February 1976 edition, organisers of carnival are encouraged to draw inspiration from the fact that colonial authorities had sought to shut down the Trinidad Carnival ("Don't Stop the Carnival" 36). The April edition of *Race Today* highlights examples of local support for the event ("Our Position on Carnival '76" 75), and an agreement was reached that the Notting Hill Carnival would go ahead and it would be organised by a new independent body, the Carnival Development Committee ("Carnival as Usual" 102) led by steel band pioneer, Selwyn Baptiste (Ferdinand 145).

The 1976 Notting Hill Carnival was already destined to be high profile given the publicity that had been generated around the lead up to the event touched upon here. The police presence from the start of the event was intense and heavy handed, with 1,500 police officers deployed (Ferdinand 145). The police undertook a series of raids of stallholders, and growing tensions spilt over into physical confrontation on the second day of carnival when a police officer made an arrest for alleged pickpocketing. Two days of rioting followed (Jackson 204).[35] Gutzmore argues that the police were "laying into black youths with their truncheons with a certain abandon" and hundreds of youths fought back (33). September's *Race Today* foregrounds that three hundred and twenty-five police officers were wounded and there were sixty reported arrests (Howe "Carnival Belongs to Us" 170). Howe made clear in an open letter to the Carnival Development Committee that the organisation had a major role to play in minimising police presence (179). Howe argues that the police had backed away from the agreement reached in April which meant that they would "recoup" at another point given that "One quarter of a million black people on the streets of Britain in 1976 is a political event" (179). Hernon argues that Senior Metropolitan Police officers "tried to play down the racial aspects of the riots" (180) and highlights press coverage which included *The London Evening Standard* reporting that "those who imbibed fascist propaganda were the aggressors" (181).

Focusing on the period of 1976–8, Pryce outlines the power dynamics and tensions in the leadership of the Notting Hill Carnival. He classifies the two years following the 1976 riots as demonstrating police crowd control but also "the potential power of blacks to resist cultural oppression by urban revolt" (40). In 1978, Howe became the first democratically elected chairman to the Carnival Development Committee (Bunce & Field 349; *Race Today* March/April 1977 27). Howe was later to refer to himself as "carnivalist to the bone, marrow and all" ("Middle Aged Spread"), and his involvement with the carnival grew from being a participant who understood its subversive potential and the value of the visibility it offered to becoming involved in its strategic and operational leadership and development. The politicisation of carnival, evident since the days of Claudia Jones, grew in response to the climate of oppression and resistance, typified by the experiences of the Mangrove Nine and attempts to shut down or move the carnival and the uprisings of 1976.

Whilst 1976 was the most significant outbreak of violence at the Notting Hill Carnival, there have been incidents of violence (including the first recorded murder at the event in 1987) and levels of crime associated with large crowds. It continues to attract criticism and challenge. On

September 7, 2023, *The Daily Mail* ran a headline story about "furious residents" who "don't feel safe letting their children walk the streets during the Notting Hill Carnival" making their concerns known during a public meeting. Reflecting wider societal trends, concerns over increased knife crime and a year-on-year increase in arrests led to the suggestion of a location switch to Hyde Park in response to some residents' safety concerns (Haigh and Stone). Here, then, is the repeat of earlier attempts to wipe the Notting Hill Carnival off the streets of Notting Hill but without an impetus likely to have any impact. Notting Hill Carnival is too well-established, too loved, too commercially viable and is too "state-sanctioned," not only in terms of permits and licencing but also in terms of it forming a celebrated part of British culture. The presence of the Notting Hill Carnival in modern British tradition is made clear in events such as Queen Elizabeth's Golden and Platinum Jubilee celebrations which included carnival parades down the Mall in front of Buckingham Palace. Commenting on her involvement in designing costumes for participants representing Notting Hill Carnival in the Golden Jubilee parade, Clary Salandy celebrated the "recognition by the establishment that we have made an artistic contribution and took carnival to people who would never go to it" (Salandy cited by Younge). King Charles III has been vocally supportive of Notting Hill Carnival for decades. When Prince of Wales, he was quoted as saying that "it's so nice to see so many happy, dancing people with smile on their faces" at the carnival (Hernon 183) and undertaking several high-profile public engagements involving the event over the years. Given the British royal family's hierarchical position and colonial legacy wealth, the celebration of, and support, for carnival, which offers sanctioned safety-valve release from the norm, may offer fruitful exploration in relation to Carnivalesque Leadership but that is beyond the scope of this current work.

The organisational and strategic leadership of the Notting Hill Carnival has continued to evolve, partly through internal conflicts and partly in response to the continuing growth of the event and corporate developments. The Carnival Arts Committee (1981–1988), Notting Hill Carnival Enterprise Limited – which then dropped the "Enterprise" tag – (1989–2002), The London Notting Hill Carnival Limited (2003–2011) and The London Notting Hill Carnival Enterprise Trust (2012–2018) (Ferdinand) have all taken turns in the organisation and management of the event. Today (as at May 2024), Carnival Village Trust and Notting Hill Carnival Limited are the current organisers of the Notting Hill Carnival, partly funded by Arts Council England (channelling government funding and National Lottery funding), The Royal Borough of Kensington and Chelsea and the City of Westminster Council.

The format of the Notting Hill Carnival is now well established. The event is heralded by steel band competitions on the Saturday with the start of carnival signalled by the throwing of colourful paints and powders for J'Ouvert at daybreak on Sunday at the top end of Ladbroke Grove. Throughout Sunday and Monday, mas' street parades, sound systems and static live stages bring together carnival traditions from Trinidad, contextualised in modern London. The standardisation of this format has helped secure the event's status, with approximately two million involved in the event as participants, general revellers and onlookers.[36] Carnival costumes have also become more standardised in terms of Pretty Mas' expectations as captured in a 2019 interview with costume designer, Allyson Williams, when she explains that "the historic traditions of mas are being replaced with so-called pretty mas, which is more popular today and has extravagantly beautiful costumes – bright colours, sequins, and beading – but they don't represent characters or themes" (quoted by Kale). As with Trinidad and Tobago carnival costumes, the dominance of Pretty Mas' has significantly lessened the subversive potential to challenge hierarchical structures through parodic play of stock characters.

The standardisation of Notting Hill Carnival is linked to its evolving economic status. The first major corporate partnership was secured in 1995 when Coca-Cola paid £1 million for a three-year sponsorship deal for Lilt to be the main brand associated with the event. A strategic review of the Notting Hill Carnival commissioned by the Mayor of London, Ken Livingstone, in 2004 highlighted positive cultural impact and the economic impact, publishing an estimated generation of £93 million in 2002 reaching an estimated £120 million added annually to London's economy by 2022 (Price). What started as a small-scale activist-driven community response to celebrate Caribbean culture, build understanding and promote racial harmony has become an industry in itself that offers safety-valve release to millions and revels in its promotion of collectivity and enjoyment through communal activities including the consumption of food and drink, dancing and music. For some, including Owusu and Ross, the event has become a "crucial antithesis to this history of state repression" (90). Notting Hill Carnival now both operates within the establishment and continues as an opportunity for subversive challenge to the establishment though its celebratory increased visibility of marginalised communities and exposure to different modes of living and alternative identities.[37]

Both Notting Hill Carnival and Trinidad and Tobago Carnival operate as sanctioned safety-valve release mechanisms that promote the dissolution of the individual within the collective through parades, costumes, dancing, music and communal consumption of food and drink. Both have operated as temporary subversive challenge to hierarchy during their evolution and reflect/impact longer-term change. The standardisation of both reflects commercial success and may, on the face of it, suggest a sanitising of subversive intent. However, it is worth noting that in Bakhtin's model, it is a *model* of carnival and therefore standardised which means that he can trace features seen in Rabelais' novels to the Saturnalian tradition. The question of whether standardisation renders the model too controlled and simply temporary party time or whether it has a longer-lasting impact forms part of the discussion around the carnivalesque model in itself that is considered throughout this book.

Raj argues that, with its capacity to bring together groups that are usually exclusive, overturn hierarchies, rearrange time and space, leaving everything playful and undefined with celebration and laughter, Notting Hill Carnival is a "direct reflection" of Bakhtin's theory of Carnival (3). This chapter has started to explore how the evolution of the two carnivals may be aligned to Carnivalesque Leadership. The history of Trinidad carnival has been explored from a limited, superficial perspective focusing on the shift from Mardi Gras carnival release aligned with European traditions and first held within the power and control of the plantocrat hierarchy to being a mechanism of resistance and a driver of change in a developing carnival model imbued with other heritage, notably African and Indian.[38] Carnivalesque Leadership is more explicitly associated with named leaders in the case of Notting Hill Carnival because of its more recent, more condensed and documented history. From the earliest indoor carnivals organised by Claudia Jones, to the first parades on the streets of Notting Hill galvanised by Rhaune Laslett, to the shift to larger scale events organised by Leslie Palmer, to the harnessing of community activist power by Darcus Howe, these leaders have all recognised the potential of carnival to bring people together, challenge existing inequalities and provide safety-valve release of pressure through communal activities. All can also be seen to employ Carnivalesque Leadership to achieve longer-term change that extends well beyond an August bank holiday weekend in London. This case study has started to explore how Carnivalesque Leadership is not simply "just" at the disposal of those at the top of power hierarchies but has proven to be a useful tool for those without such establishment power who are seeking change by securing sanctioned means for carnival expression. Of course, the contestation of that "sanctioning" process is still fraught with power tensions to be negotiated and is not a simple transactional model.

Notes

1 This chapter mostly refers to Trinidad carnival as opposed to Trinidad and Tobago carnival. My rationale for this centres on the fact that the two islands were not incorporated into a single colony until 1888 and the background of the world famous carnival is rooted in Trinidad. However, discussion of contemporary issues surrounding the carnival refers to the Trinidad and Tobago carnival.

2 There is very little use of primary sources in my discussion in this chapter, and I am indebted to the work of many other academics for my discussions of Trinidad/Trinidad and Tobago/Notting Hill carnivals.

3 In *The Trinidad Carnival; Mandate for a National Theatre*, Hill argues that carnival represents a unique form of national theatre that involves "the audience fully in the performance" (117) and includes "the ancient arts of burlesque and satire" (118).
4 See Alleyne; Pearse for typical summaries. See also de Freitas' PhD thesis exploring how attempts to determine the origins of carnival are often revealing in themselves and potential links between national identity and carnival.
5 References to emancipation and freedom in this chapter will refer to the date of 1838 rather than 1834 given this delay.
6 See Warner-Lewis' seminal work on the linguistics of this period.
7 In his discussion "Toward a Definition of Calypso," Crowley highlights that the origins of the kalenda stick fighting game are uncertain given that stick fighting was known in Africa, India and Europe.
8 See Brereton's exploration of these attempts to control Canboulay by colonial authorities.
9 Elder offers a summary of these attempts led by Sir Robert Hamilton in 1881 to outlaw Canboulay. See also Cowley for further details of legislative attempts to curb festivities.
10 This outline is not an exhaustive history of calypso but, rather, the start of an exploration of how calypso fits into carnivalesque dynamic. For a much deeper understanding of calypso and its importance in Trinidad carnival, see Fergus; Brown; Winer; Rohlehr; Cowley. Again, this is not an exhaustive list. Within these explorations there are very different perspectives on origin and identities associated with the genre.
11 Lyrics from *genius.com*
12 The word "calypso" itself is suitably polyglot as captured in Warner with Carib, Spanish and West African derivatives and Hill who focuses on the etymology of "kaiso." Elder identifies how the genre was originally sung by women during breaks in stickfighting performances, but then the genre was taken over and dominated by males and adjusted rhythmically for street parades.
13 "Chutney" is a contemporary Indian–Caribbean musical genre which accentuates the combination of Indian and Caribbean styles including Indian folk traditions, devotional songs and film music with calypso, soca and rap. See Ramnarine for a detailed exploration of the *chutney* genre.
14 In his discussion of how calypso often ridicules the very idea of hierarchy, Rohlehr refers to Bakhtin's identification of how laughter illuminates society and ridicules officialdom.
15 Also, see Crowley for a more in-depth discussion of the stock character.
16 See Kerrigan's article on "Creatures of Mas'" for a detailed consideration of these character roles and their subversive significance.
17 Gugolati explores the self-referential and visibility dynamics created by this shift to Pretty Mas' which highlights the performative practice of the masquerade.
18 See Alleyne-Dettmers for a more detailed discussion and Hill's exploration of the parody coronations which took place in carnival tents from the middle of the nineteenth century (*The Trinidad Carnival*).
19 Such a statement in itself is Eurocentric, given that European traditions, including those identified by Bakhtin as rooted in Ancient Roman Saturnalian, are also aligned to more ancient traditions of Mesopotamia and Egypt.
20 See Jha for an overview of Indian Heritage in Trinidad and Sturman for a wider discussion of Indian indentured labour around the world. See Mansingh and Mansingh for an exploration of the Hosay tradition in the Caribbean. See also

Liverpool for a discussion of the "importing" of Africans from Africa, indentured East Indians and Chinese from Asia, Portuguese from Madeira and many others from Syria and Lebanon (26).

21 Differentiating between African oppression and Indian alienation, see Sankeralli for greater exploration of the riots and the relationship between the different communities in Trinidad.

22 See Scher for an exploration of issues raised by this development.

23 See the clip of Lord Kitchener's performance on The Museum of London YouTube channel www.youtube.com/watch?v=ygBOb_XddwI.

24 See Raj for a summary of critical discussion of the origins of Notting Hill Carnival.

25 See Slepičková for an outline of Teddy Boy subculture and involvement in Notting Hill riots. See Hilliard for a detailed exploration of the 1958 riots which are sometimes seen as a turning point in British race relations.

26 See Gore; Dunstan and Owens; Schofield and Jones; Raj.

27 See Sherwood for a collection of articles centred on Claudia Jones and documents from a symposium held on September 28, 1996.

28 Skinner-Carter identifies the importance of the black beauty contest element of the event in that it challenged European standards of beauty (Skinner-Carter cited in Prescod 158).

29 See Hammond Perry 132.

30 No one was convicted for the murder of Kelso Cochrane. The significance of his murder is highlighted in Alexander and Bryne, Hernon and Hammond Perry. Journalist, Sanchia Berg, produced/presented/created a radio programme for BBC radio about the murder and the family's continuing frustrations with accessing information which could provide an understanding of the investigation that took place. Hammond Perry provides a detailed examination of Kelso Cochrane's life and death.

31 See Schofield and Jones' outline of this response.

32 See Hernon; Raj for examples of critical explorations which root the modern Notting Hill Carnival in the Caribbean Carnivals begun in 1959 which were a response to the 1958 riots.

33 See Holder for a detailed discussion of the significant organisational changes initiated led by Palmer during his tenure. Holder is a former chief executive of Notting Hill Carnival and led the event for ten years prior to an acrimonious split from the organisation. She is seen as a pivotal figure in carnival's commercial development into "Europe's biggest street party" (Muir).

34 See Smith's discussion of the publications *Race Today* and *Race & Class* within the context of activism and social unrest.

35 The term "riot" is problematic in its suggestion of one-sided criminality. Terms such as "uprising" and "resistance" reflect a different dynamic. See also discussion of term "riot" in relation to the discussion of the Stonewall "riots" in Chapter Six.

36 The blurring of the boundaries between these roles is central to Bakhtin's theory as expressed in *Problems of Dostoevsky's Poetics* (122).

37 Lending itself to a range of theoretical spheres, a detailed discussion of the potential "othering" of difference in the carnivalesque model is not within the scope of this book.

38 This statement suggests a simplistic binary of European versus African heritage of carnival. This is problematised through recognition that the European heritage of carnival is traceable to pre-European civilisations.

Works Cited

Alexander, Claire, and Bridget Byrne. "Introduction." *Ethnicity and Race in the UK: State of the Nation*. Edited by Claire Alexander et al., 1st ed. Bristol University Press, 2020, pp. 1–14. *JSTOR*. Accessed May 13, 2024.

Alleyne, Brian W. " 'Peoples' War': Cultural Activism in the Notting Hill Carnival." *Cambridge Anthropology*, vol. 20, no. 1/2, 1998, pp. 111–35. *JSTOR*. Accessed May 13, 2024.

Alleyne-Dettmers, Patricia Tamara. "Political Dramas in the Jour Ouvert Parade in Trinidad Carnaval." *Caribbean Studies*, vol. 28, no. 2, 1995, pp. 326–38. *JSTOR*. Accessed May 13, 2024.

Angelo, Anne-Marie. " 'Black Oppressed People All over the World Are One': The British Black Panthers' Grassroots Internationalism, 1969–73." *Journal of Civil and Human Rights*, vol. 4, no. 1, 2018, pp. 64–97. *JSTOR*. Accessed May 13, 2024.

Bakhtin, Mikail. *Problems of Dostoevsky's Poetics*. Edited and Translated by Caryl Emerson. University of Minnesota Press, 1984a.

Bakhtin, Mikhail. *Rabelais and His World*. Translated by Hélène Iswolsky. Indiana University Press, 1984b.

Berg, Sanchia. "The Murder of Kelso Cochrane." *BBC Radio 4*. Aug. 21, 2023. Accessed May 13, 2024.

Brereton, Bridget. "The Captain and the Canboulay." *Trinidad Express*, Jan. 31, 2012. Accessed May 14, 2024.

Brown, Ernest D. "Carnival, Calypso, and Steelband in Trinidad." *The Black Perspective in Music*, vol. 18, no. 1/2, 1990, pp. 81–100. *JSTOR*. Accessed May 5, 2024.

"Carnival". National Library and Information System Authority, nalis.gov.tt. Accessed May 13, 2024.

"Carnival as Usual". *Race Today*. Edited by Darcus Howe. May 1976, pp. 102–3. *Internet Archive*. Accessed May 13, 2024.

Charles, C. N. "Calypso Music: Identity and Social Influence: The Trinidadian Experience." PhD thesis. Leiden University, 2016.

Cohen, Abner. "Drama and Politics in the Development of a London Carnival." *Man*, vol. 15, no. 1, 1980, pp. 65–87. *JSTOR*. Accessed May 13, 2024.

Cowley, John. *Carnival, Canboulay and Calypso Traditions in the Making*. Cambridge University Press, 1996.

Crowley, Daniel J. "The Traditional Masques of Carnival." *Caribbean Quarterly*, vol. 4, no. 3/4, 1956, pp. 194–223. *JSTOR*. Accessed May 13, 2024.

Crowley, Daniel J. "Toward a Definition of Calypso (Part I)." *Ethnomusicology*, vol. 3, no. 2, 1959, pp. 57–66. *JSTOR*. Accessed May 13, 2024.

de Freitas, Patricia A. "Playing Mas': The Construction and Deconstruction of National Identity in The Trinidad Carnival." PhD thesis. McMaster University, 1994.

de Freitas, Patricia A. "Disrupting 'the Nation': Gender Transformations in the Trinidad Carnival." *NWIG: New West Indian Guide/Nieuwe West-Indische Gids*, vol. 73, no. 1/2, 1999, pp. 5–34. *JSTOR*. Accessed May 7, 2024.

Dhondy, Farrukh. "Bloody Carnival." *Economic and Political Weekly*, vol. 11, no. 39, 1976, pp. 1563–64. *JSTOR*. Accessed May 11, 2024.

"Don't Stop the Carnival". *Race Today*. Edited by Marcus Howe. Feb. 1976, pp. 36–7. *Internet Archive*. Accessed May 13, 2024.

Dunstan, Sarah, and Patricia Owens. "Claudia Jones, International Thinker." *Modern Intellectual History*, vol. 19, no. 2, 2022, pp. 551–74. *Cambridge Core*. Accessed May 13, 2024.

Elder, J. D. "Cannes Brûlées." *TDR (1988–)*, vol. 42, no. 3, 1998, pp. 38–43. *JSTOR*. Accessed May 7, 2024.

Ferdinand, Nicole. "From Port-of-Spain to Notting Hill and Beyond: The Internationalisation of the Trinidad-Style Carnival." PhD thesis. King's College London, 2014.

Fergus, Claudius. "From Slavery to Black Power: The Enigma of Africa in the Trinidad Calypso." *Transactions of the Historical Society of Ghana*, no. 16, 2014, pp. 1–26. *JSTOR*. Accessed May 13, 2024.

Gore, Dayo F. "Afterword: Centering Claudia Jones, Shifting Genealogies of Knowledge." *The Journal of Intersectionality*, vol. 3, no. 1, 2019, pp. 82–5. *JSTOR*. Accessed May 13, 2024.

Greater London Authority. *Notting Hill Carnival: A Strategic Review*. Greater London Authority, 2004. Accessed Dec. 28th 2023.

Gugolati, Maica. "Pretty Mas': Visuality and Performance in Trinidad and Tobago's Contemporary Carnival, West Indies." PhD thesis. PSL Research University, 2018.

Gutzmore, Cecil. "The Notting Hill Carnival." *Marxism Today*. Aug. 1982, pp. 31–3. *The Barry Amiel and Norman Melburn Trust*. Accessed May 13, 2024.

Guzda, John K. "The Canboulay Riot of 1881: Influence of Free Blacks on Trinidad's Carnival." *The Exposition*, vol. 1, no. 1, 2012, Article 4. *Buffalostate.edu*. Accessed May 13, 2024.

Haigh, Elizabeth, and Iwan Stone. "Furious Residents Say They Don't Feel Safe Letting Their Children Walk the Streets During Notting Hill Carnival After It Was Marred by Knife Violence – as Public Meeting with Council Over Event's Future Descends into Chaos." *The Daily Mail*, Sept. 7, 2023.

Hammond Perry, Kennetta. *London is the Place for Me – Black Britons, Citizenship and the Politics of Race*. Oxford University Press, 2015.

Hernon, Ian. *Riot! Civil Insurrection from Peterloo to the Present Day*. Pluto Press, 2006.

Hewitt, Guy, and Kevin M. Isaac. "Windrush: The Perfect Storm." *Social and Economic Studies*, vol. 67, no. 2/3, 2018, pp. 293–302. *JSTOR*. Accessed May 13, 2024.

Hill, Errol. "On the Origin of the Term Calypso." *Ethnomusicology*, vol. 11, no. 3, 1967, pp. 359–67. *JSTOR*. Accessed May 13, 2024.

Hill, Errol. *The Trinidad Carnival; Mandate for a National Theatre*. University of Texas Press, 1972.

Hill, Errol. "Traditional Figures in Carnival: Their Preservation, Development and Interpretation." *Caribbean Quarterly*, vol. 31, no. 2, 1985, pp. 14–34. *JSTOR*. Accessed May 9, 2024.

Hilliard, Christopher. "Mapping the Notting Hill Riots: Racism and the Streets of Post-war Britain." *History Workshop Journal*, vol. 93, no. 1, Spring 2022, pp. 47–68. *Oxford Academic*. Accessed May 13, 2024.

Hinds, Donald. "The West Indian Gazette." *Claudia Jones – A Life in Exile*. Edited by Marika Sherwood. Lawrence & Wishart, 1999, pp. 125–49.

Holder, Claire. "The Impact of Professionalism on Organisational Effectiveness: A Case Study of the Notting Hill Carnival." Submitted in Partial Fulfilment of the Requirements of the Degree of Professional Doctorate in the Built Environment, 2017. *Academia*. Accessed May 12, 2024.

Howe, Darcus. "Carnival Belongs to Us". *Race Today*. Edited by Darcus Howe. Sept. 1976, pp. 170–79. *Internet Archive*. Accessed May 13, 2024.

Howe, Darcus. "Middle Aged Spread – Fear of Black Youth Is to Blame for the Sudden and Sad Decline of the Notting Hill Carnival." *The Guardian*, Sept. 1, 2003. Accessed May 13, 2024.

Jackson, Nicole M. "Imperial Suspect: Policing Colonies within 'Post'-Imperial England." *Callaloo*, vol. 39, no. 1, 2016, pp. 203–15. *Project Muse*. Accessed May 13, 2024.

Jha, J. C. "Indian Heritage in Trinidad, West Indies." *Caribbean Quarterly*, vol. 19, no. 2, 1973, pp. 28–50. *JSTOR*. Accessed May 13, 2024.

Kale, Sirin. "I'm All Feathered Out' – Why Mas Is the Heart of Notting Hill Carnival." *The Guardian*, Aug. 21, 2019. Accessed May 13, 2024.

Kerrigan, Dylan. "Creatures of the Mas". *Caribbean Beat*, Jan/Feb 2004. caribbean-beat.com. Accessed May 13, 2024.

Kerrigan, Dylan. "The Economics of Pretty Mas". *Trinidad & Tobago Guardian*, n.d. guardian.co.tt. Accessed May 13, 2024.

Liverpool, Hollis Urban. "Origins of Rituals and Customs in the Trinidad Carnival: African or European?" *TDR (1988–)*, vol. 42, no. 3, 1998, pp. 24–37. *JSTOR*. Accessed May 13, 2024.

Mansingh, Ajai, and Laxmi Mansingh. "Hosay and Its Creolization." *Caribbean Quarterly*, vol. 41, no. 1, 1995, pp. 25–39. *JSTOR*. Accessed May 13, 2024.

"Mangrove Nine Protest." nationalarchives.gov.uk. Accessed May 13, 2024.

Martin, Carol. "Trinidad Carnival Glossary." *TDR (1988–)*, vol. 42, no. 3, 1998, pp. 220–35. *JSTOR*. Accessed May 9, 2024.

Muir, Hugh. "Carnival Trustees Face Legal Threat." *The Guardian*, Apr. 10, 2004. Accessed May 12, 2024.

"Our Position on Carnival '76." *Race Today*. Edited by Darcus Howe. April 1976, p. 75. *Internet Archive*. Accessed May 13, 2024.

Owusu, Kwesi, and Jacob Ross. *Behind the Masquerade – The Story of Notting Hill Carnival*. Arts Media Group, 1988.

"Peace Preservation No. 1–1884 Ordinance for the Better Preservation of the Peace." Provided by the National Archives of Trinidad and Tobago.

Pearse, Andrew. "Carnival in Nineteenth Century Trinidad." *Caribbean Quarterly*, vol. 4, no. 3/4, 1956, pp. 175–93. *JSTOR*. Accessed May 6, 2024.

Prescod, Colin. "Carnival". *Claudia Jones – A Life in Exile*. Edited by Marika Sherwood. pp. 150–62. Lawrence & Wishart, 1999.

Price, Oliver. "Ultimate Guide to Notting Hill Carnival: Festival Map, Parade Route, Event Times, Schedule and Road Closures . . . Everything You Need to Know on Party Over the Bank Holiday Weekend That Kicks Off in West London Tomorrow." *MailOnLine*, Aug. 26, 2022. Accessed May 13, 2024.

Pryce, Everton A. "The Notting Hill Gate Carnival – Black Politics, Resistance, and Leadership 1976–1978." *Caribbean Quarterly*, vol. 31, no. 2, 1985, pp. 35–52. *JSTOR*. Accessed May 13, 2024.

Raghunhandan, Kavyta. "The Body Contours of Carnival: Mas-Playing and Race in Trinidad." *Gender and Race Matter: Global Perspectives on Being a Woman,* Emerald Publishing, 2016, pp. 193–212. *ResearchGate*. Accessed May 8, 2024.

Raj, Razaq. "Carnival: Community Cohesion, Neighbourhood Identity or Political Challenge." *Journal of Hospitality and Tourism Management*, vol.13, no. 1, 2015, pp. 27–47.

Ramcharitar, Raymond. 'The Invention of Trinidad Carnival: The New World Gleichschaltung." *Caribbean Quarterly*, vol. 66, no. 1, 2020, pp. 7–28. *ResearchGate*. Accessed May 13, 2024.

Ramnarine, Tina Karina. " 'Indian' Music in the Diaspora: Case Studies of 'Chutney' in Trinidad and in London." *British Journal of Ethnomusicology*, vol. 5, 1996, pp. 133–53. *JSTOR*. Accessed May 13, 2024.

Rohlehr, Gordon. 'The Calypsonian as Artist: Freedom and Responsibility'. *Small Axe* (Number 9), vol. 5, no. 1, 2001, pp. 1–26. *Project Muse*. Accessed May 13, 2024.

Rose, Michael La. "'The City Could Burn Down We Jammin' Still!'" The History and Tradition of Cultural Resistance in the Art, Music, Masquerade and Politics of the Caribbean Carnival." Paper Presented to the International Conference on the Caribbean Carnival, 'Power, Performance and Play' at Leeds Beckett University, May 19–21, 2017.

Sankeralli, Burton. "Indian Presence in Carnival." *TDR (1988–)*, vol. 42, no. 3, 1998, pp. 203–12. *JSTOR*. Accessed May 13, 2024.

Scher, Philip W. "Copyright Heritage: Preservation, Carnival and the State in Trinidad." *Anthropological Quarterly*, vol. 75, no. 3, 2002, pp. 453–84. *JSTOR*. Accessed May 13, 2024.

Scher, Philip W. "Heritage Tourism in the Caribbean: The Politics of Culture after Neoliberalism." *Bulletin of Latin American Research*, vol. 30, no. 1, 2011, pp. 7–20. *JSTOR*. Accessed May 7, 2024.

Schofield, Camilla, and Ben Jones. "'Whatever Community Is, This Is Not It': Notting Hill and the Reconstruction of 'Race' in Britain after 1958". *Journal of British Studies*, vol. 58, no. 1, 2019, pp. 142–73. *core.ac.uk*. Accessed May 13, 2024.

Sherwood, Marika. *Claudia Jones – A Life in Exile*. Lawrence & Wishart, 1999.

Slepičková, Kristýna. "The Teddy Boy Subculture in Britain." PhD thesis. University of West Bohemia, 2020.

Smith, Evan. "Conflicting Narratives of Black Youth Rebellion in Modern Britain". *Ethnicity and Race in a Changing World: A Review Journal*, vol. 1, no. 3, 2010, pp. 16–31. *ResearchGate*. Accessed May 13, 2024.

Sturman, Rachel. "Indian Indentured Labor and the History of International Rights Regimes." *The American Historical Review*, vol. 119, no. 5, 2014, pp. 1439–65. *JSTOR*. Accessed May 13, 2024.

"Theatres and Dance Halls Act 1934." *Ministry of the Attorney General and Legal Affairs*. rgd.legalaffairs.gov.tt. Accessed May 24, 2024.

Thomas, Jeffrey. "The Changing Role of the Steel Band in Trinidad and Tobago: Panorama and the Carnival Tradition." *Studies in Popular Culture*, vol. 9, no. 2, 1986, pp. 96–108. *JSTOR*. Accessed May 13, 2024.

Tsuji, Teruyuki. "The 'Other Half': The Articulation of Carnival in Nineteenth-Century Trinidad". *Carnival Theory and Practice*. Edited by Christopher Innes et al. Africa World Press, 2013, pp. 79–91. *Internet Archive*. Accessed May 13, 2024.

Warner, Keith Q. *Kaiso! The Trinidad Calypso*. Three Continents Press, 1982.

Warner-Lewis, Maureen. *Trinidad Yoruba: From Mother Tongue to Memory*. University of Alabama Press, 2009.

Winer, Lise. "Socio-Cultural Change and the Language of Calypso." *Nieuwe West-Indische Gids/New West Indian Guide*, vol. 60, no. 3/4, 1986, pp. 113–48. *JSTOR*. Accessed May 13, 2024.

Younge, Gary. "The Politics of Partying." *The Guardian*, Aug. 17, 2002. Accessed May 12, 2024.

4 Play, Joy, Freedom and Compliance – Carnivalesque Leadership in Education

Introducing children to a model of compliance that will be unconsciously revisited throughout their lives, Carnivalesque Leadership is identifiable in schools across the world. The experience of safety-valve release; the dissolution of the individual into the collective (during a time of developing individuality); the regularity of communal eating and drinking, mask play and parody; and, if you are lucky, the social and emotional release of humour and laughter are common and naturalised elements of much school experience.[1] Typifying the early stages of my research into Carnivalesque Leadership and as a huge caveat, this chapter remains introductory in its leaping exploration of Carnivalesque Leadership in schools and the generalising links and associations started here require much deeper exploration. In teacher-talk, this is a reasonable start but further work is needed. Whilst the meta-level discussion offered in this chapter remains theoretical, this exploration is dappled with anecdotal evidence from my own experiences as a pupil, school teacher and school leader.

Some of a child's first experiences in school are based around play. Recognition of the importance of play dates back (at least) to the Ancient Greeks, and influential educational theorists and researchers have identified play as crucial in building cognitive function and as a means of learning social contracts and expectations.[2] Piaget identifies play with cognitive development and explores a framework that establishes different stages of early life development moving from "practice play," "symbolic play" to "play with rules." Vygotsky explores play as developmental through its movement beyond normal behaviours and the developed need to follow the "rules" of play. This aspect of play, in fostering rule awareness and compliance, is of particular interest from the perspective of this book as it suggests that play is a means to learn rules and understand social dynamics. In a carnivalesque model, play becomes associated with a temporary suspension of those rules, the understanding of which may have been fostered by play itself. Arguing that "play is not trivial" (cited by Musselman 25), Froebel outlined approaches based on stories, songs and games in the 1840s and

DOI: 10.4324/9781003441649-5

developed concrete material, "gifts," to promote play (Woodard 138). All three theorists – Piaget, Vygotsky and Froebel – offer a vision of play as vital in the education of young children. Whilst a detailed exploration of these developmental aspects of play and potential alignment/enabling of the carnivalesque is beyond the remit of this book, this brief outline, which superficially samples three key theorists, highlights the importance of play in schools, notably in early years and primary/kindergarten stages.[3]

In *Rabelais and His World*, Mikhail Bakhtin comments on the impact of carnival freedom on education, arguing that "[n]ot only could the students relax from the official ideological system, from scholarly wisdom and academic rules, but they were allowed to transform these disciplines into gay, degrading games, and jokes" (Bakhtin 83). The application of Bakhtin's ideas to education has taken divergent routes. Whilst the appropriation of Bakhtinian philosophy to any distinct sphere risks distorting his original concepts (this book, in itself, is a shameless example), the generation of critical dialogue between Bakhtinian philosophy and education theory opens up new insights and new potential. Critical examples of such application include DaSilva Iddings and McCafferty's exploration of how Bakhtin's carnival can be applied to second language learning in the US kindergarten environment, with the potential for the playful mocking of hierarchical order and creative language play.[4] Focusing more on the infinitely relational, White considers how the philosophical tenets of Bakhtin's dialogism (compared to a Vygotskian dialectical approach) would reposition pedagogical models away from outcomes (specific knowledge/skills acquisition) to a focus on process and making meaning through multiple discourses, with the teacher also engaging in the "unfinalised" learning process. Also breaking down the boundaries between teacher and pupil, Chen explores learning as a "side-by-side" engagement that "evokes democratization" linked to Bakhtin's emphasis on the relational (1259) and Edmiston explores an application of Bakhtin's "answerability, authorship and action" and "dialogism" along a teaching and learning path of mutual dialogic discovery through dramatic inquiry (198). Rather than focusing on the dialogic aspects of Bakhtin's philosophy and applying to school contexts, this chapter explores how school leaders across the world employ Carnivalesque Leadership components to release tension in school systems and, potentially, offer models for longer-term change through controlled subversion and breaks from the established norm. This chapter will start to map a Carnivalesque Leadership model by tracking curricular and extra-curricular routes and operationally driven mechanisms for collectivity, charting methods for embedding compliance and then subsequent planned temporary subversion as well as exploring the continuing use of folk traditions in schools that represent the continuation of alternative, "un-official" modes.

One of the most common carnivalesque components – the dissolution of the individual into the collective – is delivered globally through school curricula, with the subjects of music, drama, dance and sport all offering the potential for group interaction and performance for varying degrees of communal involvement which can be seen to prioritise the collective over the individual. The commonality of carnivalesque collectivity globally is evidenced in the increasing standardisation of school curricula. Many countries including England, Finland, Kenya and India all, to varying degrees, have centralised curriculum models.[5] Since its staggered launch from 1988, the National Curriculum in England has set out the primary curriculum to feature "foundation subjects" which include music and physical education.[6] Physical education is continued throughout the secondary curriculum in Key Stage Three and Key Stage Four, with music non-compulsory at Key Stage Four. The physical education curriculum itself includes dance as compulsory at Key Stage One, Two and Three and referenced as an option at Key Stage Four. Compulsory physical education is promoted in India's relatively new National Curriculum Framework for School Education. Music and dance are also highlighted as essential aspects of the arts education subject area for the curriculum planning. Physical education is a core subject in Kenyan upper primary, lower and upper senior schools, with dance and music available as optional subjects at secondary. At lower primary, physical education features in the Movement and Creative Arts curriculum strand and music features within the Creative Arts curriculum strand of the Kenyan upper primary.[7] One of the most influential education systems in the world over the past few decades is in Finland.[8] Physical education has been a discrete and compulsory subject within that curriculum since the mid-nineteenth century.[9] The United States does not have a national curriculum imposed by the federal government, with the closest equivalent being the Common Core State Standards Initiative introduced in 2010. The lack of a national curriculum has been identified as a barrier to ensuring that pupils undertake impactful physical education. For example, "The Society of Health and Physical Educators" 2016 report on the status of physical education in the United States identifies the diversity of state education legislative and regulatory activity as an ongoing challenge in children developing physically active behaviours.

Focusing on the building of collectivity, the first discrete discipline under consideration for potential alignment with the carnivalesque model in this chapter is physical education. From the standard timetabled school day to more high-profile performances representing the school, an individual pupil can be given opportunity within collective identity which can foster coherence, compliance and loyalty to the institution. The idea of collective identity through sport, for example, is typified by the UK's Youth Sports Trust's 2022 statement of the aim of harnessing the power of play and sport to "build belonging" (4). Personally, I have fond memories of my primary school sports day. I was in the blue team, along with Jo Wheeler and Shazza. My mate Jeanette was in the red team. This was my first conscious experience of the loss of individual in the collective. It was about the team. Was this subversive, temporary resistance to existing hierarchy? No. Was it a safety-valve release that built collectivity? Yes. Am I introducing some sleight of hand into the carnivalesque model by treating the collective and the subversive separately? Possibly. But opportunities for temporary subversion for the collective will form part of the later discussion once mechanisms for compliance through collectivity have been explored.

Globally, the rationale for teaching physical education in schools unsurprisingly focuses on the public health objectives of promoting a healthy, physically active lifestyle. Governmental and public health institution guidelines drive forward the importance of a physical education being maintained through adolescence and into adulthood.[10] In addition to being driven through national governments, the importance of physical education in school curricula is promoted globally by UNESCO,[11] the World Health Organisation[12] and the European Parliament.[13] Hardman identifies that "a majority of countries (89% primary schools; 87% secondary schools) have legal requirements for PE in schools" (7). The relative commonality of physical education within the global school curricula means that the subject is very much embedded in the lives of the majority of children across the globe. The perceived benefits of physical education as a core element of school curricular can be summarised as physical, social affective and cognitive.[14] Whilst the rationale for making physical education a core aspect of national curricular is based on health and wellbeing, rather than a carnival impulse, the break from classroom normality that physical education provides, the involvement in the collective rather than focusing on individual academic work, does provide some form of basic carnivalesque release.

I remember the relief and freedom provided by PE lessons at my primary school and the difference to how I felt after we returned to the classroom after PE. I would be refocused and refreshed from the change that PE had provided. I also remember feeling, year on year, significantly less joy about PE lessons at my secondary school given that negative body image issues had started to become more powerful than the joy of safety-valve release from the norm. My school experience as a pupil was prior to the National Curriculum, which has made it an entitlement for all state pupils to have PE as part of their core curriculum until the age of 16, and therefore I chose music instead of PE and stopped all forms of body-shaming exercise and sporting safety-valve release in my school curriculum at the end of Year 9 (aged 14 – and, *of course*, my body self-image just got worse rather than better by dropping PE).

With PE as an example, school curricular and extra-curricular activities enable school leaders to generate collectivity and, with it, a sense of belonging. Collectivity and belonging can play a significant role in building compliance within a school. Another major means of building collectivity is through the adoption of school uniform. A school leader's decision to mandate school uniform offers Carnivalesque Leadership potential. Firstly, the very uniformity of school uniform offers the potential for the dissolution of the individual into the collective. Secondly, the strategic use of exceptional non-uniform days can provide a classic safety-valve release by temporarily suspending norms of uniform requirements before the return of these expectations.

School uniforms can be traced in England back to the charitable institutions of the sixteenth century. Stephenson highlights how "charity schools supplied much-needed clothing to the children that they educated and this constitutes the first widespread use of school uniform" and that such "garments allowed those in authority to imprint their own social values upon the pupils" (7). Stephenson focuses on Christ's Hospital, which opened in Newgate Street, London in 1552 and boasts a distinctive uniform comprising long blue coat, belted at the waist, worn with matching knee breeches (boys) or skirt (girls), yellow socks and white neck bands. This uniform was introduced early in the school's history and seems to have barely changed for nearly 500 years. According to the school, which is fee paying independent and the UK's largest bursary charity school, the uniform is worn every single day of the academic year.

Stephenson focuses on the social and cultural implications of English public schools adopting uniforms, arguing that they "emphasized class-related concepts of manliness and leadership through the rules, rituals and activities associated with the public school ethos" (36). One of the most famous single-sex independent schools in the world, Eton College, famously has a uniform of black tailcoat/morning coat, black waistcoat, pinstriped trousers and white necktie with top hat for special occasions. There are also distinctions within the school uniform. Those assigned as elite prefects in The Eton Society, informally known as "Pop," don a waistcoat of their own design and checked trousers. These uniforms are worn every day except for the June 4 in recognition of the school's great patron, George III, whose birthday it is. On this day, Eton boys take part in a traditional water pageant which dates back to 1793. For these events, the boys wear naval uniforms of the mid-nineteenth century and the donning of a flower garland is common on straw boater hats. Considered the "great yearly festival of Etonians" (Collins 166), the June 4 tradition (which is not always held on that specific date) has developed into a larger event than just the water procession and now operates as an open day, with exhibitions, concerts, speeches and cricket. The change in dress code for this event signifies a break from the norm and a release from the usual constraints.[15] The first water pageants were organised by the boys themselves and operated beyond the sphere of the College to such an extent that, when asked to see the spectacle by King William IV, the disciplinarian headteacher at the time, Dr Keate, claimed not to know there was such a thing. Only later did the event come under the control of the College itself, and the adoption of the naval uniform reflects the formalisation of the previously informal event. Here, then, is an example of a potentially subversive release from the norm becoming part of the school's official traditions.[16]

Less "unique" school uniforms are the norm in British schools. The normalisation of school uniform in the British collective consciousness was brought into stark relief for me as a child when a local school adopted a non-uniform policy, pupils called teachers by their first names and they started to follow a very different curriculum. The world, it seemed, had been turned on its head. Some years later, when the leadership of the school came under significant pressure because of below national standard pupil outcomes, the adoption of a school uniform was the first of many changes.

Benefits offered by a mandated school uniform can include the embedding of a collective identity, the seeming removal of a clothing inequality which prompts envy and bullying (which, in turn, can lead to theft, abuse and violence), the removal of gang affiliation and alliance signified by clothing choices and the establishment of a "norm" of clothing that is age appropriate meaning that pupils will focus not on what they are wearing but on what they are studying. When commenting on the importance of school uniform for children in Kenya, Cabinet Secretary for Education, Professor George Magoha, stated, "School uniforms are essential for students to learn in a disciplined and orderly environment. School uniforms help to instill a sense of pride and belonging in students" (Kamau).[17] The debate surrounding the proposed institutional benefits of adopting school uniforms has been playing out in the United States over the past 30 years.

In his State of The Union Address of January 23, 1996, President Bill Clinton aligned pupil character with dress code, stating

> I challenge all our schools to teach character education, to teach good values and good citizenship. And if that means that teenagers will stop killing each other over designer jackets, then our public schools should be able to require their students to wear school uniforms.

Two years later in July 1998, the President addressed the American Federation of Teachers and stated that pupils "need to feel free" and urged for a situation whereby a "student is no longer obsessed by another student's sneakers or designer jackets, and where students are focused not on appearances but on learning, crime and violence go down, attendance and learning go up." Just over a month later, the US federal government sanctioned the distribution of a school uniform manual to all school districts which directly positioned the adoption of school uniforms as a response to growing levels of violence in American schools.[18] The manual expounds the potential benefits of school uniforms to include:

- decreasing violence and theft – even life-threatening situations – among students over designer clothing or expensive sneakers.
- helping prevent gang members from wearing gang colours and insignia at school.
- instilling students with discipline.
- helping parents and students resist peer pressure.
- helping students concentrate on their school work.
- helping school officials recognise intruders who come into school (1).[19]

There has been significant growth in schools adopting uniform policies since 1996 in the United States.[20]

Potential disadvantages of a mandated school uniform policy include the denial of the right to personal expression at a time of developing personal identity; additional financial pressure on parents and carers to purchase specific items, sometimes from specific suppliers; and the systemic processes required to check and challenge uniform infringement which are time-consuming and workload creating.

I felt nothing but acceptance and compliance towards my primary school uniform, but there was a stark difference with my feelings towards uniform at my secondary school that had nothing to do with the uniform or the school but more to do with my maturing struggle to understand individual identity. The very uniformity felt confining. Looking back, the uniform was not even that confining (black *or* blue skirt/trousers, white blouse/shirt, blue *or* black jumper; *no* tie and *no* blazer) compared to the uniform dress codes I later maintained as a school principal. Indeed, as a school principal, pupil compliance with school uniform was often seen as a direct reflection of my school leadership during quality assurance activities. Looking back, my own baggage about school uniform was probably a significant reason for resisting obsessing about the minutia of exact school uniform compliance in the way that other (more successful?) headteachers did. I was, however, always interested in the impact of non-school uniform days (one of the initial drivers for exploring Carnivalesque Leadership potential in schools). There was always a striking difference in pupil behaviour and interactions during non-uniform days. Without the uniformity of uniform, some pupils lost self-discipline as the freedom from uniform triggered the testing of normal hierarchies. Other pupils exhibited more collaborative behaviours potentially because they felt more confident in their individualised status.

But, overall, the temporary release from the norm of school uniform was a useful tool in the subsequent reinforcing of expectations.

A school leaders' decision to allow pupils not to wear school uniform for a day can have significant impact. The temporary freedom from normal routines and the eradication of normal rigid expectations and control represent a clear example of carnivalesque freedom. This, in turn, can let out pressure from within school settings simply by facilitating change. Moreover, the rigid symbolic hierarchies of power between pupils and staff are also lessened when pupils are not uniformly presented in uniform and staff adopt a more casual dress code for the day. The significant change to normal school routines through the use of non-uniform days remains a temporary release. Where this model may have more longer-term significance is the temporary removal of school uniform expectations and the sanctioning of community/cultural/heritage clothing which enables the celebration and visibility of cultural traditions. Such sanctioned subversion from standard uniform expectations is an opportunity for developing understanding and awareness. This is not a simple switch to individualism rather than the collective identity of a school but one that pauses homogenous expectations of a school body to celebrate and make visible the alignments of pupils with other collective identities.

Such community-orientated days can also include the sampling of different foods associated with different cultures. More operationally, breaks from the structures of classroom/learning space norm also happen daily through social times and the consumption of food. As a general rule, food is served communally in schools for the very practical reasons of timetable schedules, cost-efficiency and supervision. If a child brings in a packed lunch, provision will be made for the consumption of that food. Some children may consume their food in canteen-style environments whilst others may consume whilst undertaking other activities. Whatever the model, there is a break in academic routine for the consumption of food (an analysis of the subversive sneaking of a snack at non-sanctioned times is beyond the scope of this chapter). Traditional models of school dinners are therefore communal. As outlined in Chapter 2, the impact of communal eating is multifaceted and the causality of impact complex. Bakhtin's interest in communal eating is clearly rooted in festivals and carnival whilst communal eating in schools happens every day. Schools in England and Wales were given permission in law to provide food via The Education (Provision of Meals) Act (1906) which set out to make provision of meals for children attending Public Elementary Schools. The Act makes clear that a charge levied at parents for this service could be recovered as a civil debt "unless they are satisfied that the parent is unable by reason of circumstances other than his own default to pay the amount" (2.1). The Education Act 1944 made providing school meals and milk a statutory duty for local authorities (49).

There have been significant changes in school meal provision in England and around the world in line with changing eating routines in family homes. Brannen and Storey characterise the shift from school dinner as a "proper meal" without a range of choice to a market-led, choice-driven food item provision, leading to greater individualisation of food items (75). Highlighting the health mandate of school meal provision and conformity, they argue that "the social aspects of eating may also enhance (or adversely affect) health while at the same time constrain the ability of individuals to determine their own diet" (74). The tension between communal eating and individualisation is also foregrounded by Fischler who asks "Is Sharing Meals a Thing of the Past?" in his exploration of changing habits. Focusing on the rise in dietary requirements as signalling differences that can lead to alienation and individualisation, Fischler argues that eating together "is seen as bringing people together . . . it means symbolically building or rebuilding a common destiny" (5). Fischler identifies a marked different between the "communal dimension" still associated with French hospitality and social eating compared to the more "contractual" habits displayed in US and UK culture (9).

Whilst break and lunch slots are a hiatus in controlled learning within a school day, I am not suggesting they operate on an equivalent level on the safety-valve scale as calendared festivals. However, on a smaller, more regular scale, I am comfortable arguing that communal eating at break and lunch in schools does operate as a mini safety-valve release through social bonding, laughter potential and food consumption. Food is consumed in schools at social times, and it is part of the endorphin release cycle.

My personal recollections of communal eating in schools are mixed, from the shame (at that point in time) of being one of the handful of kids on free school meals and therefore the dinner ladies being so very vocal about ticking my name off the little list, to the occasional bafflement at what I was eating for desert (always with the thinnest of custards in the strangest of colours) to the occasional battleground of the boisterous secondary school canteen with the tables acquisitioned by specific friendship groups. Back then, the school canteen was frequently a venue for fights and bullying and was characterised by shouting and raucous laughter. It was a time and space for the unsanctioned, the subversive, wedged between restrictive and controlled timetabled lessons. Much has changed in English schools since the 1980s, but social times can still be testing times for school leaders in terms of ensuring decent catering services, safe and appealing serveries and canteen facilities and the fact that the pupils may not function in the same compliant way during break and lunchtime as they do in lesson time and neither may the staff.

Given that I am an ex-school teacher/leader (2002–2022) and I had my own experiences of attending primary (1977–1984) and secondary school

(1984–1988), my positioning in this chapter is dappled with anecdotal evidence. I justify the anecdotal leanings of this chapter in a reportedly academic text through its exploratory nature, its starting point for further investigation. My first memory of school isn't actually my own memory. It is my sister's. My primary school was literally at the bottom of our garden. My false memory tells me that the sounds of country dancing music blasting out on the school playground would drift across to me in my pre-school summers. As a stereotypical second child, I had two introductions to primary school: one through the eyes and experiences of my elder (by two years) sister, Julie, and one of my own. My sister definitely experienced Maypole dancing, country dancing, communal trips to the local cinema, sports day, school discos, music participation and communal eating events before I did, and therefore my anticipation was shaped by her experiences. Sports days, country dancing and discos were associated with the end of the academic year. In the English climate, there is a practical reason for the timing of country dancing and sports days in UK schools, but this increased the association with freedoms from usual constraints. I am genuinely unsure how much time was dedicated to country dancing and remember a mix of huge enjoyment and a real sense of anxiety anticipating that I would head off in the wrong direction or drop the ribbon of the school maypole. Whatever the reality, my sister and our friends, Caroline, Jeanette, Jo Wheeler, and Shazza, all joyfully country danced and circled the maypole every summer during our primary school years. Until researching Carnivalesque Leadership in education for this book, I had not realised how common maypole dancing was when I was growing up in England or, indeed, how popular it still is in many schools globally. The subversive potential of May Day and its folk traditions, including the maypole, date back centuries. In this subsection, I shall consider the subversive, safety-valve potential of sanctioned May Day traditions, particularly those associated with schools.

The maypole is associated with the festivities around May Day, the "maddest merriest day" according to Tennyson's poem "The May Queen" (1833). This combination of "maddest" and "merriest" has been a well-documented source of consternation for centuries. Philip Stubbes' "Anatomie of Abuses" (1583) is critical of festival goers who seek out a suitable tree which they "bring home with great veneration" and then cover with "floures and hearbes" and "bound round about with strings from the top to the bottome and sometimes painted with variable colours." Stubbes laments how the locals "fall they to daunce about it. Like as the heathen people did at the dedication of the Idols" (Stubbes 149). Antagonism to the maypole tradition peaked during the Commonwealth Republic (1649–1660) in England during which time maypoles were banned. The Restoration of the monarchy in 1660 signalled the reintroduction of maypoles and mayday festivities. Samuel Pepys comments on the erection of three maypoles in Deal, Kent, in his diary entry for May 1, 1660, and refers to the huge permanent maypole that had been erected at the Strand in central London in his diary entry for June 29, 1661. Here, then, in a carnivalesque topsy-turvy move, carnivalesque freedom is associated with the restoration of the monarchy rather than the puritan rule of the Commonwealth Republic.

Whilst there was much celebration of the return of May Day festivities, symbolised by the maypole and captured in Robert Herrick's poem "The Maypole" (1660) which begins "The maypole is up/Now give me the cup," the revival of such traditions did not please everyone. For example, Thomas Hall's "Funebria Flora, the Downfall of May Games" (1660) captures the disapproval of unruly peasants indulging in merrymaking and opposes "the Rascality and rout, in this their open prophanenesse, and Heathenish Customs." The associations of May Day festivities and the maypole with licentiousness and freedoms disapproved of by Puritans led to the most famous story of maypoles in recorded American history which centres on the maypole erected by early English colonist, Thomas Morton, in the colony of Wollaston on Algonquian land soon renamed Merrymount. Festivities at Merrymount drew the attention of Puritan governor, William Bradford, who labelled Morton a "Lord of Misrule" thus making clear links to ancient Saturnalian rituals and festivities (outlined in Chapter 1 in relation to Bakhtin's carnival) suggesting that the participants had "anew revived & celebrated the feasts of ye Roman Goddes Flora, or ye beasly practieses of ye madd Bacchinalians" (Bradford entry for Anno Dom: 1628).[21] Referring to the Merrymount maypole, Thompson highlights how maypoles had become "a symbol of opposition to Puritanical rule" (*Mayday Festivals in America* 43) which have been, at times, known as "Liberty Poles" and performed a role as host for nailing communications for opposition to British rule.

May Day traditions fell out of fashion in England by the eighteenth century, with many permanent maypoles falling into disrepair and not replaced. However, philosopher, John Ruskin, influenced the revival of May Day traditions in the 1880s including maypole dancing in England. In 1881, Ruskin persuaded the Principal of Whitelands College (now part of Roehampton University), John Faunthorpe, to instigate a May Day ceremony, complete with May Queen.[22] Whitelands College keeps the May Day traditions alive today and crowned the first May King in 1986 and now recognises May Monarchs. When education became compulsory in the 1880s, the relationship between folk dance and schools grew in line with the fashion for "Olde England" and, Parry argues, "the spread of ribbon Maypole dances was furthered by a new generation of lady school teachers who enjoyed such genteel exercise" (7). An alternative argument that Parry does not consider is that "lady school teachers" may have enjoyed the maypole connotations of licentious freedom and subversion as well as benefitting from the "genteel exercise."

The more general role of dance in English school life was recognised in 1952 guidance from the Ministry of Education for primary schools on "Moving and Growing" which characterised dance as an "overflow of feeling, energy or excitement" and recognised familiarity with folk dances (94). Folk dancing was relatively common in English primary schools well into the 1980s.[23] The introduction of the National Curriculum in England (mentioned earlier) is one of the reasons why folk dance is not as common as it was in my childhood. However, many primary schools in England do maintain this tradition. With the village boasting a 64-feet maypole (one of only a handful of permanent maypoles remaining in England), Offenham CE First School in Worcestershire takes part in the Wake Day celebrations including maypole dancing, and many village schools in Northamptonshire include maypole dancing as part of their curriculum.[24] For example, Paulerspury C.E. Primary School near Towcester holds a festival of dance annually, and each class learns a traditional country dance and two classes learn maypole.

Maypole dancing takes place in many countries across the world. May Day traditions involving maypole dancing remain a tradition in some US colleges and elementary schools. Thompson argues that maypole dances "were common in America in the late nineteenth century and the first half of the twentieth" ("The Plaited Maypole" 13).[25] Colleges still celebrating May Day include Bryn Mayr College, a women's college, whose traditions include crowning of two may queens, five maypoles, humorous speeches and anti-patriarchal songs.[26] The potentially subversive associations of such traditions fit neatly into the subversive potential of May Day and maypoles and, of course, to the subversive aspects of the carnivalesque.

Schools in Jamaica teach maypole dancing as a traditional dance of Jamaican culture. Maypoles, also referred to as Long Ribbon Pole, are prominent in celebrations of Jamaican independence and emancipation from British rule. During the first independence day celebrations of August 6, 1962, at least sixty-three villages included maypole dancing as part of their celebrations.[27] St Vincent and the Grenadines and Trinidad and Tobago also boast the maypole dance as a national dance. Nicaragua has a strong tradition of maypole dancing, Palo de Mayo, as does Panama, Honduras and Belize.

The presence of maypole dancing (also referred to as variants of ribbon dancing) across the world might be associated with the legacy of European colonial rule. The subsequent continuation of the folk traditions during independence celebrations therefore could represent a celebratory reframing of the tradition. However, such a Eurocentric reading belies the role played by those enslaved in Africa and transported to the regions and belies the indigenous cultures of the regions in the development of festival traditions. The origins of maypole are not "simply" European and may be as rooted in the Egyptian worship of Osiris as they are in ancient Roman celebrations of the fertility festival of Florali. Maypole traditions as we know them today can also be traced to pagan Europe, notably medieval Germany, and the addition of ribbons can be traced to Italy and promoted by the "Merry Old England" marketing of John Ruskin.[28] Maypole is both a symbol of officialdom (national dance status) and a symbol of subversion (leading to Puritan banning). The prevalence of maypole dancing as part of independence day celebrations further highlights this dual symbolism as independence days commemorate subversion of previous hierarchical status but also shows its assimilation into a new officialdom. Further associating May Day with challenges to hierarchical power structures, May Day is also known as International Workers' Day and Labour Day in some countries thereby reflecting licenced suspension of normal hierarchies as it often means a holiday from work. Haddad directly links the Russian traditions of May Day to Bakhtin's carnival and highlights how the influential Anatoly Lunacharsky argues that May Day celebrations in Russia had been subsumed into the official yet retained characteristics of the unofficial.

Whilst I am not suggesting that the gentle maypole dancing undertaken in schools represents the kind of licentious freedoms and phallic/fertility symbolism that so concerned the Puritans, I am suggesting that such activities in schools can still represent carnivalesque freedoms. For me, my sister, Caroline, Jeanette, Jo Wheeler and Shazza at primary school, it did operate as a safety-valve break from the norm and provide an opportunity for the dissolution of the individual into the collective. We danced together. And we laughed together. Such opportunities for collective fun play a significant role in school life but are usually maintained for another reason, such as cultural capital, health and fitness and collaboration. Such activities can be more significant in enabling pupils and staff to be "freed from the heavy chains of devout seriousness" (Bakhtin 83). Research into the role of laughter in delivering education has taken different forms. Wanzer et al. argue that "instructors have used humour as long as there have been educational institutions" (2) and offer a useful summary of approaches taken before specifically exploring the impact on student learning of instructor humour. Vecchio et al. offer a pragmatic exploration of why educational leaders may frequently use humour to achieve strategic aims, stating that educational leaders "have recourse to fewer extrinsic levers by which they can motivate employees" because of financial constraints, and that humour is a cheap means of establishing community and reducing tension. As such, humour "may be relied on more readily as a social influence tactic in an education setting, relative to other organizational settings, because interpersonal relations is one of the few influence mechanisms available to an educational administrator" (Vecchio et al. 173).

More specifically relevant for this book, the application of Bakhtinian laughter to the education sector is considered by Vlieghe, who analyses spontaneous laughter in formal schooling. Vlieghe explores the role of spontaneous laughter as challenge to social order and identifies its threat to the authority of teachers. Here, Vlieghe draws on Bakhtin's work on Rabelais. For Vlieghe, laughter is not a simplistic subversive challenge to social order but, rather, represents moments of self-dispossession which dissolves boundaries of identity, rank and hierarchy in entirety. Also considering the impact on established school hierarchies, White considers how Bakhtin's exploration of Rabelasian carnivalesque humour can apply to early childhood teachers who operate as dialogic partners with both horizontal and vertical roles and experiencing humour with young children outside of the hierarchical institutional scope of schooling.

My favourite personal application of Carnivalesque Leadership in my own professional career as a school leader involved laughter, specifically the subversive laughter of the pantomime. With its roots in the Italian tradition of the Commedia dell'arte, pantomime stories are based on traditional folk tales, with long-established conventions of gender role reversal, subversion of traditional power hierarchies, comic characters and slapstick physical comedy, bawdy humour and a narrative centred on good versus evil. I am not sure who benefitted more from the release offered by staff Christmas pantomimes at our school (circa 2004–7 performances of *Snow White and the Seven Teachers*, *Cinderella* and *Aladdin [A Lad in Name Only*]), staff watching, staff taking part or pupils in the audience. Experiencing seeing two very respected male senior leaders in full drag as the Ugly Sisters in Cinderella was a lived example of carnivalesque subversion. For our pupils, seeing figures of authority in slightly ridiculous situations, through the masks of drag, changed the dynamics of power momentarily. Indeed, the sanctioned booing enabled by panto, the bawdy celebration of fun can momentarily shift power dynamics and is, perhaps, some of the earliest childhood exposure to the carnivalesque spirit with its dissolution of the individual into the collective through audience participation ("he's behind you . . . oh no he isn't . . . oh yes he is"), mask wearing, gender stereotype subversion and temporary release from existing power hierarchies.[29]

School trips to the pantomime can be the first introduction to live theatre for many children (although I am not convinced that my writing and directing of school pantos delivered "in-house" didn't put children off live theatre for life). The traditional dual address of pantomime is rich with potential for Bakhtinian dialogism and double-voicing with language choices aimed at children and with bawdy potential for the adult audience. For example, Sir Ian McKellen, starring as Mother Goose in the 2022 pantomime at Duke of York's Theatre in London's West End, uttered the immortal line when pondering the local wildlife: "I'm fond of a cockatoo" to the delight of the adults whilst driving the narrative forward for the children.[30] Providing sanctioned release from normal expectations, pantomime is a commodified form of carnivalesque freedom from hierarchy.

Pupils' enjoyment of the reversal of established hierarchies and opportunities for safety-valve release in schools is evident in other "non-standard" events. Charity and community events can be rich with opportunities for school leaders to momentarily shake off the rigidity of hierarchy. I have rarely seen children as happy as when clutching a cold soggy sponge ready to be hurled (usually with some venom) at a member of school leadership voluntarily trapped in mock medieval stocks. Raising money for charity, such events have provided anecdotal evidence over the years of the advantages of momentarily enabling freedom from established power hierarchies in order to establish different relational status.

This chapter has mostly considered components of Carnivalesque Leadership as if in separate silos without much consideration of overlap. Such extrapolation can lead to seeing the carnivalesque in anything remotely fun, which is clearly not the case. In school settings, the full force and potential of Carnivalesque Leadership might best be experienced during a week that features the basics of communal eating, lessons in PE, dance, music, drama, a non-school uniform day, a community event that dissolves hierarchy and a pantomime (if around Christmas) or maypole/country dancing and/or sports day (if in the summer). As such the carnivalesque operates in a cycle of play, joy, freedom and compliance. In this exploratory model, such safety-valve experiences, such temporary subversions, release tensions from school organisations and thereby enable norms and structures to be reinstated afterwards as well as offer the potential for longer-term change through exposure to different relational modes and increased visibility of alternative collective identities.

Notes

1 The privilege involved in this statement is clear. Not every child in the world experiences education in this way. It is simplistic to acknowledge this but impossible not to.

2 See Andreu-Cabrera et al. for a detailed discussion of evidence charting ancient Greek attitudes to childhood play.

3 This shift to discussions of play may represent some slippage in the Carnivalesque Leadership model outlined here. However, references to play are relevant as they superficially operate in a binary to "non-play" which can be seen as the "norm" or the "official" and play is the sanctioned release and "unofficial." There is some troubling complexity beneath this superficiality.

4 Also see Brandist et al. for a wide-ranging exploration of more recent critical engagement with Bakhtin's philosophy and education. The significance of Bakhtin's philosophy for language and literacy education is captured in Ball and Warshauer Freedman's multidisciplinary *Bakhtinian Perspectives on Language,*

Literacy, and Learning. This chapter offers some signposting to key literature applying Bakhtin to education and does not offer a full literature review.

5 There are exceptions within these systems. In England, for example, Academies and independent schools are not constrained to the National Curriculum. However, the inclusion of these subjects in such institutions is standard.

6 Art and design and design and technology also feature as foundational subjects in the National Curriculum and can be identified as offering a form of safety-valve release for pupils. The decision to focus on music, drama, dance and PE in this chapter is based on the closer links to the traditions of festival and carnival and the collectivity in performance.

7 The shift away from the colonial legacy of an English-style curriculum and Cambridge examination boards is explored by Lillis.

8 Amongst the wealth of critical inquiry into the Finnish education system, see Kyrö and Nyyssölä for a consideration of attitudes to the curriculum. See also Hollier for an overview of explorations of the Finnish system before focusing on teacher training.

9 See Yli-Piipari.

10 For example, see US Department of Health and Human Services' 1997 publication *Guidelines for School and Community Programs to Promote Lifelong Physical Activity among Young People*. See McKenzie and Kahan for an overview of the remit of national standards for physical fitness provision in schools in the United States. The UK government's *School Sport and Activity Action Plan* was updated in 2023 and makes clear the importance of high-quality physical education to bring about a "healthier nation" and "help children into a lifetime of sport from a young age" (5).

11 See UNESCO *International Charter of Physical Education, Physical Activity and Sport* and *Quality Physical Education (QPE): Guidelines for Policy Makers.*

12 The World Health Organization's "Global Status Report of Physical Activity" considers the role of schools in the delivery and promotion of physical activity in the population.

13 The European Parliament resolution of 13 November 2007 foregrounds the EU's drive to promote physical activity that improves mental and physical wellbeing, with a focus on physical education provision in schools.

14 See Bailey et al. for a review of the evidence behind such statements.

15 Eton has potential for a fascinating examination of the carnivalesque as harnessing safety-valves not only in terms of uniform and so on but also through sanctioned subversion such as examples of the boys rallying to the cry of *Floreat seditio* (Let sedition flourish), a parody of the school motto *Floreat Etona* highlighted by Collins. Collins highlights Eton boys' rebellion against Headmaster Keate's disciplinarian approach expressed through the boys' use of umbrellas despite them being banned and uniform flouting (102).

16 Other examples of this movement from subversion to tradition include "egging" which involves pupils hurling of eggs at each other. Such traditions are increasingly assigned back to subversion rather than sanctioned, given wider prioritising of wellbeing and safety and recognition that activities such as "egging" represent sanctioned bullying and assault.

17 Evans et al. explore the impact of a Kenyan non-governmental organisation distributing free school uniforms in poor communities. The findings conclude that giving a child a uniform reduces school absenteeism by more than a third, with even greater impact for those children without uniforms to begin with in the short-term. Such a study might offer resonance with the collective identity

or simply be a very practical response to removing one of the most significant costs for Kenyan families to send their children to school. Two of the researchers involved in the 2008 study, Evans and Ngatia, then undertook an evaluation of the long-term impact on attendance of providing free school uniform to some poor pupils in Kenya but could not draw firm conclusions.

18 See Mitchell and Knechtle; DaCosta.

19 The manual provides case study examples of where and when the implementation of uniform has made a significant contribution to school district communities including Long Beach, California; Seattle, Washington; and Richmond, Virginia citing decreases in theft, assault, vandalism and truancy. See Brunsma and Rockquemore for an exploration of the validity of such claims. They report a failure to conclude on the direct effect of uniforms on behavioural outcomes or academic achievement and question why uniform is identified as a "sole factor causing a variety of positive educational outcomes" (60) when the adoption of uniform may be one aspect of a multifaceted school improvement drive. In a separate study, Brunsma also highlights the relationship between schools that introduce zero-tolerance policies and security measures such as security guards, metal detectors, sign-in policies and limited toilet breaks and school uniform policies and explores the detrimental effect of school uniform policies. The continuing lack of empirical inquiry into the advantages and disadvantages of school uniforms prompted Ansari et al.'s research into the potential link between school uniform and student behaviour. The outcomes of their work suggested no conclusive evidence to suggest that students in schools employing a uniform policy demonstrated stronger social-behavioural and engagement outcomes than those from schools without a uniform policy. Moreover, students themselves reported a lower sense of school belonging.

20 Indicator 20 of the National Center for Education Statistics' *Indicators of School Crime and Safety: 2016* outlines the levels of growth in uniform policy adoption in the United States.

21 William Bradford's *Of Plimouth Plantation* (1651) provides a first-hand account of settlement of the Puritan Pilgrims. Nathaniel Hawthorne's short story, "The May-Pole of Merry Mount" (1836) provides a fictionalised version of this history played out to reveal the tensions of Puritanism and morality.

22 The University's website features a section on the history of this tradition – "May Day at Whiteland's College."

23 See Middleton-Metcalfe's overview of research evidence for this popularity which includes reference to the 1989 Pagan report into folk activities provided a snapshot survey covering twenty-five primary schools, twenty of which taught folk dance (Dashwood 6). Badrick tracks the declining presence of folk dancing in English schools.

24 See the Offenham Village website for a brief history of the traditions of maypole.

25 Thompson challenges the commonly held post-Freudian belief that May Day maypoles are phallic symbols derived from pagan fertility.

26 See Thompson's *May Day Festivals in America* for an overview.

27 See "Maypole: Jamaica Traditional Dance" On about-jamaica.com website.

28 For more detailed explorations of the history of the maypole and its potential origins, see Parry and several texts by Thompson.

29 Wilson comments that pantomime belongs to Bakhtin's category of mocking laughter (78). Hassan et al.'s exploration of the carnivalesque in Derek Walcott's play "Pantomime" is a multilayered interrogation of relationship between the carnivalesque and pantomime. See also Jun.

30 This version of Mother Goose was written by Jonathan Harvey and directed by Cal McCrystal. See *Evening Standard* review by Curtis for other examples of bawdy punning.

Works Cited

About Jamaica. "Maypole: Jamaica Traditional Dance." *about-jamaica.com*. Accessed Jul. 25, 2024.

Andreu-Cabrera, Eliseo et al. "Play and Childhood in Ancient Greece." *Journal of Human Sport and Exercise*, vol. 5, no. 3, 2010, pp. 339–47. *JSTOR*. Accessed May 24, 2024.

Ansari, Arya, et al. "School Uniforms and Student Behavior: Is There a Link?" *Early Childhood Research Quarterly*, 1st Quarter, vol. 58, 2022, pp. 278–86. *National Library of Medicine*. Accessed May 16, 2024.

Badrick, Kate. 'Folk Dancing & the School Curriculum – A Study of the Undervaluation of Part of the English Cultural Heritage in the Education System." Study Report for the Teaching Fellowship Scheme of the Essex Institute of Higher Education, December 1986.

Bailey, Richard, et al. "The Educational Benefits Claimed for Physical Education and School Sport: An Academic Review." *Research Papers in Education*, vol. 24, no. 1, 2009, pp. 1–27. *ResearchGate*. Accessed May 16, 2024.

Bakhtin, Mikhail. *Rabelais and His World.*. Translated by Hélène Iswolsky. Indiana University Press, 1984.

Ball, Arnetha F., and Sarah Warshauer Freedman. *Bakhtinian Perspectives on Language, Literacy, and Learning*. Cambridge University Press, 2004.

Bourne, Paul Andrew, and Ruth Owen-Wright. "Education in Jamaica: A Need for Redefinition and a Changing of the Old Philosophy of Education." *International Journal of Research in Humanities and Social Studies*, vol. 5, no. 2, 2018, pp. 36–41. *ResearchGate*. Accessed May 16, 2024.

Bradford, William. History of "Plimouth Plantation." *The Project Gutenberg*. E-Text Prepared by Juliet Sutherland and Leonard Johnson. 2019. *gutenberg.org*. Accessed May 16, 2024.

Brandist, Craig, et al. "Bakhtin in the Fullness of Time – Bakhtinian Thought and the Process of Social Education." *Educational Philosophy and Theory*, vol. 49, 2017. *Taylor and Francis Online*. Accessed May 16, 2024.

Brannen, Julia, and Pamela Storey. "School Meals and the Start of Secondary School." *Health Education Research*, vol. 13, no. 1, 1998, pp. 73–86. *JSTOR*. Accessed May 16, 2024.

Brunsma, David. "School Uniform Policies in Public Schools." *Principal*, vol. 85, no. 3, Jan-Feb. 2006, pp. 50–3.

Brunsma, David, and Kerry A. Rockquemore. "Effects of Student Uniforms on Attendance, Behavior Problems, Substance Use, and Academic Achievement." *The Journal of Educational Research*, vol. 92, no. 1, 1998, pp. 53–62. *ResearchGate*. Accessed May 16, 2024.

Chen Johnsson, Mary. "Practitioner Meets Philosopher: Bakhtinian Musings on Learning with Paul". *Educational Philosophy and Theory*, vol. 45, no.12, 2013, pp. 1252–63. Accessed May 16, 2024.

Clinton, President William Jefferson. "State of the Union Address." Jan. 23, 1996. *Clintonwhitehouse4.archives.gov*. Accessed May 16, 2024.

Clinton, President William Jefferson. "Remarks by the President to the 75th Annual Convention of the American Federation of Teachers." July 20, 1998. *Clinton-whitehouse6.archives.gov*. Accessed May 16, 2024.

Collins, William L. *Etoniona Ancient and Modern, Being Notes of the History and Traditions of Eton College*. Legare Street Press, 2022.

Curtis, Nick. "Mother Goose at Duke of York's Theatre Review: Ian McKellen Makes a Triumphant Return to Panto." *The Standard*, Dec. 12, 2022. standard.co.uk. Accessed May 16, 2024.

DaCosta, Kneia. "Dress Code Blues: An Exploration of Urban Students' Reaction to a Public School Uniform Policy." *The Journal of Negro Education*, vol. 75, no. 1, 2006, pp. 49–59. *JSTOR*. Accessed Nov. 9, 2023.

Dashwood, Janet. "Folk Education in Primary Schools." *English Dance and Song*, vol. 51, no. 3, Oct. 1989.

DaSilva Iddings, Ana Christina, and Steven G. McCafferty. "Carnival in a Mainstream Kindergarten Classroom: A Bakhtinian Analysis of Second Language Learners' Off-Task Behaviors." *The Modern Language Journal*, vol. 91, no. 1, 2007, pp. 31–44. *JSTOR*. Accessed Feb. 19, 2024.

Edmiston, Brian. "Playing with Children, Answering with Our Lives: A Bakhtinian Approach to Coauthoring Ethical Identities in Early Childhood." *British Journal of Educational Studies*, vol. 58, no. 2, 2010, pp. 197–211. *JSTOR*. Accessed Feb. 19, 2024.

Education Act 1944. legislation.gov.uk. Accessed Feb. 19, 2024.

Education (Provision of Meals) Act. 1906. legislation.gov.uk. Accessed May 16, 2024.

European Parliament. " 'Role of Sport in Education." 2007. europarl.europa.eu. Accessed Feb. 19, 2024.

Evans, David K., and Mũthoni Ngatia. "School Uniforms, Short-Run Participation, and Long-Run Outcomes: Evidence from Kenya." *The World Bank Economic Review*, vol. 35, no. 3, 2021, pp. 705–19. Accessed Feb. 19, 2024.

Evans, David K., et al. "The Impact of Distributing School Uniforms on Children's Education in Kenya." 2008. edu-links.org. Accessed Feb. 19, 2024.

Fischler, Claude. editor. *Selective Eating: The Rise, Meaning and Sense of Personal Dietary Requirements*. Odile Jacob, 2015.

Haddad, Laura. "A May Day Reclamation Project." *Landscape Journal*, vol. 18, no. 2, 1999, pp. 119–36. *JSTOR*. Accessed Feb. 19, 2024.

Hall, Thomas. "Funebraie Flora, The Downfall of May Games." *Internet Archive*. Accessed May 5, 2024.

Hardman, Ken. "Physical Education in Schools: A Global Perspective." *Kinesiology*, vol. 40, no. 1, 2008, pp. 5–28. *ResearchGate*. Accessed May 5, 2024.

Hassan, Asrar, et al. "Postcolonial Carnival: The Carnivalesque Subversion in Derek Walcott's Play *Pantomime*". *Journal of Xi'an Shiyou University, Natural Science Edition*, vol. 19, no. 3, 2023. *xisdxjxsu.asia*. Accessed May 5, 2024.

Hawthorne, Nathaniel. "The May-Pole of Merry Mount." *ibiblio.org*. Accessed Jul. 25, 2024.

"The History of Eton's 4th June Celebrations." *New & Lingwood*. newandlingwood.com. Accessed May 3, 2024.

HM Government. *School Sport and Activity Action Plan 2023*. assets.publishing.service.gov.uk. Accessed May 16, 2024.

Hollier, David R. "Are We Finnished Yet? Teacher Preparation and the Rise of 'Glocalization.'" *The Journal of Education*, vol. 198, no. 2, 2018, pp. 127–35. *JSTOR*. Accessed Dec. 28, 2023.

"Jamaica Traditional Dance". *About Jamaica*. about-jamaica.com. Accessed Dec. 28, 2023.

Jun, Joon-Taek. "The Evolution of Peter Pan as a Carnivalesque Pantomime (II)—The Endings of The Manuscript, The Lord Chamberlain's Copy and The Premier of Peter Pan." *Journal of Modern English Drama*, vol. 29, no. 1, 2016, pp. 123–56. Accessed Dec. 28, 2023.

Kamau, Winnie. "Kenya's Standardized School Uniform Conversation Draws Mixed Reactions." *Talk Africa*, Oct. 27, 2023. Accessed Dec. 28, 2023.

Kyrö, Matti, and Kari Nyyssölä. "Attitudes Towards Education in Finland and Other Nordic Countries." *European Journal of Education*, vol. 41, no. 1, 2006, pp. 59–70. *JSTOR*. Accessed Dec. 28, 2023.

Lillis, Kevin M. "Processes of Secondary Curriculum Innovation in Kenya." *Comparative Education Review*, vol. 29, no. 1, 1985, pp. 80–96. *The University of Chicago Press Journals*. Accessed Dec. 28, 2023.

McKenzie, Thomas L., and David Kahan. "Physical Activity, Public Health, and Elementary Schools." *The Elementary School Journal*, vol. 108, no. 3, 2008, pp. 171–80. *The University of Chicago Press Journals*. Accessed Jan. 13, 2024.

Middleton-Metcalfe, Chloe. "Douglas Kennedy and Folk Dance in English Schools." *The Routledge Companion to English Folk Performance*. Routledge, 2021, pp. 261–76.

Ministry of Education and the Central Office of Information. "Physical Education in the Primary School Part One: Moving and Growing." 1952. education-uk.org. Accessed Jan. 13, 2024.

Mitchell, Harold, and John Knechtle. "Uniforms in Public Schools and the First Amendment: A Constitutional Analysis." *The Journal of Negro Education*, vol. 72, 2004. Accessed Jan. 13, 2024.

Musselman, Frances. "Play as Fundamental in Education." *Francis W. Parker School Year Book*, vol. 3, 1914, pp. 25–36. *JSTOR*. Accessed May 25, 2024.

National Center for Education Statistics. "Indicators of School Crime and Safety: 2016". 2017. nces.ed.gov. Accessed Jan. 13, 2024.

O'Connell, Rebecca, and Julia Brannen. "Children's Experiences of School Meals." *Families and Food in Hard Times: European Comparative Research*. UCL Press, 2021, pp. 207–30. *JSTOR*. Accessed May 16, 2024.

Offenham Village. "Offenham Wake." *offenhamvillage.co.uk*. Accessed May 16, 2024.

Parry, Caroline Balderston. "The Maypole Is Up, Now Give Me the Cup . . ." *Records of Early English Drama*, vol. 11, no. 1, 1986, pp. 7–9. *JSTOR*. Accessed May 16, 2024.

Piaget, Jean. *Play, Dreams and Imitation in Childhood*. Translated by C. Gattegno and F. M. Hodgson. Routledge, 1999.

Society of Health and Physical Educators. *Shape of the Nation*. 2016. shapeamerica.org. Accessed May 16, 2024.

Stephenson, Kate. *A Cultural History of School Uniform*. University of Exeter Press, 2021.

Stubbe, Philip. *Anatomy of the Abuses in England in Shakespeare's Youth*, A.D. 1583. Edited by Frederick J. Furnivall. wellcome collection.org. Accessed May 16, 2024.

Thompson, Allison. *Dancing Through Time – Western Social Dance in Literature, 1400–1918: Selections*. McFarland & Company Inc., 1998.

Thompson, Allison. "The Plaited Maypole Dance in America, Part 1." *Country Dance and Song Society News*, no. 190, May/Jun. 2006.

Thompson, Allison. *May Day Festivals in America, 1830 to the Present*. McFarland & Company, 2009.

UNESCO. *International Charter of Physical Education, Physical Activity and Sport*. 2015. unesdoc.unesco.org. Accessed Jul. 25, 2024.

University of Roehampton. "May Day at Whitelands College." roehampton.ac.uk.

US Department of Health and Human Services. "Guidelines for School and Community Programs to Promote Lifelong Physical Activity Among Young People." *Morbidity and Mortality Weekly Report*, vol. 46, no. RR-6, 1997. cdc.gov. Accessed May 16, 2024.

US Government. *Manual on School Uniform*. NCJRS Virtual Library, 1996. Accessed Nov. 8, 2023.

Vecchio, Robert P., et al. "The Influence of Leader Humor on Relationships between Leader Behavior and Follower Outcomes." *Journal of Managerial Issues*, vol. 21, no. 2, 2009, pp. 171–94. *JSTOR*. Accessed Jan. 13, 2024.

Vlieghe, Joris. "Laughter as Immanent Life-Affirmation Reconsidering the Educational Value of Laughter Through a Bakthinian Lens." *Educational Philosophy and Theory*, vol. 46, no. 2, 2012, pp. 148–61. *Academia*. Accessed May 16, 2024.

Vygotsky, Leo. "Play and Its Role in the Mental Development of the Child". *eric.ed.gov*. Accessed May 24, 2024.

Wanzer, Melissa Bekelja, et al. "An Explanation of the Relationship between Instructor Humor and Student Learning: Instructional Humor Processing Theory." *Communication Education*, vol. 59, no. 1, Jan. 2010, pp. 1–18. *ResearchGate*. Accessed May 16, 2024.

White, Elizabeth Jayne. "Are You 'Avin a Laff?: A Pedagogical Response to Bakhtinian Carnivalesque in Early Childhood Education." *Educational Philosophy and Theory*, vol. 46, 2014a, pp. 898–913.

White, Elizabeth Jayne. "Bakhtinian Dialogic and Vygotskian Dialectic: Compatabilities and Contradictions in the Classroom." *Educational Philosophy and Theory*, vol. 46, no. 3, 2014b, pp. 1–17.

Wilson, Robert R. "Play, Transgression and Carnival: Bakhtin and Derrida on 'Scriptor Ludens.'" *Mosaic: A Journal for the Interdisciplinary Study of Literature*, vol. 19, no. 1, 1986, pp. 73–89. *JSTOR*. Accessed May 16, 2024.

Woodard, Carol. "Gifts from the Father of the Kindergarten." *The Elementary School Journal*, vol. 79, no. 3, 1979, pp. 136–41. *JSTOR*. Accessed May 25, 2024.

World Health Organization. *Global Status Report on Physical Activity*. 2022. iris.who.int. Accessed May 16, 2024.

Yli-Piipari, Sami. "Physical Education Curriculum Reform in Finland." *Quest*, vol. 66, no. 4, Oct. 2014, pp. 468–84. *ResearchGate*. Accessed May 16, 2024.

Youth Sports Trust. "Inspiring Changemakers, Building Belonging – Our Strategy 2022–35." youthsportstrust.org. Accessed May 16, 2024.

5 Corporate Carnivalesque

The "Carry On" series of British films may seem an unlikely and somewhat controversial starting point for considering "Corporate Carnivalesque."[1] However, with its bawdy physicality, subversive potential and raucous laughter, *Carry on at Your Convenience* (1971) leads us neatly into exploring mechanisms used by leaders in the commercial and corporate world accelerated during the industrial revolution to provide safety-valve release, enable and then contain subversion *and* accommodate change in the workforce and society. *Carry on at Your Convenience* stars Sid James as a middle manager trying to balance the needs of a heavily unionised workforce with the capitalist drive of the bosses at W. C. Boggs' toilet manufacturers. Having suffered a series of "walk out" strikes led by a heavily parodied union official, tensions are running high on the factory floor and the obstinate bosses, led by the lampooned boss, Mr Boggs, played by Kenneth Williams, are digging their heels in and not engaging with the workforce until, that it, the annual works outing to Brighton. Leaving tensions and hierarchy at the factory gates, Mr Boggs enthusiastically embarks on the works outing and is temporarily absolved of all responsibility. He has raucous fun and copious drinks with his previously antagonistic workforce on Brighton pier before returning to the works' coach covered in balloon animals and draped over colleagues. Hierarchy is momentarily dissolved on the pub crawl back to the W. C. Boggs factory and, once back at the works, tensions have been resolved and relations at the factory are harmonious.

Whilst such a simplistic approach to industrial disputes is wondrously naive, works outings were a popular and relatively common feature of English industrial relations in the nineteenth century and for several decades of the twentieth century. Nannestad argues that such outings had become an established feature of the social calendar and "were seen as an occasion for promoting good staff relations by providing opportunities for management and employees to socialise" (15). The suspension of hierarchy during such events offers clear affiliation with Carnivalesque Leadership as the temporary release of hierarchical structures, and prioritising of socialising

DOI: 10.4324/9781003441649-6

opportunities enables shared fun, laughter, food, drink and the dissolution of the individual into the collective. Food was such a key part of the works outing that by 1895 excursions were sometimes referred to as "bean-feasts" (15). Bass Brewery of Burton-on-Trent provides a useful case study with "Bass Excursions" recognised as the world's largest company outings (Owen 132). In fact, so famous are the Bass Excursions, which started in 1860 and continued until the outbreak of the First World War in 1914, that they feature on their own Wikipedia page.[2] From 1889 to 1914, Bass Excursions were run on a four-year cycle to Liverpool, Blackpool, Yarmouth and Scarborough (Owen 131). The Brewery paid for the entire event which also included the families of workers. Bass even employed a "Traffic Manager," Mr William Walters, whose responsibility was to organise the annual big day out. On Friday July 24, 1914, fifteen trains set off from Burton station to Scarborough and transported ten thousand people to the seaside. In his guide to the event, Walters offers a final reminder of expectations:

> I trust that every Employee, and everyone else going with us, will again cheerfully display that spirit of good fellowship which has always characterised Bass' outings, and that the general behaviour will be of the same high standard as formerly, not only for individual reputation and comfort, but for the credit of Bass, Ratcliff and Gretton, Limited.
>
> (Walters 40)

Whilst the great Bass Excursions ended with the First World War, the practice of works outings did continue in the British workplace. For example, peddle bicycle manufacturer, Raleigh UK of Nottingham, paid for and organised a day out to London for all of its 8000 staff in 1958 (Smart 2018).

However seemingly outdated the "Carry On" version of the works day out may be, such outings offer some affiliation with the strategically driven "team building" strategies we might recognise today. Moreover, it is possible to identify themes of group social interaction, temporary suspension of hierarchy, communal food and drink consumption and collective fun within these works outings that not only resonate with modern group dynamic interventions but also resonate with ancient, medieval and contemporary carnivalesque. This chapter begins an exploration of how leaders utilise Carnivalesque Leadership techniques to achieve temporary safety-valve release and/or bring about longer-term change in corporate and commercial environments.

The works outing is an example of temporary subversion of hierarchy and a clear break from the norm. Significantly, it also offers insight into the evolving relationship between employer and employee during the industrial revolution. The freedom offered by a works outing was in stark contrast to the increasing levels of standardisation and control exerted over the workforce from the mid-nineteenth century in England. Employers had fought hard to standardise working practices to improve productivity and move away from previous working patterns that tended to exhibit extremes of idleness and intense work (Thompson 73). This shift towards standardisation of working hours and practice is demonstrated by the eradication of the phenomena of "Saint Mondays" which were evident in many countries including Mexico, France, Prussia, Belgium and England (Thompson 74) in the seventeenth, eighteenth and nineteenth centuries. During this time, Mondays were so often a "spill over" from weekend festivities that either there was high absenteeism or there was low productivity or both. As such, the phrase "Saint Mondays" reflected an attitude to work that would normally be seen on a feast day, that is, holiday time.[3] So entrenched were Saint Mondays that steel mills in Sheffield would schedule machinery repairs for a Monday in "honour" of the Saint (Thompson 74), and it was so widespread amongst colliers in Scotland and South Staffordshire that a Monday holiday was generally taken fortnightly (Kirby 963). The custom of Saint Mondays came under increasing attack in the nineteenth century from two angles: employers determined to drive productivity and religious organisations concerned about moral standards (Reid 99). The temperance movement focused on the hangover factor of Saint Mondays whilst employers, such as Josiah Wedgwood who had transformed industrial organisation in his factories during the eighteenth century, operated a work regime that did not have scope for wakes, fairs or Saint Mondays (McKendrick 51). Formal changes to work patterns began with a focus on Saturdays in the retail sector. The Early Closing Association 1842 argued for Saturday afternoons to be kept free for leisure in return for a full day on Monday as summed up by Reid's comment that "half a day was given in exchange for a whole one" (Reid 101). For Reid, the resultant conformity marks the submission "to the norms of industrial capitalism" (101).[4] The Factory Act of 1850 determined that working day in factories was also set to end at 2 p.m. on Saturdays.

The increasing standardisation of working practices was combined with the standardisation of supervision and managerial processes in a more rigid, transparent hierarchy.[5] This is, perhaps, most famously encapsulated in F. W. Taylor's mechanised approach to work operations through his "Scientific Management" theory in which "managers assume new burdens, new duties, and responsibilities never dreamed of in the past" (36).[6] Whilst Taylor famously standardises working practice in new depths of exactitude towards the end of the nineteenth century, guidance about the disciplined management of workers was found in wider discussions of maximising factory productivity and profitability long before Taylor. The books of James Montgomery were popular in the United States and Germany as well as in his native Great Britain in the first half of the nineteenth century. Writing in

1832, Montgomery offers guidance on the management of spinning factories which reflects the drive for discipline and balance. He argues

> I do not hesitate to assert, that a Spinning Factory can never be managed more profitably, and more to the satisfaction of the proprietors, than when there exists a good feeling and a good understanding between the manager and workers.
>
> (224)

Montgomery argues that this "good feeling" is easier to establish in the spinning department than the carding department because in the latter "they are mostly women on set wages, whom it is difficult to make sensible of their responsibility, and the evils resulting from carelessness on their part; and, therefore, they require to be constantly looked over" and that the "carding master must act with the utmost vigilance and promptitude, and sometimes with a degree of seeming severity, that is not so necessary in the other" (226). Here, then, Montgomery is clear that the manager has a particularly key role to play in preserving the discipline of the female workers.[7]

Increased discipline, spreading standardisation and greater layers of rigid management hierarchy were therefore increasingly evident in the workplace in the nineteenth century. Whilst detailed exploration of such changes in the formalisation of working patterns, drawing on eminent authors including Barnard, Weber and Blau and tracing pre-industrial formalisation of labour such as that evident in Ancient Egypt, is beyond the remit of this book, the potential for exploring traits and patterns of organisational practices is worth considering in relation to Carnivalesque Leadership elements. Whilst not delving into the details beyond such generalised references to Taylor and Montgomery above, it is possible to relate aspects to the model of Carnivalesque Leadership considered in this book. The "periodic release necessary in a rigidly hierarchical society" which had been provided previously by the Saturnalia or feasts in pre-industrial society (Henricks 53) was transformed into standardised and regular access to commodified communal events which offered regular safety-valve release and a refreshing break from the norm. Griffin argues that in place of the annual cycle of feasts and festivals, governed by seasons and harvests, were to be found modern spectator sports and commercial music thereby demonstrating the commodification of leisure/pleasure release and providing an example of how "the traditional sing-along of the local beerhouse had been transformed into the commercial music" ("Popular Culture" 621).[8]

Here, then, we can identify a pattern of standardisation and commodification not only in work and leisure patterns but also in the standardisation and commodification of carnivalesque safety-valve mechanisms. The standardised half-day finish on a Saturday significantly increased the capacity of the masses to partake in organised leisure on a Saturday afternoon. One of the most significant examples of this in Great Britain is football. The Football Association was formed in 1863 and led the standardisation of the game. Whilst its origins may be in "melee" games that regularly took place on feast days (Kitching 130), football became regulated and standardised in the second half of the nineteenth century and yet also maintained the capacity for safety-valve release through the dissolution of the individual in the collective experience, communal consumption of food and drink and collective singing and laughter (usually both being more prevalent when your team is winning – as a Tottenham Hotspur fan, my experience of such joy is sadly intermittent).

The standardisation of football also provides an insight into the growing functions of "works teams." Five high profile football teams in the English football leagues have their roots in employment:

- Arsenal Football Club's origins are in the Woolwich Arsenal Armament Factory.[9]
- Manchester United was originally formed by the Lancashire and Yorkshire Railway Company in 1878 named Newton Heath LYR.
- West Ham United's origins are from the Thames Ironworks and Shipbuilding Company.
- Coventry City was originally a club for workers of Singers (bicycle manufacturers).
- Crystal Palace was formed by the company managing the world-famous Victorian exhibition building originally designed to house the Great Exhibition of 1851.[10]

In the Netherlands, PSV Eindhoven grew out of the Philips Sports Association which was a club for employees of The Philips Company. In Germany, Bayer 04 Leverkusen was formed at Friedrich Bayer and Co after employees wrote a letter to the board of directors for a gymnastics club which then spawned the formation of a football team in 1907. Verein für Leibesübungen (VfL) Wolfsburg grew out of the sports club set up for Volkswagen workers in Wolfsburg.

Works football teams (a tiny minority of which have grown into professional clubs as the above examples) show how leaders have harnessed the potential for carnivalesque safety-valve release through building collective group dynamics and promoting opportunities for fun and laughter. The standardisation of working patterns enabled a more standardised and regular carnivalesque release for football fans through group spectatorship and team alignment. Marples traces the potential roots of football in Britain to the Roman Saturnalia through to the mass football festivals of Shrovetide and directly to a "carnival spirit" (21). Offering the only recognition of women playing football in his book *A History of Football*, Marples highlights a Shrove Tuesday football match between married women and "spinsters" that would take place annually in Inveresk in which the married women would "always" win (13).[11]

Association football is not the only sport with a history of works teams, of course. American football also has a history of works teams, most notably The Columbus Panhandlers, a team initiated by workers from the Pennsylvania Railroad. American football also provides an example of how works team sports continue to be supported by employers through the National Public Safety Football League of American Football. Operating on a voluntary basis and raising funds for charity, the league is open to teams of full-time police officers, firefighters, emergency medical technicians, military firefighters, correction officers and other full-time first responders. The continuing appeal of works teams is also reflected in the existence of The World Federation for Company Sports (WFCS) which promotes and hosts games specifically to provide a collective event for company sports. The WFCS states its aims to support "corporate culture, health, social responsibility, individual and collective performance" and to "build stronger bonds among colleagues" and "enhance team cohesion" and lists "improved employee morale," "team building" and "wellbeing" as some of the benefits of competing.[12]

From a proposed Carnivalesque Leadership perspective, works sports teams offer safety-valve release, dissolution of the individual within the collective and opportunities for collective fun. The above offers historical examples of how this has been harnessed by leaders and employers over the last couple of centuries. Such activities can temporarily suspend the hierarchical power dynamic between managers and the managed (there is nothing quite as "levelling" or subversive as a two-footed sliding tackle into the ankles of the boss during a staff football match after a difficult day at work). Indeed, the temporary suspension of hierarchy through activities like sport can lead to opportunities to build a different group dynamic, create greater understanding about the capabilities of each other and establish different relationships (rather than simply exacting petty revenge).

The carnivalesque safety-valve effect of organised works sporting activities does not necessarily end at the final whistle, with the potential for subsequent communal consumption of food and drink. Communal eating has a long history in employee relations, with examples including sanctioned tea breaks, subsidised lunches in works canteens, luncheon voucher coupons which enabled off-site communal consumption (an early childhood memory from the mid-1970s was of pink paper luncheon vouchers bandied about by family friend, Shirley), informal after-hours get-togethers and organised events centred on annual calendars (i.e. Christmas) and celebrations of organisational success. Within the history of work relations, food and drink has been an opportunity for building relationships and benefitting from endorphin release. Building on the earlier identification of the importance of communal eating during works outings or "beanfeasts" (Nannestad 15), there are multiple other examples from the start of the Industrial Revolution in England that place food and drink as central to communal activities and registering the impact on employee relations. These include the "Cromford Feast," established by industrialist Richard Arkwright for his workers and the villagers of Cromford near Matlock, Derbyshire, which involved festivals and celebrations held in the village for mill workers and the general public. *The Derby Mercury*, September 19, 1776, reported an annual festival of candlelight at Cromford with

> 500 workmen and children led by a band and a boy working on a weavers loom. They paraded from the mills round the village . . . returning to the mill for a feast of buns, ale, nuts and fruit followed by music and dancing.[13]

In a Carnivalesque Leadership model, the role of food and drink in such an event contributes to safety-valve release and incentivises compliance with the subsequently reinforced hierarchy.

A very different drinking custom, the Japanese tradition of *nomikai*, seemingly bears little resemblance to Bakhtin's exploration of feast and carnival. However, *nomikai*, which involves sanctioned drinking with colleagues after work, offers potential for temporary safety-valve release from rigid hierarchical structures in a controlled, "official" manner and therefore offers an extreme example of the mechanism. The expected aim of this structured drinking culture is to strengthen camaraderie between bosses and employees. This concept is called *nominication*, with the drink (*nomu*) and the (commun)ication taking place simultaneously (Yamauchi & Orr). When surveyed by Japan's Census Bureau, 73.2% (80.9% for males) of Japanese believed that drinking helps smooth people's relationships through *nominication* (Kato 12). During these periods of suspended hierarchy, there is an acceptance of people behaving freely and behaviours that occur during this time of *nominication* are expected to be forgotten/forgiven (within reason) in the custom of *breiko*. This drinking norm assumes that all that happened at the drinking place was like a dream – an occasion detached from the real world which makes people feel relieved and consequently unites the group on an intimate level (Kato 72 and 74). *Nomikai* is just one example of a communal activity that is part of Japanese corporate life focusing on building team relationships and providing safety-valve release. Other established traditional communal corporate opportunities include Year-End (*Bōnenkai*), New Year (*Shinnenkai*), Farewell and Welcome Parties (*Sōbetsukai*), Sports Days (*Undōkai*) and Cherry Blossom viewing (*Hanami*).

Other, less obviously boozy, examples of mechanisms to generate comradery, reassess working relationships, increase effectiveness and let out pressure from an organisation can be seen in formalised "team building" activities and events. The "team building" industry has commodified this process to create a break from the norm and provide bonding opportunities. These opportunities can involve outdoor physical challenges, such as abseiling, rafting and hiking, which may represent individual and collective challenge, or communal art/craft/performance events which enable a realignment in creativity, or a theme-focus event offering exposure to a chosen subject, with any variety of these usually coupled with communal eating and drinking. Academic interest in team building activities tends to fall under the remit of organisational development (OD) which has attracted academic interest since the 1920s (Shuffler et al. 366). This work is multifaceted, from studying how group cohesiveness impacts performance (Mullen and Copper), how happiness makes people more productive (Oswald et al.) and the exploration of the measurability of the effectiveness of team building.[14] Most OD/team building rationale is driven by the pursuit of greater understanding and cohesiveness that could lead to productivity gains and greater efficiency in organisations. Increasingly, wellbeing and mindfulness have become a feature of commercial corporate team building as has the commodified pursuit of a perceived sense of belonging. From a Carnivalesque Leadership perspective, typical team building activities help release the pressure and tension that build within any organisation through the employment of carnivalesque components.

To provide a framework for this initial exploration of OD and Carnivalesque Leadership, I shall use a framework developed by Pasmore who argues that most effective organisations "are those which produce excellent results by any measure of costs, quality, or efficiency while simultaneously enhancing the energy and commitment of organizational members to the success of the enterprise" (1).[15] Such commitment from organisational members is established through a combination of individual intrinsic and extrinsic motivation with individual motivation, "the engine that drives organizations to success" (Pasmore 26).[16] Challenging the "over-reliance on the ability of supervisors to control employee behaviour" (90), Pasmore's work identifies two approaches in organisational leadership: the first of which emphasises control, which can lead to an oppressive, control-orientated structure, whilst the second is calculated to produce commitment among employees (40–1). In the model developing in this book, Carnivalesque Leadership can be associated both with an attempt to control employee behaviour (by offering temporary safety-valve release that enables reinforcement of the subsequently restored hierarchy) *and* with an attempt to produce commitment amongst employees through offering fun, laughter, food and drink and collectivity in a break from the norm. Here, hierarchical models are reinforced through the strategic employment of carnivalesque components that provide safety-valve release and quell potential rebellion through temporary, sanctioned subversion. In the process, Carnivalesque Leadership components provide motivational and communal opportunities which contribute to the building of commitment and compliance amongst employees.

Recognising a shift from leaders getting work done through others to getting work done with others (White 4), organisational models that are not reliant "just" on hierarchy can also be related to Carnivalesque Leadership. At a basic level, we have recognition of the "power" of the worker to grant or withhold full compliance as opposed to a singular model focusing on the power of the boss. Barnard argues that organisations are cooperative systems based on the "willingness" of worker participation rather than "just" the authority from above. He emphasises the importance of willingness to cooperate and argues that "the decision as to whether an order has authority or not lies with the person to whom it is addressed"; there must be assent (163). The hierarchical structures explored by Bakhtin, wherein feasts and carnivals play a major role in releasing tensions in society and offer a continuation of subversive folk traditions, may not easily fit into Barnard's model. Indeed, I am not proposing a seamless alignment. There is, however, some value in recognising the role of the follower in the granting/acceptance of authority for full compliance within a Carnivalesque Leadership model. Firstly, there is pure transaction (salary for effort/delivery) which is then eased/smoothed/promoted by carnivalesque components that release the pressure from such a system and bring pleasure, happiness and, potentially, a perceived sense of belonging that eases full compliance with authority.[17] In this model, the follower must be willing to give full compliance and Carnivalesque Leadership can offer a means to achieve this.[18]

The role of happiness as a motivator in worker/employee participation, compliance and alignment is complex.[19] A starting complexity is the definition of happiness in itself and whether this is rooted in the intrinsic and/or the extrinsic. The satisfaction of the need for self-actualisation, the role of self-esteem and the predisposition towards an optimistic or pessimistic outlook (potentially informed by trauma) are likely contributory factors or shifting paradigms when considering the role of happiness at work/in employment. Family and social situations and psychological factors impacting happiness are tricky variables in terms of individual positionality for happiness. The subsequent intersection of personal factors with a plethora of work factors (conditions and compensation, leadership hierarchy, work environment, power dynamics, colleague relations and job fulfilment, inclusivity, potential for self-actualisation, belonging) therefore can offer more variables than non-variables.

Whilst the definition of happiness when applied to a specific work context is just the starting point of complexity, a (albeit problematic) working definition of happiness is useful for the subsequent discussion in this chapter. Freud offers a definition of happiness that resonates with safety-valve release:

> What is called happiness in its narrowest sense comes from the satisfaction – most often instantaneous – of pent-up needs which have reached great intensity, and by its very nature can only be a transitory experience. (27)

A full exploration and evaluation of the definition of happiness are beyond the scope of this text, but Freud's definition here appeals in its specific presentation of happiness being the satisfaction of pent-up needs as if a safety valve has been loosened and therefore resonates with carnivalesque release. Moreover, Freud's definition reflects the transitory nature of moments of happiness which links to carnivalesque components that are generated at distinct, temporary moments. For the purposes of this discussion, the subtleties of happiness and its application to a work context will only be engaged with superficially as a starting point for exploration. As a result, the argument that Carnivalesque Leadership, by utilising many components that can be linked to happiness (laughter, food, drink, break from the norm, subversion of hierarchy, prioritising of the collective and, of course, festivities and carnival *in themselves*), needs further exploration from this starting point. For the purposes of this initial exploration, there is naive "acceptance" of causality: that happiness is quantifiable and, moreover, that happiness makes employees more productive. Here, I am relying on researchers who have grappled with this complexity and secured quantifiable outcomes including Oswald et al.'s study on "Happiness and Productivity" which registered a 12% increase in productivity (789) and Bellet et al.'s report that determined "a strong causal effect of positive affect on productivity" (32).[20]

Despite the difficulty of quantifying internal and external happiness, corporations and organisations themselves readily make links between the place of work and employee happiness with both explicit and implicit suggestion of benefits to the organisation. The concept of "Corporate Happiness" is now in parlance, and the ability to quantify and promote strategies for happiness has generated much interest. Moss describes happiness as "intangible" and "sequential" and considers how happiness can be achieved through the building of traits like hope, efficacy, resilience, optimism, gratitude and empathy (1). She argues that happiness in work environments can be achieved through habitual practicing of these traits by individuals in an organisation and promoted by leaders. The traits identified by Moss are not, on the face of it, aligned with Carnivalesque Leadership components. Indeed, Saturnalian "mindlessness" and freedom from restraint seem polar opposite from the restrained mindful traits identified by Moss. However the employee achieves happiness, whether through carnivalesque safety-valve release provided by boozy celebration, sporting communal effort, shared food, days out, team-building, fun and humour or through meditative gratefulness, the proposed outcome for employers is implicitly the same: increased effectiveness and productivity. Many successful business leaders have emphasised the role of happiness in their organisations. For example, Tony Hsieh outlines how an understanding of positive psychology led to his reframing of the focus of his company to "Zappos is about delivering happiness in the world" (261) and prompting a commitment to focusing on employee as well as customer happiness. Hsieh outlines frameworks for happiness which he subdivides into three types: pleasure (stimuli reliant), passion (flow peak performance) and high purpose (being part of something bigger than yourself that has meaning to you (269). For Hsieh, happiness, which is driven by pleasure, passion and purpose, is the goal of all of us even if the mechanism that brings that happiness is different. It is significant that business leaders like Hsieh identify the importance of happiness in their organisations and seek means to quantify what happiness is and offer some guidance on how to achieve it within organisations. The subtitle of Hseih's book *Delivering Happiness – a Path to Profits, Passion, and Purpose* makes explicit the suggested link between employee happiness and business success.

The business of promoting workplace happiness has seen a growth in business consultants and specialists and the development of support organisations offering expertise to help businesses and organisations prioritise happiness. LinkedIn reflects this increasing focus with specialist contributors discussing the importance of employee happiness in corporate success with accompanying hashtags including #workplacehappiness, #joyatwork, #happinessatwork and #happinessmatters.[21] The importance and impact of workers/employees' happiness are directly recognised by others in the corporate world including Google. Lara Harding, people programmes' manager at Google, states "We have also noticed that employees who are happy . . . demonstrate increased motivation" (cited by Oswald et al. 789). The increased focus on "happiness" in organisational culture is evident in the attention paid to company rankings for happiness. *Comparably.com* operates a "Happiness" ranked list which identifies the happiest employees, with the subsequent top companies highlighting their success in the ranking including Zoom and HubSpot.[22]

Modern corporate strategising for employee happiness tends to focus on health, wellbeing and job satisfaction and strives for long-term, sustainable impact. A Carnivalesque Leadership model for happiness employs a very different set of mechanisms and most obviously focuses on the strategic but temporary subversion of hierarchy, break from the norm, laughter and fun, opportunities for extreme collectivity and food and drink consumption. The contemporary health and wellbeing focus is likely to mean alcohol consumption is not featured on corporate lists of the mechanisms employed to promote happiness (the teetotal Bakhtin may have been showing even greater foresight in not focusing on alcohol consumption too much as part of his study of carnival). On the face of it, happiness brought about by Carnivalesque Leadership is most obviously related to the temporary (but repeatable) stimuli of pleasure, that is laughter, parody, fun, break from the norm, collectivity and communal food and drink. Such a reading of Carnivalesque Leadership is rooted in the carnivalesque as "just" temporary and short-term only and ignores the potential longer-term impact of shifting power dynamics and the potential longer-term impact from the employment of safety-valve mechanisms and follower compliance/sense of communal belonging. Moreover, longer-term passion and purpose are also intertwined with examples of Carnivalesque Leadership, from Claudia Jones' organisation of the Caribbean Carnival from 1959 to educational leadership approaches that value safety-valve release and communal bonding, from the challenge to hierarchy evident in the history of the Trinidad and Notting Hill carnivals to the subversive role of the carnivalesque in the development of the Pride movement discussed in the next chapter.

At its basest level, Carnivalesque Leadership's impact on happiness could simply be seen as a manipulative means to improve productivity and achieve corporate objectives through the strategic use of carnivalesque components. However, this belies the very human need which drives this dynamic and has done since humans evolved in family units, tribes and groups. Carnivalesque Leadership offers a means to achieve a chemical messenger boost from serotonin, dopamine, oxytocin and endorphins and to satiate the human craving for being part of something bigger than oneself. As such, Carnivalesque Leadership can be of particular interest in enhancing communal relations and potentially "belonging" in a workplace environment. Recognising belonging as "a cloud of connected concepts" (Filstad et al. 117), the application of "belonging" here is, again, acknowledged as a starting point for exploration and is not exhaustive. The starting point for this exploration of belonging and carnivalesque is rooted in Maslow's "hierarchy of need" wherein if physiological and safety needs are "fairly well gratified, then there will emerge the love and affection and belongingness needs" (380). In this model, once salary has taken care of basic need (security, warmth/shade and food), the need for belonging and self-actualisation become more prevalent in the workplace. As such, the communal components of Carnivalesque Leadership come to the fore. Practical examples already considered in this chapter include the Cromford Feast, the Bass Excursions, support for works sports teams and team building activities which represent physical, concrete examples used by employers for people to feel as if they belong in a unit. Whilst an organisation can, of course, seek to generate a sense of belonging through its culture, driven by its vision/

mission rooted in ethos without such concrete, physical manifestations, for centuries, leaders have chosen the physicality of carnivalesque components to generate physical and emotional safety-valve release and physical and emotional compliance and belonging.

Given its carnivalesque roots, the concept of "belonging" referenced here is not only linked to the joy of the communal but also linked to the dissolution of the individual into the collective. There are different dynamics at play here and some potential for slippage between the communal (community-based experiences) and collectivity (in which boundaries are dissolved allowing the individual dissolution into the mass body). The casual linking of belonging to the dissolution of the individual into collectivity has multiple repercussions, two of which are explored here (again offered only as a starting point). Firstly, the individual is lost within the larger group in which the individual is engulfed. As such, the loss of individuality, and associated different characteristics, can represent a means to disempower the individual and promote homogeneity. The potential consequence of such homogeneity is, ironically, in its shaping by the most powerful. Secondly, it could be argued that the loss of individual status offers a means to dissolve barriers between individuals and subvert power dynamics akin to Bakhtin's exploration of feast and carnival offering temporary loss of the individual which enables power redress and subversion of hierarchy.

An alternative reading of belonging and the communal/collectivity switches focus on the potential for alignment between an individual's ethos and corporate ethos. Offering greater agency for the individual, such alignment is increasingly seen as a determining factor in workplace cohesion and effectiveness.[23] Whether generated by harmonious matching of ethos or through communal bonding or through other more earthy means of dissolution of the individual into collectivity, extremes of alignment are not always helpful. Teams can be highly dysfunctional and can develop a "group think" mentality that can be problematic. Deliberately offering connotations with George Orwell's "doublethink" and "crimethink" from his novel *Nineteen Eighty Four*, Janis introduced the term "groupthink" to refer to "a mode of thinking that people engage in when they are deeply involved in a cohesive in-group, when the members' strivings for unanimity override their motivation to realistically appraise alternative courses of action" (9).

The dissolution of the individual into collectivity in a corporate environment is complex. In terms of power differentials, if an individual is aligned with the values of the organisation, the dissolution of the individual into collectivity can be a positive if there is alignment rather than sublimation. A sense of belonging through communal alignment is more straightforward (but not without its own complexities). In both the communal and collectivity, the temporary status of the impact is called into question. Leadership deployment of carnivalesque strategies can lead to the loss of everything individual in an unhelpful power dynamic and/or constitute a moment of subversive belonging with far-reaching consequences for individual and collective happiness and bring about long-term change.

The importance of the communal and the value of opportunities for collectivity in organisations was brought to the fore during, and as part of the legacy of, the coronavirus (COVID-19) pandemic and global responses to it. Lockdowns, social distancing and self-isolation were key strategies employed by countries around the world to minimise the spread of the virus. Forbes et al. outline how approximately half of all workers in the UK work from home at least some of the time since the initial lockdown in 2020. Eddy's research into the impact of the pandemic finds prolonged homeworking to be associated with greater anxiety around social interaction post-pandemic and that even those with regular attendance at the workplace still report feelings of social isolation. Despite the use of technology to ease communication, the absence of regular and routine face-to-face communication has foregrounded its importance of human connection in the workplace as well as in family and wider social groups. Haider et al. highlight evidence that the response to the SARS (severe acute respiratory syndrome) outbreak in Hong Kong in 2003 had already demonstrated the long-term potential for a significant impact on mental health, PTSD (post-traumatic stress disorder) and depression.[24]

The lack of opportunity for the physicality of communal carnivalesque safety-valve release due to the measures brought in to minimise the spread of the virus impacted not only work organisations but society more generally. Despite the legal framework around the restrictions, subversive opportunities for collective revelry still took place. Media reports identified global examples of curfew-breaking revelry such as those in Madrid and reported that, in Berlin, the police made clear its intentions to break up "corona speakeasies" which were springing up in the city despite restrictions.[25] In the UK, the media updated on arrests made for breaching lockdown rules, with BBC News reporting on arrests. Significantly, the centre of UK government, No. 10 Downing Street, became notoriously known as one of the locations being investigated for employee revelry during restrictions. The media reported that staff were reportedly encouraged by the Prime Minister, Boris Johnson, to "let off steam" during "wine time Fridays."[26] The allegations and revelations prompted media commentators to cast Mr Johnson as a carnivalesque Lord of Misrule, a bringer of chaos and revelry. Journalist and political commentator for *The Guardian* newspaper, Andrew Rawnsley, for example, argued that "Britain is presided over by a Lord of Misrule" whilst, when reviewing a new biography of Johnson for the *Times Literary Supplement*, ex-Tory MP, Rory Stewart, asked "Is he a carnival lord of misrule allowing us to rebel against the oppressive expectations of our age, or a hand-grenade to be thrown at the establishment?" In *Twelfth Night*, Shakespeare's Sir Toby Belch, a classic literary Lord of Misrule, asks jumped-up, would-be authoritative servant Malvolio "Dost thou think because thou art virtuous there shall be no more cakes and ale?" (Act 2, Sc III) in a symbolic challenge to those who would dampen a carnivalesque spirit. The carnivalesque Lord of Misrule figure represents more than just the licence for "cakes and ale," however. If Mr Johnson did, as Prime Minister, temporarily sanction carnivalesque safety-valve release in No 10, this could be seen as a limited example of Carnivalesque Leadership but only in an elite sphere far, far removed from mass communal impact. Indeed, the Carnivalesque Leadership identified in this text would suggest that Mr Johnson cannot be a carnivalesque Lord of Misrule as that specific role is filled by a member of the lower orders of society who is temporarily promoted to a position of mocking authority. While Mr Johnson has some affinities with the role of Lord of Misrule through a tendency to mock others in authority and the temporary nature of his stay at the highest position of power, he was never in a lowly position to be subverting hierarchy. Moreover, one cannot be a Lord of Misrule ***and*** the substantive boss. It is simply impossible. You cannot have your cake and eat it. Sir Toby Belch is a Lord of Misrule only. He is not the boss and does not want to be. He only wants the cake and to eat it (literally not metaphorically).

The impact of COVID-19 and the global response to it will continue to be investigated and research undertaken in many different formats as its legacy continues to be seen globally in schools, places of work and wider society.[27] In the corporate world, the pandemic triggered a mass social experiment in working arrangements (Barrero et al. 2). Adisa et al. consider the implications for new working practices informed by responses to the pandemic in relation to shifts to working from home and subsequent blurring of boundaries between home and work life with exploration of perceived flexibility. Such blurring of boundaries, with working not only at home but on the move facilitated by technology, impacts both standardised and non-standardised work patterns. Here, I am using Kalleberg et al.'s definition of standardised work as "work done on a fixed schedule – usually full-time – at the employer's place of business, under the employer's control, and with the mutual expectation of continued employment" (258) and non-standardised work as all other types of work including self-employment.[28] Cappelli and Keller identified as early as 2013 (pre-COVID-19, of course, and pre-working from home drive) that up to 20% of individuals undertaking economic work in the United States did so in alternatives to traditional employment, with an even higher percentage in other countries. Barrero et al. updated these statistics to state that "Full days worked at home account for 28 percent of paid workdays among Americans 20–64 years old, as of mid 2023" (1).

Earlier in this chapter, the link was made between the growth of standardised work patterns and the growth of standardised and commodified leisure activities that provide opportunities for commodified carnivalesque safety-valve release. Therefore, any consideration of the impact of growing non-standardised work may suggest a compromising impact on opportunities for carnivalesque communal activities which operate as a safety-valve release. Given the remit of this study, four hypotheses are offered at this point for further exploration:

- firstly, the transformation of working practices brought about by the response to the pandemic may mean that there is less of a need for carnivalesque safety-valve release as there is potentially greater freedom experienced by employees in some sectors.
- secondly, the transformation of working practices brought about by the response to the pandemic may mean that there is more of a need for carnivalesque safety-valve release through temporary subversion and the communal/collectivity.
- thirdly, the logistical opportunity for partaking in standardised (and commodified) carnivalesque activities is minimised by the rise of non-standard working patterns.
- fourthly, logistical opportunity for partaking in standardised (and commodified) carnivalesque activities is maximised by the rise of non-standard working patterns.

As evident at several points in this text, this discussion represents a starting point for exploring Carnivalesque Leadership in the commercial and corporate sectors and raises more questions than it answers. As a starting point, this chapter offers no measurement of effectiveness and no measurement of productivity impact. Whilst such quantifying is beyond the remit of this book, I am actively piggybacking on the work of those acknowledged in this chapter as I have starting to map where Carnivalesque Leadership can be aligned to approaches associated with work relations and power dynamics. The development of safety-valve mechanisms such as the annual works outing, the organisation of leisure time by employers and proactive "team building," all contribute to carnivalesque release within standardised, sanctioned times. The shift away from such standardised patterns has been radical, accelerated recently by the response to COVID-19. How significant was the temporary hiatus in carnivalesque communal safety-valve release during the pandemic? What might the need be going forward, given the increased isolation in the workplace enabled, in part, by technology? Is a Carnivalesque Leadership strategy likely to have the same kind of impact that it has had for centuries? Could it be less impactful? Or could it be more?

The contemporary corporate focus on individual wellbeing seemingly offers little alignment with carnivalesque extremes of dissolution of the individual within the collective, potentially rumbustious consumption of food and drink and subversive humour and parodic impulse. Employers and researchers "have long been aware of the extensive costs, in both human and financial terms, attributable to dysfunctional well-being. . . . In turn, these variables have been related to decrements in important work outcomes" (Wright and Huang 1189). There are many contributory factors to employee disengagement, disconnection and disenfranchisement. "Quiet quitting," a phrase and attitude that arrived in parlance via the Tik Tok platform in 2022, formed part of the Gallup "State of the Global Workplace: 2023 Report," with 59% of the respondents identifying as "Quiet Quitters" and 18% identifying as "Loud Quitters" whose direct actions directly harm their employing organisation.[29] Whilst a blunt application of a Carnivalesque Leadership approach is not offered as a simple solution to address corporate alienation, a deeper understanding of how temporary, licenced carnivalesque subversion has helped human beings to operate in groups for centuries may offer insight to bring about short-term release and longer-term change.

Notes

1 "Carry On" films now generally come with a warning regarding the out-of-date world views and attitudes evident in the films.
2 See https://en.wikipedia.org/wiki/The_Bass_Excursions
3 See Reid; Thompson; Tiratelli for more detailed explorations of Saint Mondays.
4 Whilst entrenched behaviours had been significantly disrupted, Saint Mondays were still part of the British working life into the early twentieth century. Harris cites an employer in 1906 complaining that "the average British workman . . . generally is more interested in the next football match and the nearest public house than he is in his work . . . some trades suffer much from St Monday" (135).
5 See Reid; Clark; McKendrick.
6 See Fry; Littler; Watanabe for samples of academic responses to Taylor. A further interest in Taylor's work from a Carnivalesque Leadership perspective is through his discussion of the "initiative and incentive model" that he is seeking to replace with his "scientific management" given the potential scope that Carnivalesque Leadership may be aligned to an incentive-based model.
7 A detailed examination of such an attitude is beyond the scope of this text but is worth highlighting here as a reminder of perceptions of women in the workplace as tricky to control.
8 See also Alexander; Marrus; Henricks. Griffin offers an overview of the historiographical shift from positing industrialisation as threatening popular culture to a model which recognises the resilience and continuation of popular culture.
9 As an already declared supporter of Tottenham, the north London rival to Arsenal, it pains me to acknowledge AFC in this text. My team morphed from a cricket team rather than a works team which is not reflective of our subsequent

success (or relative lack of) nor any potential links to work rate, teamwork or fun – although, at times, even the most ardent of us might wonder.

10 See Marples for a discussion of team formation and club websites for background summaries. Please note Marples assigns Manchester City's origins to the workers of the Lancashire and Yorkshire Railway. As fans of both Manchester clubs will be aware, this is not the case as Manchester City developed out of a church cricket team. More significantly, Marples' book exhibits outdated comments about the spread of football across the globe in his text and his general ignoring of female participation in the sport is indicative of dominant ideologies.

11 As above in relation to Montgomery's commentary of needing to discipline female workers in the carding department, a detailed exploration of Morris' reasons for ignoring the history of women's football is beyond the scope of this text. For alternative perspectives on the women's game, see Petty and Pope; Williams and the FA's website section on Women's and Girls' Football.

12 See the WFCS website.

13 See the Cromford Mills website.

14 See also Buller and Bell; Svyantek et al.; White. This is not a comprehensive list of key academic work as that is beyond the capacity and scope of this book.

15 There are multifarious versions and adaptions of motivational models explored by research-informed literature. An in-depth review is beyond the remit of this work. See Steers et al. for a historical overview of the development of work motivation theory; Steel and König for an overview that proposes integration of different disciplinary approaches; Michaelson for an exploration of the ethics of work motivation theory.

16 See Bénabou and Tirole; Prendergast for explorations of the tension between leaders employing mechanisms for extrinsic motivation and the potential impact on intrinsic motivation.

17 See Burns for a detailed consideration of transactional leadership.

18 The proposition of this book is an extreme extrapolation from Bakhtin's philosophy of carnival. His carnival is located in a Rabelaisian world of the Middle Ages and largely models of authoritarian leadership which are shored up through safety-valve release.

19 See Spicer and Cederström for a lively overview of the tensions and problems of applying happiness to a causal relationship with work.

20 Whilst their specific work registers weather as the stimulant for positive mood change, Bellet et al.'s literature review provides an overview of the development of research into the link between productivity and happiness. See Ledford for an exploration of the appeal of identifying a causal relationship and an overview of approaches that have sought to debunk a happiness–productivity causal connection.

21 For example content see Gordon; Lambert.

22 See the comparably, hubspot and zoom websites.

23 See Rubino; Baumgartner for sample approaches.

24 See Haider et al.; Brooks et al. for sample approaches. See Eddy's literature review which covers the impact of loss of in-person human contact, loss of social interaction and physical distancing.

25 See Parra; Tolosa and Estebanez.

26 See Duncan et al. for an overview timeline including referencing to the PM's alleged encouragement. See Crerar's article in *The Mirror*.

27 See Jack and Oster; Williams; Millar et al. for sample overviews of the impact on school pupils' mental wellbeing.

28 See Broschak and Davis-Blake; Davis-Blake et al. for greater exploration of the impact on relationships within models blending standard and non-standard workers.

29 See Morgan for an overview of the "Quiet Quitting" movement and Mahand and Caldwell for an exploration which seeks to locate the root cause of the decline of employee commitment in the failure of many managers and supervisors "to engage, empower, and inspire employees" (9).

Works Cited

Adisa, T.A., et al. "Exploring the Impact of COVID-19 on Employees' Boundary Management and Work–Life Balance." *British Journal of Management*, vol. 33, 2022, pp. 1694–709. *Wiley Online Library.* Accessed May 18, 2024.

Aggarwal, Deepak, et al. "Team Building Intervention." *Indian Journal of Industrial Relations*, vol. 42, no. 3, 2007, pp. 445–53. *JSTOR*. Accessed Apr. 2, 2024.

Alexander, Sally. *St Giles Fair, 1830–1914: Popular Culture and the Industrial Revolution in Nineteenth-Century Oxford.* History Workshop, 1970.

Bakhtin, Mikhail. *Rabelais and His World.* Translated by Hélène Iswolsky. Indiana University Press, 1984.

Barnard, Chester I. *The Functions of the Executive.* Harvard University Press, 1938. *Internet Archive.* Accessed Mar. 24, 2024.

Barrero, Jose Maria, et al. "The Evolution of Work from Home." Working Paper 31686, 2023. *nber.org.* Accessed May 18, 2024.

"The Bass Excursions." *wikipedia.org.* Accessed May 18, 2024.

Baumgartner, Natalie. "Build a Culture That Aligns with People's Values." *Harvard Business Review.* April 2020. *nbr.org.* Accessed May 17, 2024.

Bellet, Clement, et al. "Does Employee Happiness Have an Impact on Productivity?" Saïd Business School WP 2019–13, Oct. 14, 2019. *papers.ssrn.* Accessed May 18, 2024.

Bénabou, Roland, and Jean Tirole. "Intrinsic and Extrinsic Motivation." *The Review of Economic Studies*, vol. 70, no. 3, 2003, pp. 489–520. *JSTOR*. Accessed Apr. 2, 2024.

Blau, Peter M. *Bureaucracy in Modern Society.* Random House, 1956.

Blau, Peter M. "A Formal Theory of Differentiation in Organizations." *American Sociological Review*, vol. 35, no. 2, 1970, pp. 201–18. *JSTOR*. Accessed Apr. 2, 2024.

Briggs, Jo. "Ballads and Balloon Ascents: Reconnecting the Popular and the Didactic in 1851." *Victorian Studies*, vol. 55, no. 2, 2013, p. 253–66. *Project MUSE.* Accessed May 18, 2024.

Brooks, Samantha K., et al. "The Psychological Impact of Quarantine and How to Reduce It: Rapid Review of the Evidence." *Lancet*, vol. 395, 2020, pp. 912–20. Accessed May 18, 2024.

Broschak, Joseph P., and Alison Davis-Blake. "Mixing Standard Work and Nonstandard Deals: The Consequences of Heterogeneity in Employment Arrangements." *The Academy of Management Journal*, vol. 49, no. 2, 2006, pp. 371–93. *JSTOR*. Accessed Apr. 2, 2024.

Buller, Paul F., and Cecil H. Bell. "Effects of Team Building and Goal Setting on Productivity: A Field Experiment." *The Academy of Management Journal*, vol. 29, no. 2, 1986, pp. 305–28. *JSTOR*. Accessed Apr. 2, 2024.

Burns, James MacGregor. *Leadership.* Harper & Row, 1978.

Cappelli, Peter, and J. Keller. "Classifying Work in the New Economy." *Academy of Management Review*, vol. 38, 2012, pp. 575–96. *ResearchGate.* Accessed May 18, 2024.

Carry on at your Convenience. Directed by Gerald Thomas and produced by Peter Rogers. Rank Organisation, 1971.

Christensen, Paul. "Real Men Don't Hold Their Liquor: The Complexity of Drunkenness and Sobriety in a Tokyo Bar." *Social Science Japan Journal*, vol. 15, no. 2, 2012, pp. 239–54. *JSTOR*. Accessed Apr. 2, 2024.

Clark, Gregory. "Factory Discipline." *The Journal of Economic History*, vol. 54, no. 1, 1994, pp. 128–63. *JSTOR*. Accessed May 18, 2024.

Comparably.com. "Happiest Employees." *comparably.com.* Accessed May 18, 2024.

Connolly, Kate. "Fears 'Lockdown Parties' Will Increase Global Spread of Coronavirus". *The Guardian*, Mar. 18, 2020. Accessed May 18, 2024.

"Coronavirus: 13 Arrested After Two Lockdown Parties." *BBC News*, 2020. Accessed May 18, 2024.

Crerar, Pippa. "Boris Johnson's 'wine time Fridays' – No10 staff held drinks EVERY week during pandemic'. mirror.co.uk. Jan. 15 2022. Accessed Aug. 14 2024.

Cromfordmills.org.uk. "Information Sheets." www.cromfordmills.org.uk/wp-content/uploads/2021/11/KS-3-4-Information-Sheets.pdf. Accessed May 18, 2024.

Davis-Blake, Alison, et al. "Happy Together? How Using Nonstandard Workers Affects Exit, Voice, and Loyalty among Standard Employees." *The Academy of Management Journal*, vol. 46, no. 4, 2003, pp. 475–85. *JSTOR*. Accessed May 18, 2024.

Duncan, Pamela, et al. "How No 10's Alleged Parties Took Place as UK Covid Death Toll Rose." *The Guardian*, Jan. 15, 2023. Accessed May 18, 2024.

Eddy, Clare Margaret. "The Social Impact of COVID-19 as Perceived by the Employees of a UK Mental Health Service." *International Journal Mental Health Nursing*, vol. 30, 2021, pp.1366–75. *ResearchGate.* Accessed May 18, 2024.

Filstad, Cathrine, et al. "Belonging at Work: The Experiences, Representations and Meanings of Belonging." *Journal of Workplace Learning*, vol. 31, 2019, pp. 116–42. *ResearchGate.* Accessed May 17, 2024.

Forbes, S., et al. "Managing Employees During the COVID-19 Pandemic: Flexible Working and the Future of Work". 2020. pure-oai.bham.ac.uk. Accessed May 18, 2024.

Freud, Sigmund. *Civilization and Its Discontents.* Hogarth Press, 1930. *Internet Archive.* Accessed Mar. 24, 2024.

Fry, Louis W. "The Maligned F. W. Taylor: A Reply to His Many Critics." *The Academy of Management Review*, vol. 1, no. 3, 1976, pp. 124–29. *JSTOR*. Accessed May 18, 2024.

Gallup. "State of the Global Workplace." 2023. Accessed Mar. 23, 2024.

Gatenby, Mark. "Teamworking: History, Development and Function A Case Study in Welsh Local Government". PhD thesis. 2008. *orca.cardiff.ac.uk.* Accessed May 18, 2024.

Gordon, Cindy. "Employee Happiness is a Leading Indicator of Profitability and Productivity." *Forbes*, Oct. 30, 2022. forbes.com. Accessed May 19, 2024.

Gordon, Cindy. *LinkedIn.* www.linkedin.com/in/cigordon. Accessed May 18, 2024.

Griffin, Emma. "Popular Culture in Industrializing England." *The Historical Journal*, vol. 45, no. 3, 2002, pp. 619–35. *JSTOR*. Accessed May 18, 2024.

Griffin, Emma. "Work and Leisure". *A Cultural History of Work in the Age of Enlightenment.* Edited by D. Simonton and A. Montenach, vol. 4. Bloomsbury Academic, 2020. ueaeprints.uea.ac.uk. Accessed May 18, 2024.

Haider, I. I., et al. "Impact of the COVID-19 Pandemic on Adult Mental Health." *Pakistan Journal of Medical Sciences*, vol. 36, 2020, pp. S90–4. *National Library of Medicine.* Accessed Mar. 23, 2024.

Harris, Jose. *Private Lives, Public Spirit: Britain 1870–1914.* Penguin, 1993.

Henricks, Thomas S. *Disputed Pleasures: Sport and Society in Pre-industrial England.* Greenwood Press, 1991. *Internet Archive.* Accessed May 18, 2024.

Hsieh, Tony. *Delivering Happiness – A Path to Profits, Passion and Purpose.* Grand Central Publishing, 2010.

Hubspot.com." Comparably Awards." www.hubspot.com/company-news/comparably awards. Accessed May 19, 2024.

Hutton, Ronald. *The Rise and Fall of Merry England. The Ritual Year, 1400–1700.* Oxford University Press, 1994.

Jack, Rebecca, and Emily Oster. "COVID-19, School Closures, and Outcomes." *The Journal of Economic Perspectives*, vol. 37, no. 4, 2023, pp. 51–70. *JSTOR*. Accessed May 18, 2024.

Janis, I. L. *Victims of Groupthink: A Psychological Study of Foreign-policy Decisions and Fiascoes.* Houghton Mifflin, 1972. *Internet Archive.* Accessed Mar. 20, 2024.

Kalleberg, Arne L., et al. "Bad Jobs in America: Standard and Nonstandard Employment Relations and Job Quality in the United States." *American Sociological Review*, vol. 65, no. 2, 2000, pp. 256–78. *JSTOR*. Accessed May 18, 2024.

Kato, K. *Necktie-Alcoholics: Cultural Forces and Japanese Alcoholism.* Washington State University, Master of Arts, 2000. Rex.libraries.wsu.edu. Accessed May 18, 2024.

Kirby, Peter. "Attendance and Work Effort in the Great Northern Coalfield, 1775–1864." *The Economic History Review*, vol. 65, no. 3, 2012, pp. 961–83. *JSTOR*. Accessed Apr. 2, 2024.

Kitching, Gavin. "The Origins of Football: History, Ideology and the Making of 'The People's Game.'" *History Workshop Journal*, no. 79, 2015, pp. 127–53. *JSTOR*. Accessed Apr. 2, 2024.

Kozlowski, Steve W. J., and Daniel R. Ilgen. "Enhancing the Effectiveness of Work Groups and Teams." *Psychological Science in the Public Interest*, vol. 7, no. 3, 2006, pp. 77–124. *JSTOR*. Accessed Apr. 2, 2024.

Lambert, Louise. *LinkedIn.* www.linkedin.com/in/dr-louise-lambert-89434927/?originalSubdomain=ae. Accessed May 18, 2024.

Ledford, Gerald E. "Comment: Happiness and Productivity Revisited." *Journal of Organizational Behavior*, vol. 20, no. 1, 1999, pp. 25–30. *JSTOR*. Accessed Apr. 2, 2024.

Littler, Craig R. "Understanding Taylorism." *The British Journal of Sociology*, vol. 29, no. 2, 1978, pp. 185–202. *JSTOR*. Accessed May 18, 2024.

Lowenthal, Leo. "Historical Perspectives of Popular Culture." *American Journal of Sociology*, vol. 55, no. 4, 1950, pp. 323–32. *JSTOR*. Accessed May 18, 2024.

Mahand, Thalmus, and Cam Caldwell. "Quiet Quitting -Causes and Opportunities." *Business and Management Research*, vol. 12, no. 1, 2023. *ResearchGate.* Accessed May 18, 2024.

Marples, Morris. *A History of Football.* Secker & Warburg, 1954.

Marrus, Michael, editor. *The Emergence of Leisure.* Harper & Row, 1974.

Maslow, A. H. "A Theory of Human Motivation." *Psychological Review*, vol. 50, no. 4, 1943, pp. 370–96. *Academia.* Accessed May 18, 2024.

McKendrick, Neil. "Josiah Wedgwood and Factory Discipline." *The Historical Journal*, vol. 4, no. 1, 1961, pp. 30–55. *JSTOR*. Accessed Apr. 2, 2024.

Michaelson, Christopher. "Meaningful Motivation for Work Motivation Theory." *The Academy of Management Review*, vol. 30, no. 2, 2005, pp. 235–38. *JSTOR*. Accessed Apr. 2, 2024.

Millar, R., et al. *Considering the Evidence of the Impacts of Lockdown on the Mental Health and Wellbeing of Children and Young People within the Context of the Individual, the Family, and Education*. Menta l Health Foundation, 2020. mentalhealth.org.uk. Accessed Apr. 2, 2024.

Montgomery, James. "James Montgomery on Factory Management, 1832." *The Business History Review*, vol. 42, no. 2, 1968, pp. 219–26. *JSTOR*. Accessed May 18, 2024.

Morgan, Kate. "Quiet Quitting Is the Status Quo': Workers Are Still Proud to Do the Bare Minimum". 2023. bbc.com. Accessed May 18, 2024.

Moss, Jennifer. *Unlocking Happiness at Work*. Kogan Page Limited, 2016.

Mullen, Brian, and Carolyn Copper. "The Relation Between Group Cohesiveness and Performance: Am Integration." *Psychology Bulletin*, vol. 115, no. 2, 1994, pp. 210–27. *ResearchGate*. Accessed May 18, 2024.

Nannestad, Eleanor. "Working-Class Pleasure Excursions to and from Lincoln 1846–1914." *Proceedings of the Lincolnshire History and Archaeological Society*, vol. 26, 1991, pp. 12–20. *slha.com*. Accessed May 18, 2024.

Oswald, Andrew J. "Happiness and Economic Performance." *The Economic Journal*, vol. 107, no. 445, 1997, pp. 1815–31. *JSTOR*. Accessed May 18, 2024.

Oswald, Andrew J., et al. "Happiness and Productivity." *Journal of Labor Economics*, vol. 33, no. 4, 2009, pp. 789–822. *ResearchGate*. Accessed May 18, 2024.

Owen, Colin C. *'The Greatest Brewery in the World': A History of Bass, Ratcliff & Gretton*. Derbyshire Record Service, 1992. *Internet Archive*. Accessed May 18, 2024.

Parra, Aritz. "In Rule-abiding Europe, Partygoers Flock to Madrid for COVID Relief." *Los Angeles Times*, Mar. 30, 2021. Accessed May 18, 2024.

Pasmore, William A. *Designing Effective Organizations – The Sociotechnical Systems Perspective*. John Wiley and Sons, 1988.

Petty, Kate, and Stacey Pope. "A New Age for Media Coverage of Women's Sport? An Analysis of English Media Coverage of the 2015 FIFA Women's World Cup." *Sociology*, vol. 53, no. 3, 2019, pp. 486–502. *JSTOR*. Accessed Apr. 2, 2024.

Pollard, Sidney. "Factory Discipline in the Industrial Revolution." *The Economic History Review*, vol. 16, no. 2, 1963, pp. 254–71. *JSTOR*. Accessed Apr. 2, 2024.

Prendergast, Canice. "Intrinsic Motivation and Incentives." *The American Economic Review*, vol. 98, no. 2, 2008, pp. 201–5. *JSTOR*. Accessed Apr. 2, 2024.

Rawnsley, Andrew. "Tories Made a Faustian Bargain When They Gave Us This Lord of Misrule." *The Guardian*, May 30, 2021. theguardian.com. Accessed May 18, 2024.

Reid, Douglas A. "The Decline of Saint Monday 1766–1876." *Past & Present*, no. 71, 1976, pp. 76–101. *JSTOR*. Accessed Apr. 2, 2024.

Rubino, John. "Aligning Personal Values and Corporate Values: A Personal and Strategic Necessity." *Employment Relations Today*, vol. 25, 1998, pp. 23–35. *Scribd*. Accessed May 18, 2024.

Shuffler, Marissa L., et al. "There's a Science for That: Team Development Interventions in Organizations." *Current Directions in Psychological Science*, vol. 20, no. 6, 2011, pp. 365–72. *JSTOR*. Accessed Apr. 2, 2024.

Singh, Rajesh. "The Impact of Intrinsic and Extrinsic Motivators on Employee Engagement in Information Organizations." *Journal of Education for Library and Information Science*, vol. 57, no. 2, 2016, pp. 197–206. *JSTOR*. Accessed May 18, 2024.

Smart, Andy. "The Day 8,000 Raleigh Workers Went on a Staff Outing to London." *Nottinghamshire Live*, May 28, 2018. nottinghampost.com. Accessed May 17, 2024.

Spicer, André, and Carl Cederström. "The Research We've Ignored About Happiness at Work." *Harvard Business Review*, July 21, 2015. hbr.org. Accessed May 17, 2024.

Steel, Piers, and Cornelius J. König. "Integrating Theories of Motivation." *The Academy of Management Review*, vol. 31, no. 4, 2006, pp. 889–913. *JSTOR*. Accessed May 18, 2024.

Steers, Richard M., et al. "Introduction to Special Topic Forum: The Future of Work Motivation Theory." *The Academy of Management Review*, vol. 29, no. 3, 2004, pp. 379–87. *JSTOR*. Accessed May 18, 2024.

Stewart, Rory. "Lord of Misrule." *Time Literary Supplement*, Nov. 6, 2020. the-tls.co.uk. Accessed May 18, 2024.

Svyantek, Daniel J., et al. "The Relationship between Organizational Characteristics and Team Building Success." *Journal of Business and Psychology*, vol. 14, no. 2, 1999, pp. 265–83. *JSTOR*. Accessed May 18, 2024.

Taylor, Frederick Winslow. *The Principles of Scientific Management*. Harper & Brothers Publishers, 1911. *Internet Archive*. Accessed May 18, 2024.

Thompson, E. P. "Time, Work-Discipline, and Industrial Capitalism." *Past & Present*, no. 38, 1967, pp. 56–97. *JSTOR*. Accessed May 18, 2024.

Timinsky, Samuel J. 'The Nation That Never Rests: Japan's Debate Over Work-Life Balance and Work That Kills'. *The Asia-Pacific Journal – Japan Focus*, vol. 17, no. 10, 2019. apjjf.org. Accessed May 18, 2024.

Tiratelli, Matteo. "The Working Week in the Long Nineteenth Century: Evidence from the Timings of Political Events in Britain." *Social Science History*, vol. 46, no. 2, 2022, pp. 1–23. *ResearchGate*. Accessed May 18, 2024.

Tolosa, Lucí, and Elisa Tasca y Diego Estebanez, trans. Melissa Kitson. "Madrid's Nightlife Rages on Despite Pandemic: 'These Parties Give Me Life'". *EL PAÍS*, Mar. 29, 2021. *english.elpais.com*. Accessed May 18, 2024.

Tucker, Barbara M. "The Merchant, the Manufacturer, and the Factory Manager: The Case of Samuel Slater." *The Business History Review*, vol. 55, no. 3, 1981, pp. 297–313. *JSTOR*. Accessed May 18, 2024.

Voth, Hans-Joachim. "Time and Work in Eighteenth-Century London." *The Journal of Economic History*, vol. 58, no. 1, 1998, pp. 29–58. *JSTOR*. Accessed May 18, 2024.

Walsh, Aidan, and Malcolm Brady. "Chester Barnard Revisited: Spontaneous Orders and the Firm." *Journal of Institutional Economics*, vol. 15, no. 6, 2019, pp. 951–62. cambridge.org. Accessed May 18, 2024.

Walters, William. *Bass Ratcliff & Gretton Limited Excursion to Scarborough*. The Bass Museum, 1977.

Watanabe, Masao. "Taylorism: A Critical Reassessment." *Hitotsubashi Journal of Social Studies*, vol. 23, no. 2, 1991, pp. 69–84. *JSTOR*. Accessed May 18, 2024.

Weber, Max. *Essays in Sociology*. Oxford University Press. 1946. *Internet Archive*. Accessed May 18, 2024.

White, Michael R. "Team Building: A Management Technology for Improving Productivity." *The Journal of Epsilon Pi Tau*, vol. 13, no. 2, 1987, pp. 4–10. *JSTOR*. Accessed May 18, 2024.

Williams, Jean. "An Equality Too Far? Historical and Contemporary Perspectives of Gender Inequality in British and International Football." *Historical Social Research/Historische Sozialforschung*, vol. 31, no. 1 (115), 2006, pp. 151–69. *JSTOR*. Accessed May 18, 2024.

Williams, Zoe. *Review of the Impact of Mass Disruption on the Wellbeing and Mental Health of Children and Young People, and Possible Therapeutic Interventions.* Welsh Government, GSR report number 62/2020. gov.wales. Accessed May 18, 2024.

"Women's and Girls' Football". *The Football Association.* thefa.com. Accessed May 19, 2024.

World Federation for Company Sports. *worldcompanysport.org/what-is-the-wfcs.* Accessed May 19, 2024.

Wright, Thomas A., and Ching-Chu Huang. "The Many Benefits of Employee Well-Being in Organizational Research." *Journal of Organizational Behavior*, vol. 33, no. 8, 2012, pp. 1188–92. *JSTOR*. Accessed May 20, 2024.

Yamauchi, Kazuaki, and Thomas Orr. "Nominication for Strategic Leadership: Best Practices in Japanese-Style Communication for Managerial Purposes." Professional Communication Conference (IPCC), 2011 IEEE International. *ResearchGate.* Accessed May 19, 2024.

Zoom.com. "Zoom Employee Happiest." www.zoom.com/en/blog/zoom-employees-happiest. Accessed May 19, 2024.

6 Pride

From Riot to Carnival

The subtitle of this chapter "From Riot to Carnival" focuses on a shift from triggered, reactive violence and protest to planned, calendared, carnival-style events. Both mechanisms, riot and carnival, offer safety-valve release, but only one is sanctioned and therefore fits the Carnivalesque Leadership model. This chapter considers how the shift from unsanctioned protest to sanctioned and contained safety-valve release has caused contention and consternation over the decades, with the criticism that Pride events have become too contained, too celebratory and too carnival. For some, Pride events have morphed into increasingly standardised, commercialised and, potentially, commodified products. The Carnivalesque Leadership model explored in this book means that even standardised, commercialised and commodified Pride events employ carnivalesque components that not only offer temporary safety-valve release but also still signal, reflect and determine longer-term change.

The starting point for this discussion is the Stonewall riots of 1969, which provided the stimulus for Pride marches and added a driving narrative to protest and visibility events globally.[1] In tracking the transition from unsanctioned riot (Stonewall) to sanctioned, temporary subversion (Pride), this chapter highlights that the very fact of Pride means that it remains a subversive challenge to hierarchy in many parts of the world despite its seemingly temporary, safety-valve status. Indeed, the potential tension between the controlled standardisation and protest activism will be considered in this chapter, thus drawing out some of the tensions of the "temporary" status of controlled subversion at the centre of Carnivalesque Leadership.

Riot!

"Something like a carnival" erupted into what became known as the Stonewall riots outside the eponymous New York gay bar following a police raid on the hot night of June 27 and the early hours of June 28, 1969 (Duberman 250). The Stonewall Inn's reputation at the time did not

DOI: 10.4324/9781003441649-7

suggest it would occupy a significant place in history or become associated with political and social movements that have challenged discrimination in many countries around the world. Located on Christopher Street in New York City's Greenwich Village, the Stonewall Inn was opened as a "private" gay bar in 1966 by "Fat" Tony Lauria who was part of a mafia crime family (Todd 58). The outlawing of homosexual acts meant that gay bars provided vital outlets for personal expression and social/sexual associations and, from the Mob's perspective, they were incredibly profitable. The Stonewall Inn had no running water behind the bar and no fire exit. To avoid the need for a liquor licence, the Stonewall Inn was registered as both a "private" club and a "bottle bar," which meant that patrons were supposed to bring their own alcohol and sign in at the door (Todd 59.) Despite its lack of finery or, indeed, basic necessities, the Stonewall Inn established a welcoming reputation for its (mainly) gay male regulars, drag queens and drag kings and transvestites many of whom were not welcome elsewhere given New York state's "gender appropriate" clothing legislation. This "Masquerade" law dated back to the 1845 introduction of the "anti-loitering" legislation, New York Penal Law 240.35(4) which included an anti-disguise element. The New York State Assembly Bill (Memo No A10446A), when seeking to repeal paragraph 4 of this law, acknowledges in 2020 that "the law has been used to criminalize protest, as well as to arrest New Yorkers 'masquerading' as a different gender" (New York State Assembly). By the 1960s, this part of the law had commonly become known as the "three-item rules" or "three-piece law," which was generally understood to mean that people must wear at least three pieces of clothing associated with their perceived gender.[2] The Stonewall Inn's welcoming attitude to those who did not confirm to these rules was part of its appeal and popularity. Significantly, Stonewall was also one of the only gay clubs in New York that allowed dancing. As such, the Stonewall Inn became established as one of the most popular gay bars in Greenwich Village and was seen as safe retreat from the harassment of everyday life (Duberman 225).

The Stonewall Inn, like other gay bars, was subject to regular police raids and, only the week before the riots, the NYPD had raided the place. The impetus for the raid on the night of the riots was seemingly to gather evidence for liquor being sold, drugs being traded and cross dressing (Todd 67). The well-recognised network of police corruption meant that the management usually received tip offs and could subsequently prepare for a visit by the police. On the night of the June 27, 1969, however, no tip off was received. Police officers stormed the bar at 1.20 a.m. and arrested thirteen people, including those violating the state "gender appropriate" clothing law. Significantly, patrons and locals did not just disperse as would normally be expected but remained gathered outside the bar. The crowd and the agitation grew as knowledge of unfolding events began to spread in the local area. The violent arrest and manhandling of a butch lesbian (potentially Drag King, Stormé DeLarverie) is sometimes identified as the "tipping point" which led the crowd to act (Todd 72 and 242).[3] Details of the specific events and the responsible actors vary in different accounts. In some versions, trans women Marsha P. Johnson and Sylvia Rivera led the uprising (Todd 76), despite other accounts that suggest that Johnson took a major role but Rivera was not present at the start of the first night (Cohen 90) and another focuses on Craig Rodwell's yelling of "Gay Power" as a key trigger (Todd 72). Rodwell himself states that there were multiple triggers and that there was no "one thing" that happened or one person, "there was just . . . Flash of group – of mass – anger" (Duberman 243).

Missiles, including bottles, coins and stones, started to be launched from the crowd at the police. Marsha P. Johnson was seen climbing a lamp post and dropping "a bag containing a heavy object" on a police car windshield and shattering it (Cohen 90). Mark Segal, an eighteen year old who had been in the bar that night and went on to play a major role in the subsequent response, describes the importance of protecting the Stonewall Inn by its patrons, stating, "Whoever assumes that a swishy queen can't fight should have seen them, makeup dripping and gowns askew, fighting for their home and fiercely proving that no one would take it away from them" (Segal 154). When they perceived the threat levels from the missile-hurling crowd to be too dangerous, the police officers took refuge in the Stonewall Inn itself and barricaded the doors to protect themselves from the advancing crowds. What has become known as the Stonewall riots had begun as the crowds swelled to a mob (Duberman 244). The crowds attempted to breach the barricades multiple times, and there were numerous attempts to set fire to the bar with the police officers inside. The arrival of the fire department and riot squad eventually forced the dispersal of the crowd at approximately 3.30 a.m. on June 28.

News of the events on that Friday night spread quickly by word of mouth and gained immediate local newspaper, radio and TV coverage. Rodwell created a leaflet highlighting the police action and set out demands for the future such as "Get the Mafia and the Cops out of Gay Bars" (Barnes). During the following day, crowds started to gather at the Stonewall Inn and along Christopher Street including some of those who had been involved with previous night's events, notably a "fearless chorus line of queens . . . kicking their heels high in the air, as if in direct defiance" (Duberman 251). A story frequently related about the Stonewall riots features this impromptu troupe of drag queens in chorus line formation facing down the police with Rockettes-style high kicks and chanting:

"We are the Stonewall girls
We wear our hair in curls

> We wear no underwear
> We show our pubic hair
> We wear our dungarees
> Above our Nelly knees!"
>
> (Duberman 247; Todd 77)

The police's Tactical Patrol Force was deployed in readiness for a potential repeat of public non-compliance. By the evening and into the night, the crowd had swelled to many hundreds of people. When the police advanced, the crowd tactically retreated down different sideroads before returning. During the resulting skirmishes, missiles were thrown, lamp posts were climbed and there was damage to police vehicles. The destruction of the night lasted until approximately 4 a.m. The following Sunday and Monday nights saw some further interactions between groups of protestors and the police, but the wet weather helped dampen the tinderbox tensions on the streets surrounding the Stonewall Inn. The immediate riotous uprising had peaked, but the challenge to hierarchical power would continue. Segal comments on the atmosphere of the uprising:

> There were a lot of people running around having fun. It was probably the most joyous riot you have ever seen, because the heavy weight of oppression lifted that night. We felt that that oppression was being lifted by our very actions.
>
> (Segal cited by Teeman)

Here, Segal captures a sense of safety-valve release during the Stonewall uprising. In the context of the argument here, this safety-valve release does not represent carnivalesque safety-valve release as it is unsanctioned. Temporary licence was taken not granted by the hierarchy.

Recognition of the significance of the Stonewall uprising was mixed at the time and retrospectively depending on perspective. Trans icon, Jayne County, highlights the role of the "street queens" who "took the lead in the Stonewall Riots. They walked around in semi-drag with teased hair and false eyelashes on and they didn't give a shit what anybody thought about them." She adds "Nowadays, the Stonewall Riots are regarded as the birth of gay liberation, but for me and the other street queens, it wasn't such an amazingly important thing; we were already out there" (County 168). For others, the Stonewall uprising was the rebellion that changed everything. Segal argues that in the nights that followed the Stonewall uprising, various different organisations started to come together publicly which was significant, given that "until that moment, LGBT people had simply accepted oppression and inequality as their lot in life. That all changed. There was a spirit of rebellion in the air" (155). Attempts at organising a collective response had begun.

The Stonewall riots provided a galvanising energy. Capturing and spreading this impulse, Rodwell and Fred Sargeant published a flyer on behalf of the Homophile Youth Movement in Neighborhoods stating that the "nights of Friday, 27 June 1969 and Saturday, 28 June 1969 will go down in history as the first time Homosexual men and women went out into the streets" (Todd 80). The history of the Stonewall riots and their impact have been reviewed and revised many times and will continue to be. Stein highlights that the dominant narrative has positioned Stonewall riots "as the first act of lesbian and gay resistance *ever*" (Stein cited by Hall 546). The Stonewall riots were not, in fact, the first gay rights street protests in the U. S. In August 1966, there had been protests against police harassment led by drag queens at Gene Compton's Cafeteria 6 in San Francisco. This is widely regarded as the first LGBTQ-related riot in the United States, but it gained no mainstream media coverage (Hillman 161). Prior to this, a sit-in and subsequent demonstration outside Dewey's restaurant in Philadelphia on April 25, 1965 was a response to the denial of service to "homosexuals," "masculine women," "feminine men," and "persons wearing non-conformist clothing" (Stein).

Whilst these incidents show that there had been gay rights protests before the Stonewall uprising, the development of a coherent, organised, multifaceted and ongoing response to Stonewall was a turning point. There was a multiple and wide-ranging domino effect that followed the events at the Stonewall Inn. Multiple organisations were founded, and existing organisations were given tighter focus in the subsequent months. The Gay Liberation Front (GLF) was formed by collective in July 1969 with its first editorial published in the magazine *Come Out!* in September of that year. Some members of the GLF broke away from the organisation six months after its formation to instigate the Gay Activists Alliance (GAA) to solely focus on homosexual liberation (Bell 17).[4] Martha Shelley and Karla Jay broke away to form Lavender Menace which became Radicalesbians in response to perceived "male chauvinism" in the GLF (*Gay Youth's Gay Journal* cited in Cohen 31). The GLF also formed sub-cells, with Segal driving the formation of the Gay Youth New York in February 1970. Another organisation, the Christopher Street Liberation Day Committee, was established as a direct consequence of events at the Stonewall Inn. During a meeting in Rodwell's flat in November 1969, it was proposed that a demonstration should "be held annually on the last Saturday in June in New York City to commemorate the 1969 spontaneous demonstrations on Christopher Street and this demonstration to be called CHRISTOPHER STREET LIBERATION DAY" (Todd 82).[5]

Providing an example of the further domino effect from the activism at Stonewall, Street Transvestite Action Revolutionaries (STAR) was also founded in its wake after Sylvia Rivera conceived the idea for STAR during a sit-in occupation of the Weinstein Hall of NYU Washington Square campus on September 20–25, 1970. The occupation had been initiated following the university's decision to cancel the last in a series of four gay community dances organised by the Christopher Street Liberation Day Committee with support of members from the Gay Student Liberation of NYU, GLF, GAA and Radicalesbians (Bell 111). Amongst those that joined for the protest was Rivera, who started formulating STAR as a direct result of the sit-in and the police response to it. Offering practical help, Rivera and Marsha P. Johnson set up the STAR House on East Second Street to provide shelter and sustenance to transvestite youths and "fought against abuse perpetrated by prison officials, mental institutions, police, and the legal system" (Cohen 90). STAR, along with GLF and GAA, also organised pickets, visited prisons and helped form the Gay Community Prison Committee, and they publicly supported the Young Lords and the Black Panthers (Cohen 93). STAR and GLF maintained a multi-issue, intersectional approach to liberation, whereas the GAA was tightly focused on gay rights. Rivera had previously been involved in the Black Liberation Movement and commented in interview that "The people at them bars, especially at the Stonewall, were involved in other movements" (Rivera 175). The GLF's support for the Black Panthers contributed to the GAA's split from the organisation (Driskill 46). Apart from the GAA, the LGBTQ+ protest movements at this time "were closely tied to other social movements, including civil rights and women's rights, antiwar, and poor people's struggles" (Ashley 28).[6] Moreover, the involvement and leadership of street transvestites, Rivera and Johnson, in the Stonewall uprising and the subsequent action reflect that the riots were, to an extent, a rebellion of the poorest and most marginalised among the gay community, who were the patrons of the Stonewall Inn (Ashley 28).

Alongside the new organisations fighting for change, the Queens Liberation Front had already been announced by trans activist, Lee Brewster, just prior to the Stonewall uprising. Brewster had originally been part of the established left-wing Mattachine Society which had been founded by Harry Hay in Los Angeles in 1950 before splintering into different regions of the country. The name of this organisation derives, via the French *Société Mattachine*, from the Italian *mattachino* meaning a "court jester who dared to tell the truth to the king" (Cohen 14). The subversive challenge to hierarchy captured in the name of the organisation was hampered during the fearful McCarthy-era persecution, and the organisation became less radical and grew "increasingly circumspect" (Cohen 15). Another well-established homophile group, The Daughters of Bilitis (DOB), had been founded by Phyllis Lyon and Del Martin in San Francisco in 1955 with the aim of helping lesbians "adjust to society" and "working towards the goal of educating the public toward an acceptance of the homophile in society" (*D.O.B. News* cited by Cohen 15).[7] In its September 1969 Newsletter, DOB proclaimed

"The Birth of Gay Power," outlining the events at Stonewall Inn on the Friday and Saturday nights and the gatherings and speeches held at Washington Square on the Sunday of that weekend (1).

Both DOB and Mattachine Society were relatively well established in New York prior to the Stonewall uprising. Whilst the September 1969 Newsletter of DOB reflects a positive view of the activism around Stonewall and outlines DOB involvement on the Sunday of that weekend, Mattachine Society adopted a very different approach, criticising the image created by "a bunch of drag queens in the Village acting disorderly and tacky and cheap" (Duberman 255). Whilst at odds with the Mattachine Society on many levels, prominent activist in the homophile movement, Randy Wicker, also believed that the much publicised events at the Stonewall Inn were "setting back the gay liberation movement twenty years" as it counteracted the "work" done "to try to establish legitimacy of the gay movement that we were nice middleclass people . . . . And suddenly there was all this, what I considered riffraff" (Wicker interviewed with Johnson by Marcus 139). Capturing the tensions he felt at the time, Wicker adds that he was considered "the first militant and a visionary leader of the gay movement" but did not realise that that the "revolution" he thought would never come *was* actually happening and that "a small nuclei of people" were becoming "a mass social movement." He retrospectively admits "I was against it. Now I'm very happy Stonewall happened. I'm very happy the way things worked out" (140).

Martha Shelley of DOB played another more immediate key role in shaping the community response to the Stonewall uprising. Very shortly after the uprising, Shelley liaised with the Mattachine Society members who agreed to a proposed protest march despite concerns over the uprising. The group of people who then gathered together to plan and organise this demonstration collectively became the Gay Liberation Front. Organised by Shelley, the GLF march took place in July 1969 as an immediate response to the Stonewall uprising ("Cross Currents" 227). Therefore, the first demonstration marking the uprising at Stonewall Inn was not the Christopher Street Liberation Day march on the anniversary weekend June 1970 but the GLF protest march one month after the event.

Relations between the different LGBTQ+ organisations that were spawned by, or refocused from, Stonewall provide examples of clear co-operation such as STAR's first dance being supported by Gay Youth and co-sponsored by Gay Liberation Front with whom it also joined to organise the short-lived Gay Community Center (Cohen 33). There are also multiple examples of differing priorities with resultant tensions that led to some of the breakaways from the GLF as identified earlier. Arthur Bell of GAA also highlighted tensions, mainly focusing on the trans community among the LGBTQ+ organisations and that "STARs" were the "great unwanteds"

(Bell cited in Cohen 127). The fight for gay rights prior to, during and after the uprising at Stonewall was not a unified collective effort carried out by a homogenised group. The power of the collective did, however, come to the fore in the organisation of the first Christopher Street Liberation Day demonstration, with previously misaligned groups working together (Sergeant).

Two key figures in the gay liberation movement, Rodwell and Ellen Broidy, who was an early member of the GLF and took part in the Lavender Menace action of May 1970, were driving forces behind the co-ordinated next stage response to Stonewall which involved transforming existing "Annual Reminder" events (Todd 82). Rodwell and Broidy met with their partners Fred Sergeant and Linda Rhodes at Rodwell's flat. Between the four of them, the plans for a demonstration to mark the first anniversary of the uprising at Stonewall started to take shape over dinner. Rodwell's Oscar Wilde Bookshop, which had been opened in 1967 and was the first gay bookshop in the United States, became a central meeting place for planning the event. In November 1969, Broidy presented a resolution to the Eastern Regional Conference of Homophile Organizations for the creation of the Christopher Street Liberation Day march instead of the established "Annual Reminder" format.[8] Previously, the East Coast Homophile Organization (ECHO) – the forerunner to the Easter Regional Conference of Homophile Organizations (ERCHO) – had been the umbrella organisation overseeing the Annual Reminders which had been originally instigated by Rodwell to commemorate the Mattachine Society's picket of the White House in April 1965. These Annual Reminders took place outside Philadelphia's Independence Hall and were strategically sedate and non-confrontational. They were conservative to the point of requiring a formal dress code for participants. The proposal for the Christopher Street Liberation Day protest was to establish a new version of this Annual Reminder event which would, from the outset, be less reserved, less driven by an urge for conformity and assimilation and less conservative in approach. Whilst the Annual Reminders sought to downplay difference from heterosexual "norms," the new annual event sought to increase the visibility of difference (McFarland Bruce 106).

The proposal submitted to ERCHO set out Resolution #1:

> that the Annual Reminder, in order to be more relevant, reach a greater number of people, and encompass the ideas and ideals of the larger struggle in which we are engaged – that of our fundamental human rights – be moved both in time and location
>
> (cited by Armstrong and Crage 738).

The proposal was accepted and the march was therefore sanctioned by ERCHO. Whilst the initial plans were for the march to take place on Saturday 27, it was shifted to Sunday 28. Three dozen people were involved in the planning committee for New York (Rodwell). The Christopher Street Liberation Day Umbrella Committee was formed with the aim of holding a massive march at the culmination of a Gay Pride Week ("The History of Pride" – Library of Congress). The scale of the plans was bigger than just New York City, however, and aimed for national recognition as captured in the proposal: "We also propose that we contact Homophile organizations throughout the country and suggest that they hold parallel demonstrations on that day. We propose a nationwide show of support" (Todd 82).

The start of this chapter has offered a summary of events leading up to the Christopher Street Liberation Day march and the beginnings of "Pride" events as we know them today. It is not offered as an exhaustive account but, rather, to enable the exploration of a carnivalesque model for short-term safety-valve release and longer-term change. The origins of Pride are in unsanctioned demonstration, in protest and in temporary subversion. Events from the first Christopher Street Liberation Day March in 1970 to the official calendared Pride events globally today are sanctioned through the hierarchical bureaucratic systems of host cities. The subsequent tension between sanctioned protest/demonstration and the potential commodification of Pride will be considered during the second section of this chapter which starts to explore if a carnivalesque model enables containment and nullification of subversive protest or whether it facilitates longer-term change.

The Christopher Street Liberation Day March 1970

Approximately 5,000 people took part in the Christopher Street Liberation Day March in Greenwich Village, New York City, on Sunday June 28, 1970. Reflecting on events, Fred Sergeant who is credited as one of the four founding organisers of the event as discussed earlier, explains "There were no floats, no music, no boys in briefs. The cops turned their backs on us to convey their disdain, but the masses of people kept carrying signs and banners, chanting and waving to surprised onlookers" (Sergeant). The comparison that Sergeant offers here is very much aimed at highlighting the differences between the first demonstration in 1970 and later developments and standardised expectations of the Pride march as an event.

The march route began on Washington Place between Sheridan Square and Sixth Avenue in Greenwich Village, moved north up Sixth Avenue, and ended with a "Gay-In" in Central Park's Sheep Meadow (Shockley). Reflecting the collaborative planning of the march, it was led by a representative from each of the contributing organisations. The official chant had been decided before the event: "Say it clear, say it loud. Gay is good, gay is proud" (Sergeant). The sense of freedom and release is palpable in the first-hand accounts from those who participated in the event. Trans activist, Victoria Cruz, recalls:

> As we were marching, more and more people joined the parade. We got to Central Park. It was like a spectacle. We were so happy, free, and liberated. It was a different feeling. Nobody was ashamed to be out and be themselves. It was just an uplifting feeling of freedom.
>
> (Cruz cited in Teeman)

At an individual level, the decision to participate in the march may not have been taken lightly, given the potential for backlash following exposure/disclosure. Perry Brass, who took part in the march and wrote about it for GLF's *Come Out!* publication, was clear on the bravery of participants:

> The courage that it took for some people to make those first steps from Sheridan Square into Sixth Avenue and out of the Village was the summoning up of a whole lifetime's desire to finally come clear, to say the truth as it is, to expose themselves nakeder than any pinup boy in any flesh book.
>
> (215)

Brass discusses the week leading up to the march: "It was Gay Pride Week, just like the coming of a holiday you've never heard about and suddenly discovered and the holiday became a time and feeling, a mass feeling, like Mardi Gras" (216). In making links to a feeling of Mardi Gras, Brass offers us an easy alignment with the carnivalesque. Whilst joy and freedom may have been experienced by some during the 1969 Stonewall uprising (see Segal above), it was not sanctioned and therefore does not align with a carnivalesque model. Participation in the Christopher Street Liberation Day march does, however, represent carnivalesque safety-valve release, given that it is sanctioned, temporary and communal.

The Christopher Street Liberation Day March was not the first LGBTQ+ commemorative march that anniversary weekend, with events taking place on Saturday June 27 in Chicago and San Francisco. There had been a week of events leading up to the march in Chicago, including a "Gay Dance" at the Aragon Ballroom and a series of workshops on a range of legal and social issues relating to the communities involved. Approximately 150 people gathered at Bughouse Square in Chicago and then embarked on the first steps of a Pride march on June 27, the day before the New York event. Following tone-setting speeches, banner waving and communal chanting of "Gay Power," the march set off along Dearborn to Chicago Avenue, east to the Water Tower, then south on Michigan Avenue to the Civic Center (now Daley Plaza) for more speeches (de la Croix). One of the participants,

Albert Williams, commented "We ended up with a speech and did a circle dance around the Picasso, which I always thought Pablo would have liked" (cited by Lawrence). San Francisco hosted a small march (roughly 30 participants) on the Saturday before a "Gay-In" that attracted approximately 200 people at Golden Gate Park on the Sunday. The arrival of mounted police at the "Gay-In" was reported by Pukas in the counter-culture underground newspaper, the *Berkeley Barb* (July 3–9), which describes how participants were searched and harassed.

The events in San Francisco and Chicago were not on the same scale as the Christopher Street Liberation Day march in New York. However, the Christopher Street West (CSW) equivalent in Los Angeles, which also took place on Sunday June 28, was significant in terms of participation, with approximately 2000 involved (Perry in *Advocate*). Morris Knight, who had formed the Los Angeles section of the Gay Liberation Front in October 1969, had been contacted by the New York organisers and convened a group of key Los Angeles activists, including Reverend Troy Perry and Reverend Bob Humphries, to plan an event (Armstrong and Crage 740). Whilst the other cities held protest marches, Los Angeles adopted a slightly different approach. During initial discussions with Knight and Reverend Humphries about how the city should contribute, Perry recollects asking the other two men "Why don't we just hold a parade?" He explains how they then went to the police commission to fill out an application for a parade permit and answered questions for about two hours before the Chief of Police, Ed Davis, asked, "Did you know that homosexuality was illegal in the state of California?" Perry replied "No, sir, it's not." Davis then reportedly went on to state

> Well, I'll tell you something, as far as I'm concerned, granting a parade permit to a group of homosexuals to parade down Hollywood Boulevard would be the same as giving a permit to march to a group of thieves and murderers!
>
> (Perry in *Advocate*).

Ensuing legal challenges eventually led to the parade permit being issued, with agreement for police protection. The presiding Judge Schauer made clear the right to protection and the right to demonstrate, formally stating "wherever people are attempting to demonstrate peacefully to petition their government for redress of grievances, it is the duty of the police that are paid by the taxpayer – including the demonstrators – to protect them" (McFarland Bruce 46). There had been a long history of resistance by the gay community in Los Angeles and a long history of police antagonism, making this ruling even more significant. The brutal police raid on the city's Black Cat Tavern in 1967 had left a legacy of distrust. The peaceful protests subsequently undertaken at the Black Cat Tavern had led to the formation of a new group named Personal Rights in Defense and Education (P.R.I.D.E.). This had been the first time "Pride" was formally used in the context of LGBTQ+ rights (Todd 28–9).

Whilst the decision to adopt the form of a parade was to prove influential in the development of Pride in subsequent years, in 1970, the first, relatively basic, parade set off from the point of Hollywood Boulevard and McCadden Place. Perry states:

> We couldn't get the bands we wanted to have, nor the horsemen, nor a lot of the floats, but we did exceptionally well anyway. The parade started with Willie Smith driving his VW Microbus, and playing some recordings of World War II German marches over an amplification system he had hooked up.
>
> (Perry "The Lord Is My Shepherd" 204)

The choice of the music parodied the perceived oppressive attitudes of the police towards the LGBTQ+ community (Perry in *Advocate*). Capturing the subversive good humour of the event, Perry recollects how a

> conservative gay group from extremely conservative Orange County brought a large sign that read "Homosexuals for Ronald Reagan" and heard a woman on the sidewalk say, "I can forgive them for being homosexual, but I will never forgive them for supporting Ronald Reagan"
>
> (Perry in *Advocate*).

The Christopher Street Liberation Day march in New York, the CSW parade in Los Angeles and the smaller scale events in Chicago and San Francisco set in motion the Pride phenomenon. Publishing an account of CSW in *Gay* published in July 1970, Pedersen states

> On Sunday all was festive, militant, gay and determined . . . . We now have, thanks to our brothers' and sisters' activities in New York, Chicago and elsewhere, an established National gay holiday. And just wait 'till next year.
>
> (4)

Pedersen was right to imply the impetus had come from that first set of protest displays. The following year, more cities got involved both in the United States and beyond. Boston, Dallas, Milwaukee, Paris, West Berlin and Stockholm were all added to the existing active cities (Todd 87). The following year, 1972, saw Brighton and London in the UK; Atlanta, Buffalo, Detroit, Washington DC, Miami and Philadelphia in the United States also join in.

London Pride provides a useful case study for exploring tensions between the more potentially "frivolous" aspects of Pride and its protest status as well as the potential impact of commercialisation and commodification. London Pride grew out of the recently formed UK Gay Liberation Front which had been very much influenced by the United States models of activism. The UK GLF co-founder, Bob Mellors, had spent the summer of 1970 in New York and had become involved with the city's GLF. He met Aubrey Walter at the Revolutionary Peoples' Constitutional Conference in Philadelphia sponsored by the Black Panther Movement. When they returned to England, Bob and Aubrey set up the UK Gay Liberation Front and held its first meeting on October 13, 1970, at the London School of Economics, where Mellors was studying. The UK GLF held its first demonstration on November 27, 1970, in Highbury Fields to protest about the police arrest at that location of liberal activist, Louis Eakes, for "indecency" (Walter 13). In August 1971, the GLF youth group organised a demonstration march starting from four different points in London and congregating for a rally in Trafalgar Square to protest about the age of consent for gay men being 21 which represented the first organised LGBTQ+ public march in the UK. Global activist, Peter Tatchell, joined GLF in 1971 and was part of the group organising and planning the first "Gay Pride" march in London on July 1, 1972. Tatchell outlines the initial aims of the event as generating visibility and breaking down barriers. He describes how the event started with approximately 1000 people marching in a "joyful, carnival-style parade" (Tatchell 2022), and Walter characterises the event as a "carnival-type demo" (Walter 25). Expression of affection was illegal for homosexual men at this time, and Tatchell reports multiple incidents of police homophobia and abuse and how participants received a combination of overt hostility from the public and overt support. The event culminated at Hyde Park with a "Queer picnic" (Tatchell *Pride before Pride*). Here, communal food, drink, music and party games created what Tatchell describes as a "carnival atmosphere" (*Pride before Pride*). The carnivalesque relevance and safety-valve mechanisms outlined here are obvious. For Tatchell, the event was both a joyful celebration and a visibility-raising protest. By 1987, the number of participants in London's Pride reached approximately 15,000. Significantly, the following year, the British government, led by Margaret Thatcher, introduced The Local Government Act 1988 which included Section 28, stating:

> A local authority shall not –
>
> (a) intentionally promote homosexuality or publish material with the intention of promoting homosexuality.
> (b) promote the teaching in any maintained school of the acceptability of homosexuality as a pretended family relationship.[9]

Tatchell describes how, as a direct consequence of the unpopularity of Section 28, public support and participation in Pride demonstrations saw a doubling of participants in 1988 (Tatchell 2022). At a time when the LGBTQ+ community was faced with legislation which effectively prevented teachers from talking about same-sex relationships in schools, forcing teachers back into the closet, or out of their job, and scarred a generation of LGBT people (Stonewall), Pride provided a rallying call against oppressive legislation and safety-valve release. The 1988 Pride was "angry and political" (Tatchell 2022). Every subsequent year, the marches increased, reaching peak participation in 1997, which saw over 100,000 marching with 300,000 at the after-march party on Clapham Common. From the outset, Pride in London combined carnival mode with protest. Over the course of its history, the London event has developed and, at various points, has overtly aligned itself with carnival. For example, the 1978 event was presented as a "Gay Pride Carnival" with the stated aim, in response to increased physical attacks on the gay community and the increasing attacks from the media, to "show the positive side of being gay; GAY IS FUN; GAY IS PROUD; GAY IS BEAUTIFUL!" The planned week included discos, theatre, exhibitions and workshops, "climaxing with a Carnival parade and March through West London" ("Gay Pride Week 1978"). The Carnival was advertised as featuring floats, steel bands, fancy dress and street theatre.

Arguing that Pride was hijacked by commercial interests, Tatchell states that there was a "takeover by gay businesspeople at the turn of the century" which "rebranded Pride as a 'Mardi Gras' party and started charging for the post-march festival" (Tatchell 2022). He laments that there are only 30,000 people allowed on the march, making it "one of the smallest Prides of any Western capital city" (Tatchell 2022). For Tatchell, such limits on numbers goes against the original premise of Pride. In response to what he sees as a significant shift away from its founding aims, Tatchell initiated the "Reclaim Pride" London march in 2021 which has no attendance limits, no fees, no commercialisation and is putting "the politics back into Pride" (*Pride before Pride*).[10]

The development of an alternative "Pride" event in London follows a New York model also born from an increasing backlash to the perceived commercialisation and limitations of Pride.[11] In New York, the Reclaim Pride Coalition claims the tagline "No corps, no cops, no bs!" (*Reclaim Pride Coalition – NYC*) and the alternative Queer Liberation March in 2019 followed the same route as the original Christopher Street Liberation Day March in 1970. Criticism of Pride and mainstream LGBTQ+ activism is ongoing. DeFilippis argues that "Stonewall was a rebellion against the police and the criminal legal system" (95) and that the "mainstream LGBT movement of the next fifty years failed, spectacularly, to follow through" and argues that "to claim that the last fifty years of activism has been inspired by Stonewall is disingenuous at best" (DeFilippis 96 and 100). Alternate readings of the meanings and aims of Pride focus on its genesis being on cultural change. McFarland Bruce, for example, argues that unlike most mass demonstrations, "Pride gives casual participants a central role and focuses on changing culture instead of state laws and policies" (7) and that the aim of Pride is "to change the heteronormative cultural meanings that render LGBT people symbolically inferior to heterosexuals" (8). Here, McFarland Bruce offers alignment with a Carnivalesque Leadership model that offers Bakhtinian merging of the spectator and participant (see Chapter 1) and challenge to existing hierarchies through enabling visibility of those with less power.

The tensions foregrounded by the Reclaim Pride movement include concerns about the commodification and commercialisation of Pride. Commercial links are well established with Salarvand highlighting that "Gay Pride events across North America present an impressively long list of corporate sponsors" (35). The tensions generated by commercial alignment date back to the early years of Pride, with Maccubbin highlighting that, by 1978, tensions around the balance between sponsorship and protest were surfacing. Whilst an in-depth exploration of the commercial tensions that exist around Pride is beyond the remit of this book, it is worth (inevitably problematically) summarising some of these in relation to the carnivalesque. Firstly, the commodification of Pride can be seen as an extension of the commodification of gay identity with potential for both exploitation and validation. McFarland Bruce argues that commercial "businesses that sell LGBT-themed items serve as community resources that enable participants to make their identities visible" (150). Sears lists commercialised, corporately sponsored Pride Day celebrations as one example of the way in which open gay and lesbian life has "thrived" in commodified forms.[12] There is an established argument that corporate sponsorship of Pride increases visibility (McFarland Bruce 150) and that the support of corporations has helped normalise LGBTQ people and families (Roth and Paisley 2019). In a Carnivalesque Leadership model, the temporary subversion of dominant heterosexual hierarchy and exposure to alternative lifestyles through increased visibility and joyous celebration have had, and continue to have, longer-term impact on individuals involved and increased cultural and social awareness more widely thereby representing the potential for longer-term change.

The commercialisation of Pride through corporate sponsorship and affiliation has been a focus of critical attention and accusations of manipulative tokenism, the potential for compromise on message leading to movements such as Reclaim Pride and subdivisions of Pride to focus on underrepresented members of LGBTQ+ communities.[13] Alternative marches with a more specific focus within LGBTQ+ communities, including Dyke Marches, Trans Marches, and Black and Latino Gay Pride events, are increasingly evident (McFarland Bruce 7). As early as 1973, tensions between different communities within the gay community were surfacing with different priorities and agendas. McFarland Bruce captures the perception that "middle-class white men have played leading roles organizing and participating in Pride – leaving women, transgender individuals, people of color, and the working class to feel excluded" (7). The brief summary of the founding of Pride events offered at the opening of this chapter shows the leading involvement of women, black communities and trans communities and the intersectionality of those involved. However, recognition and underrepresentation reflect wider inequalities.[14]

Tensions around the commercialisation/commodification of Pride and its protest/challenge to hierarchy can be explored within a carnivalesque framework. Pride is a sanctioned event that temporarily disrupts the norm, offers safety-valve release and utilises a range of carnivalesque components including communal gatherings, dance, music, costumes (including the parodic), drink and food consumption. In doing so, it draws attention to alternative, marginalised identities that are temporarily prioritised and made more visible. Involvement in and commercial support for Pride events, Pride weeks, Pride months and Pride flags can be seen to represent corporate tokenism due to its "seemingly" temporary status. Just as the mechanisms of carnival offer short-term safety-valve release *and* enable long-term change through both reinforcing compliance and enabling sanctioned subversion that can inform longer-term change, the corporate support for Pride events and the Pride events, in themselves, are not restricted in impact purely because of their temporary status. The impact can last longer than a singular Pride event.

The potential tension between the seemingly "frivolous" aspects of Pride and the drive for meaningful protest can also be aligned to the carnivalesque. From the starting point of a riot, the trajectory of Pride towards festive carnival has been controversial. Troy Perry's suggestion of a parade for the first Los Angeles CSW event in 1970 has become folklore and set off this trajectory. The parade status added expectation of carnivalesque components. When describing the CSW parade in Los Angeles, the *Advocate* ran a heading "In Hollywood: pride, joy, a touch of Mardi Gras" and Duberman argues that the CSW parade constituted "a political Mardi Gras"(342). The affiliations between Pride marches/parades and Mardi Gras were also identified by Brass (highlighted earlier). The first official Pride event in Australia was held on June 24, 1978 and was labelled as "the Sydney Gay Mardi Gras" (Markwell and Waitt 152).[15] This book is presenting a model of Carnivalesque Leadership in which subversive components of the carnivalesque associated with Mardi Gras-style events may be temporary, but they also readily combine for social impact and should not naively be dismissed as "just" frivolous. As Perry points out, "That first LGBT parade in Los Angeles put a political edge on our fight" (Perry in *Advocate*).

The celebratory tone of the Christopher Street Liberation Day (CSLD) march in New York and the CSW parade in Los Angeles were tonally very different to traditional protest marches and very different to the staid respectability of the Annual Reminders which had sought to prove respectability and potentially ease assimilation and disprove perceptions of social deviance. The celebratory model established in New York and Los Angeles was to set the tone for global Pride events to come by combining protest and carnivalesque freedoms.[16] Organiser of a Pride parade in Detroit, Susan Williamson captured this combination, stating "Though this will be a serious demonstration, we do not intend to lose our sense of humor . . . The atmosphere will be festive, with floats and a good bit of camp" (cited by McFarland Bruce 84). The decision to adopt a festive parade model over a more traditional protest march model proved significant early in the history of Pride. McFarland Bruce argues that, from 1973 to 1975, Pride solidified in form as a parade with a "contentious purpose" and the full transfer to parade format was complete by 1975 (86).

Pride has become a sustained social action and has become embedded, standardised and, to some extent, commodified. From that first anniversary commemoration of the Stonewall uprising on Christopher Street, New York City, Pride has undoubtedly increased the visibility of LGBTQ+ communities. Focusing on the Roma and LGBTI communities, McGarry concludes that, whether or not Pride parades "will lead to a fundamental change in societal attitudes, to inclusion in socio-economic and political life and to a reduction of discriminatory treatment" of both communities, "it does herald an affirmation of presence in public life" (McGarry 270). A perceived shift from "contentious cultural protests to benign community celebrations" (McFarland Bruce 225) has been claimed and not welcomed, with resultant campaigns to "reclaim" that original contentious protest status, particularly when the power differentials between different intersections of LGBTQ+ communities are not fully represented, seen or heard. Significantly, Pride is not established as a "benign community celebration" throughout the world and is a contentious site of conflict in many countries. In recent years, crackdowns against Pride events in some countries including Russia, Türkiye and Poland have brought condemnation by human rights groups and international communities. Amnesty International has led calls against crackdowns on protest generally, including Pride, and launched a campaign "Protect the Protest" in 2022.[17] The status of Pride in the country of its origin is also still contentious at times. Several US states have sought to ban the display of Pride flags in schools, and there has been the blocking of displaying Pride flags on government buildings and US embassies (Faguy). However, Pride parades have been recognised as a key indicator of human rights and democratisation in the European Union (EU). Kahlina argues that Pride marches have been recognised by the EU as an important marker of democratisation and human rights promotion and became "one of the central events in the struggle for equal citizenship status of sexual minorities" (15–16). International attention on curbs of Pride events means that Pride is still driving an LGBTQ+ visibility campaign without anyone being sanctioned to take to the streets.

The style and tone of Pride parades have been the focus of contention as highlighted earlier. References aligning Pride parades with Mardi Gras do not diminish its potential for subversion when viewed through a carnivalesque lens. There can be a tendency to view carnival, Mardi Gras and celebration as having less credibility or impact than a traditional protest march. This sets up a binary opposition between protest march and carnival that a Carnivalesque Leadership approach will inevitably trouble. McFarland Bruce, for example, states that "at first glance, many may view Pride parades as frivolous public parties, more like a Mardi Gras celebration than a march on Washington" (McFarland Bruce 13). As we have started to explore in this book, however, Mardi Gras is not simply a frivolous public party. Such carnivals play a key role in society not only to offer safety-valve release through all the component benefits of the carnivalesque but also to provide a means for subversive challenge and visibility that can lead to longer-term social and cultural change. Communal cheering, dancing, singing, costumes, masks, food and drink consumption, laughter, parody, joy and fun are a carnivalesque means of challenge to existing authority and hierarchy.

From the moment organiser, Troy Perry, determined the tone of the CSW event on Sunday June 28, 1970, it set in motion the trajectory of Pride. Even that first Los Angeles event was "a full-blown parade" with *Advocate* painting a picture: "Flags and banners floated in the chill sunlight of the late afternoon; a bright red sound truck blared music; drummers strutted; a horse pranced; clowns cavorted" ("1200 Parade in Hollywood" in Stein 279). McFarland Bruce rightly argues that as well as the high-minded talk about changing the world, Pride parades are "a hell of a lot of fun" (20). By adopting a Carnivalesque Leadership lens, the binary distinction falls apart. The fun is part of how leaders of Pride are seeking to change the world. It is one of the component carnivalesque tools that leaders can choose to drive change. As a communal event, Pride brings people together in a celebratory tone that increases visibility of LGBTQ+ communities (although not all equally). In doing so, Pride offers a safety-valve release from the norm and challenges that norm. The temporary status of Pride does not mean that this challenge stops the moment the bands stop playing, the make-up is sweated off and the streets swept clear of debris. Moreover, through its symbolic representation of liberation expressed through carnivalesque components, Pride offers challenge to hierarchy in countries where is it currently banned through its noisy, jubilant, communal absence.

Notes

1 The terminology applied to events at the Stonewall Inn is subjective and contentious. The term "riot" is loaded and has simplistic associations of wrongdoing without regard for context. Reflecting the fight against oppression, alternatives such as "uprising" and "rebellion" are mainly chosen for discussions of the events within the body of the chapter. However, for the purposes of accentuating the dynamics of Carnivalesque Leadership and the scale of the shift to sanctioned subversion, the term "riot" will also be strategically employed. The significance of language when discussing Stonewall is extended to an awareness of language choices in discussions of LGBTQ+ communities. The discussion of the lead roles in the Stonewall uprising taken by trans women and trans men, self-labelled drag queens and kings, for example, means that I draw on a range of contemporary discourse as well as later critical responses, and therefore this discussion reflects a range of language choices. I use the collective LGBTQ+ as a collective acronym throughout including references during a time frame in which it was not in parlance.

2 Whilst acknowledging the complexity of its usage, a discussion of the term "gender" and its application is beyond the remit of this book.

3 DeLarverié was explicit about being at least partly responsible for igniting the response to the police action – see Feinberg for comments by DeLarverié and Starfire's dedicated website's article on "Stonewall and Stormé."

4 See Bell for a first-hand account of the rationale behind the establishment of the GAA.

5 See Cohen's Table of the Evolution of Selected Gay Liberation and Homophile Groups (32).

6 See Corrigan for an exploration of the relationship between gay liberation and black liberation movements.

7 The organisation's name relates to the fictional lesbian, Bilitis, who had been created by the French poet, Pierre Louys, in his pseudo translation work *The Songs of Bilitis* (1894) as a contemporary of Greek poet, Sappho.

8 See Broidy interview transcript.

9 The campaign against Section 28 led to the formation of the Stonewall organisation in the UK in 1989 by Peter Ashman, Deborah Ballard, Michael Cashman, Duncan Campbell, Olivette Cole-Wilson, Fiona Cunningham Reid, Simon Fanshawe, Dorian Jabri, Ian McKellen, Matthew Paris, Lisa Power, Dr Peter Rivas, Pam St Clement and Jennie Wilson.

10 Reclaim Pride is listed as an initiative of the Peter Tatchell Foundation and its website outlines Reclaim Pride as "a community-led march to get back to the roots of Pride, being both a celebration and a protest for LGBT+ rights, ditching the corporate sponsors and commercialism" ("Reclaim Pride").

11 Other "Reclaim Pride" initiatives are seen in Brighton, England, and Oslo, Norway. This list is not exhaustive at the time of writing.

12 See Salarvand for an overview of some of the academic literature on the corporate involvement in Pride. See Hennessey for a Butlerian discussion of the commodification of gay styles and identity related to the positioning of postmodern gay/queer subjectivity and ambivalent gender coding. This discussion is offered only as a signposting and is not exhaustive.

13 For a sample critique of the commercialisation of Pride, see Brammer and see Davies and McDonald's discussion of the commercialisation of Pride in the mainstream media. The commercialisation of Pride offers associations with the

commercialisation of the gay identity more generally. Chasin explores the commercial marketing of a homogenising, ultimately discriminatory "gay identity." D'Emilio links the development of capitalism with the development of a lesbian/gay identity. Valocchi draws on D'Emilio's work to frame a discussion of gay and lesbian movements within capitalist political economy.

14 In her study of six Pride parades, McFarland Bruce concludes that whilst all six officially cited themselves as LGBT, but "it was clear that transgender people were not fully part of the celebration" (197).

15 Markwell and Waitt explore the role of gay pride festivals within the context of international tourism and their role in social change. They draw on the work of Foucault via Hetherington to discuss ambiguous liminal spaces that generate "heterotopia" in festivals and make reference to Bakhtin to highlight how festivals operate as temporary "ritualized transgression" (146) that enable letting off of steam in the momentary overturning of the status quo (146).

16 See McFarland Bruce for an in-depth exploration of the tensions amongst Pride organisers and different communities when it comes to celebratory/"frivolous" models for visibility and advancing cultural change.

17 Amnesty's "Protect the Protest" campaign identifies peaceful protest as a human right and is not solely focused on Pride.

Works Cited

"1200 Parade in Hollywood; Crowds Line Boulevard". *The Advocate*, July 22, 1970. *The Stonewall Riots – A Documentary History*. Edited by Marc Stein. New York University, 2019, pp. 279–80.

Amnesty International. "Protect the Protest." amnesty.org. Accessed May 23, 2024.

Armstrong, Elizabeth A., and Suzanna M. Crage. "Movements and Memory: The Making of the Stonewall Myth." *American Sociological Review*, vol. 71, no. 5, 2006, pp. 724–51. *JSTOR*. Accessed Apr. 17, 2024.

Arnold, Shayna Rose. "We're Going to do a Parade. This Is Hollywood." *Los Angeles Magazine*, Jun. 10, 2015. lamag.com. Accessed May 23, 2024.

Ashley, Colin P. "Gay Liberation: How a Once Radical Movement Got Married and Settled Down." *New Labor Forum*, vol. 24, no. 3, 2015, pp. 28–32. *JSTOR*. Accessed Apr. 3, 2024.

Barnes, Eric Lane. "The Stonewall Riots of 1969." esuc.org. Accessed May 23, 2024.

Bell, Arthur. *Dancing the Gay Lib Blues*. Internet Archive, 1971. *archive.org*. Accessed May 23, 2024.

Brammer, John Paul. "Priced Out." *The Washington Post*, 2019. washingtonpost.com. Accessed Mar. 19, 2024.

Brass, Perry. "We Did It". *The Stonewall Reader*. Edited by Jason Baumann. Penguin, 2019, pp. 214–6.

Broidy, Ellen. "Live from NYPL: 50 Years of Marching for Pride." *New York Public Library Transcript*, Jun. 22, 2020. nypl.org. Accessed May 23, 2024.

Chasin, Alexandra. "Interpenetrations: A Cultural Study of the Relationship between the Gay/Lesbian Niche Market and the Gay/Lesbian Political Movement." *Cultural Critique*, no. 44, 2000, pp. 145–68. *JSTOR*. Accessed Apr. 13, 2024.

Cohen, Stephen L. *The Gay Liberation Youth Movement in New York – "An Army of Lovers Cannot Fail."* Routledge, 2008.

Conway, Daniel. "The Politics of Truth at LGBTQ+ Pride: Contesting Corporate Pride and Revealing Marginalized Lives at Hong Kong Migrants Pride."

International Feminist Journal of Politics, 25, no. 4, 2023, pp. 734–56. *Taylor & Francis Online*. Accessed May 23, 2024.

Corrigan, Lisa M. "Queering the Panthers: Rhetorical Adjacency and Black/Queer Liberation Politics." *QED: A Journal in GLBTQ Worldmaking*, vol. 6, no. 2, 2019, pp. 1–25. *JSTOR*. Accessed Apr. 6, 2024.

County, Jayne. "Except from *Man Enough to Be a Woman*." *The Stonewall Reader*. Edited by Jason Baumann. Penguin, 2019, pp. 166–9.

"Cross Currents." *The Ladder*, Oct. 1969. *The Stonewall Riots – A Documentary History*. Edited by Marc Stein. New York University Press, 2019, pp. 227–8.

Davies, Caroline, and Henry McDonald. "Pride in London Organisers Fend off Pinkwashing Claims". *The Guardian*, Jul. 6, 2019. theguardian.com. Accessed Mar. 24, 2024.

DeFilippis, Joseph Nicholas. "Betraying the Legacy of Stonewall." *QED: A Journal in GLBTQ Worldmaking*, vol. 6, no. 2, 2019, pp. 95–103. *JSTOR*. Accessed Apr. 3, 2024.

de la Croix, Sukie. "A Look Back at Chicago Pride Parade: 1970–2022" *GoPride*, Jun. 25, 2022. chicago.gopride.com. Accessed Mar. 20, 2024.

D'Emilio, John. "Capitalism and Gay Identity." *The Lesbian and Gay Studies Reader*. Edited by Abelove et al., Routledge, 1993, pp. 467–76.

Driskill, Qwo-Li. "All Power to the People: A Gay Liberation Triptych." *QED: A Journal in GLBTQ Worldmaking*, vol. 6, no. 2, 2019, pp. 44–53. *JSTOR*. Accessed Apr. 6, 2024.

Duberman, Martin. *Stonewall – The Definitive Story of the LGBTQ Rights Uprising that Changed America*. Plume, 2019.

Duberman, Martin, and Andrew Kopkind. "The Night They Raided Stonewall." *Grand Street*, no. 44, 1993, pp. 120–47. *JSTOR*. Accessed May 20, 2024.

Dunham, Cyrus, Grace. "Stuck in Stonewall." *The New Yorker*, Nov. 18, 2015. newyorker.com. Accessed Mar. 23, 2024.

Emerson, Caryl. *The First Hundred Years of Mikhail Bakhtin*. Princeton University Press, 1997.

Faguy, Ana. "Embassies Banned from Flying LGBTQ Pride Flags, House DEI Office Closed By Spending Bill." *Forbes*, Mar. 24, 2024. forbes.com. Accessed Mar. 20, 2024.

Feinberg, Leslie. *Transgender Warriors: Making History from Joan of Arc to Dennis Rodman*. Beacon Press, 1996.

Flores, Andre R., et al. *Democratic Backsliding and LGBTI Acceptance*. UCLA School of Law Williams Institute, 2023. williamsinstitute.law.ucla.edu. Accessed Mar. 20, 2024.

"Gay Pride Week 1978." *Gay Pride Committee*. museumoflondon.org.uk. Accessed May 20, 2024.

Genter, Alix "Appearances Can Be Deceiving: Butch-Femme Fashion and Queer Legibility in New York City, 1945–1969." *Feminist Studies*, vol. 42, no. 3, 2016, pp. 604–31. *JSTOR*. Accessed Apr. 3, 2024.

Hall, Simon. "The American Gay Rights Movement and Patriotic Protest." *Journal of the History of Sexuality*, vol. 19, no. 3, 2010, pp. 536–62. *JSTOR*. Accessed Apr. 3, 2024.

Hennessy, Rosemary. "Queer Visibility in Commodity Culture." *Cultural Critique*, no. 29, 1994, pp. 31–76. *JSTOR*. Accessed May 20, 2024.

Hillman, Betty Luther. "'The Most Profoundly Revolutionary Act a Homosexual Can Engage in': Drag and the Politics of Gender Presentation in the San Francisco

Gay Liberation Movement, 1964–1972." *Journal of the History of Sexuality*, vol. 20, no. 1, 2011, pp. 153–81. *JSTOR*. Accessed Apr. 3, 2024.

"The History of Pride – How Activists Fought to Create LGBTQ+ Pride." *Library of Congress*. loc.gov. Accessed May 23, 2024.

"In Hollywood: Pride, Joy, a Touch of Mardi Gras." *The Advocate*, vol. 4, no. 11, Jul. 22–Aug. 4. advocate.com. Accessed May 23, 2024.

Johnson, Marsha P., and Randy Wicker. "From Interview with Eric Marcus." *The Stonewall Reader*. Edited by Jason Baumann. Penguin, 2019, pp. 135–40.

Kahlina, Katja. "Contested Terrain of Sexual Citizenship: EU Accession and the Changing Position of Sexual Minorities in the Post-Yugoslav Context (2013). CITSEE Working Paper 2013/33. Papers.ssrn.com. Accessed Mar. 21, 2024.

Lawrence, Curtis. "150 Marchers Set the Pace." *Chicago Sun-Times*, Jun. 27, 2004. suntimes.com. Accessed Mar. 20, 2024.

Local Government Act 1988. legislation.co.uk. Accessed May 23, 2024.

Maccubbin, Deacon. "Gay Pride Day." *Off Our Backs*, vol. 8, no. 8, 1978, p. 21. *JSTOR*. Accessed May 20, 2024.

Markwell, Kevin, and Gordon Waitt. "Festivals, Space and Sexuality: Gay Pride in Australia." *Tourism Geographies*, vol. 11, no. 2, 2009, pp. 143–68.

McFarland Bruce, Katherine. *Pride Parades – How A Parade Changed the World*. NYU Press, 2016.

McGarry, Aidan. "Pride Parades and Prejudice: Visibility of Roma and LGBTI Communities in Post-Socialist Europe." *Communist and Post-Communist Studies*, vol. 49, no. 3, 2016, pp. 269–77. *JSTOR*. Accessed Apr. 7, 2024.

New York State Assembly. "An Act to Repeal Subdivision 4 of Section 240.35 of the Penal Law, in Relation to the Crime of Loitering." May 18, 2020. nyassembly.gov. Accessed Mar. 19, 2024.

Pedersen, Lyn. "Christopher Street West – Los Angeles Liberation Day". *Gay*. Jul. 27, 1970.

Perry, Troy D. Rev. "Troy Perry's Pride." *Advocate*, May 18, 2007. advocate.com. Accessed May 23, 2024.

Perry, Troy D. Rev. "From the Lord Is My Shepherd and He Knows I'm Gay." *The Stonewall Reader*. Edited by Jason Baumann. Penguin, 2019, pp. 203–13.

Peter Tatchell Foundation. "Reclaim Pride." petertatchellfoundation.org. Accessed May 23, 2024.

Pukas, Paul. "Lonely Porkers Crash Gay-In." *Berkeley Barb*, vol. 10, no. 26 (255), Jul. 1970. *JSTOR*. Accessed Apr. 10, 2024.

Reclaim Pride Coalition. reclaimpridenyc.org. Accessed May 23, 2024.

Rivera, Sylvia. "Interviewed by Eric Marcus." *The Stonewall Reader*. Edited by Jason Baumann. Penguin, 2019, pp. 141–7.

Rodwell, Craig. "Extract from the Gay Crusaders." *The Stonewall Reader*. Edited by Jason Baumann. Penguin, 2019, pp. 87–95.

Roth, Timothy, and David Paisley. "Corporate Allies." *The Washington Post*, 2019. washingtonpost.com. Accessed May 20, 2024.

Russell Frederix, et al. "The Detroit Liberator." *The Detroit Liberator*, vol. 1, no. 4, Aug. 1970. *John J. Wilcox, Jr. Archives at the William Way LGBT Community Center. Independent Voices. Reveal Digital*, *JSTOR*. Accessed May 20, 2024.

Salarvand, Heyla. "(Re)Locating Pride: Borders, Space, and Policing at Los Angeles Pride." *Aleph, UCLA Undergraduate Research Journal for the Humanities and Social Sciences*, vol. 19, 2022. escholarship.org. Accessed Mar. 20, 2024.

Sears, Alan. "Queer Anti-Capitalism: What's Left of Lesbian and Gay Liberation?" *Science & Society*, vol. 69, no. 1, 2005, pp. 92–112. *JSTOR*. Accessed Apr. 12, 2024.

Segal, Mark. "Except from *And Then I Danced*." *The Stonewall Reader*. Edited by Jason Baumann. Penguin, 2019, pp. 119–27.

Sergeant, Fred. "One Year After the Stonewall Riots: Fred Sergeant Remembers." *Outhistory*, 2019. outhistory.org. Accessed May 24, 2024.

Shockley, Jay. "NYC Pride March." *NYC LGBT Historic Sites Project*, 2022. nyclgbtsites.org. Accessed May 24, 2024.

Starfire, Chris. "Stonewall and Stormé." www.storme-delarverie.com. Accessed May 24, 2024.

Stein, Marc. "Dewey's Sit-In in Philadelphia, 1965". *OutHistory*, Apr. 20, 2015. outhistory.org. Accessed May 24, 2024.

Stonewall. "Our History." www.stonewall.org. Accessed May 20, 2024.

Tatchell, Peter. "Stonewall Sparked a Global LGBT Freedom Movement – Today's Activists Have Lost the Stonewall Vision." Jun. 19, 2019. www.petertatchellfoundation.org. Accessed May 20, 2024.

Tatchell, Peter. "Fifty Years of Pride and Prejudice." *Index on Censorship*, vol. 51, no. 2, 2022, pp. 14–6. journals.sagepub.com. Accessed May 20, 2024.

Tatchell, Peter. "Pride Before Pride." *British Library*. living-knowledge-network.co.uk. Accessed May 20, 2024.

Tatchell, Peter. "Reclaim Pride." petertatchellfoundation.org. Accessed May 20, 2024.

Teeman, Craig. "They Marched in America's First Pride Demonstrations in 1970. They're Still Out, Loud, and Proud." *The Daily Beast*, 2020. thedailybeast.com. Accessed May 20, 2024.

Todd, Matthew. *Pride: The Story of the LGBTQ Equality Movement*. Wellbeck, 2021.

Valocchi, Stephen. "Capitalisms and Gay Identities: Towards a Capitalist Theory of Social Movements." *Social Problems*, vol. 64, no. 2, 2017, pp. 315–31. *JSTOR*. Accessed Apr. 14, 2024.

Walter, Aubrey, editor. *Come Together – The Years of Gay Liberation 1970–1973*. Verso, 2018.

Conclusion

Carnivalesque components have their origins in the oldest of civilisations, with festivals and carnivals evident in studies of Mesopotamia and ancient Egypt. Mikhail Bakhtin's carnivalesque is rooted in the Middle Ages of François Rabelais and informed by the Roman Saturnalia, but the folklore customs date back further. Imbued with the past, Carnivalesque Leadership is still evident today, and there is clear value in exploring how its naturalised components are employed for strategic effect. Recognition that strategic temporary licence may be being sanctioned to shore up existing power structures in return for compliance can provide significant insight. Moreover, recognition of the potential for transformation through exposure to alternatives to official "norms" as sanctioned by such temporary licence can similarly be empowering.

This book is the starting point of an exploration centred on the components that constitute Carnivalesque Leadership and the potential for short- and long-term subversion and challenge to established power and hierarchy. There are exploratory leaps made in this application, and there are problems galore with some of the extrapolation and brevity of debate. But it is a starting point. The conclusion offered here is even more explorative and initiates a consideration of the potential for the strategic employment of Carnivalesque Leadership models to release pressure from an organisation/society and therefore prevent unsanctioned subversion. In this book, I have argued that this safety-valve release provides a means to shore up existing hierarchy and power structures whilst also enabling an impetus for longer-term change. The case studies offered in this book show how this carnivalesque power dynamic can support both seemingly contradictory impulses. Leaders in official power structures can recognise the "very human need" to release pressure via carnivalesque means and, in doing so, be confident that this can help build a sense of communal belonging, enjoyment and fun which may, in turn, bring about greater "happiness" and commitment in those being led. This model can seem bluntly manipulative or transactional (short-term, temporary carnivalesque release is sanctioned

DOI: 10.4324/9781003441649-8

by leaders in return for compliance). However, the model is more subtle, and Carnivalesque Leadership has been shown to offer significantly more than simple safety-valve release and shoring up of existing power hierarchies. Whilst the subversion is sanctioned, the impact is not restricted to its temporary status. Sanctioned subversive challenge to normal hierarchies, structures and modes of living, through communal play, fun, humour, laughter, parody, mask, dance, food and drink, can draw attention to alternative structures, different traditions and expressions and provide exposure to usually marginalised modes of living. Whilst the return to normal signals an end to the temporary carnivalesque release, the impact is not restricted to that designated time frame.

The use of the phrase "very human need" earlier is an unacademic, unsubstantiated shorthand for the communal need satisfied by the carnivalesque. A leader's recognition of this "very human need" may well be rewarded through the release of pressures that have built within the system but that may not be the driving force of the sanctioning of carnivalesque release. Such a leader may not be sanctioning release "just" to reinforce their own power hierarchy but rather to enable release and transformation beyond the temporary. Indeed, the strategic employment of carnivalesque release may result in greater compliance in a transactional model, but it can also offer an opportunity to temporarily explore alternative modes, power structures and group dynamics that may have longer-term impact. The hedging around these suggestions reflects the need for much greater enquiry beyond the case studies explored in this book.

I have argued that the employment of carnivalesque components as a means to fulfil "very human needs" and release pressure from a system is so common as to be naturalised. Chapter 4 explores how schools, for example, provide safety-valve mechanisms so regularly as to be ubiquitous, partly through curricular breadth but partly through the ways in which communal organisations operate for ease of scale. Moreover, schools can be the repository of traditions and customs offering carnivalesque release, with the maypole being the example considered in Chapter 4. In terms of the carnivalesque in education, will such folk customs and traditions continue to be enjoyed by school children around the world as a calendared break from the norm? As curricula continue to evolve, will the opportunities for safety-valve release, humour and fun continue to play a significant role in pupils' school experiences? How might the impact from the isolationism of technology be offset (at least in some degree) by carnivalesque components that have formed part of child-rearing for millennia? These unanswered questions again reflect the need for much greater enquiry beyond the case studies explored in Chapter 4.

The "frivolous" aspects of carnivalesque does not mean that the potential impact is frivolously minimal. Carnivalesque components meet "very human needs" for communal belonging, safety-valve release and the generation of the chemical messengers: serotonin, dopamine, endorphins and oxytocin. Moreover, the temporary subversion of normal hierarchies offers exposure to alternative modes of living which may challenge the existing official hierarchy. The return to the normal can be brutal, and the picture offered in this book of the potential for change is undoubtedly idealistic. However, carnival does have a history of driving and reflecting change. The discussion of the history of carnivals in Trinidad and Notting Hill in Chapter 3 provides a case study for how the subversive parody of dominant hierarchy and challenge to official social/cultural norms and power dynamics can lead to greater cultural expression and longer-term transformation. Notting Hill Carnival's origins can be traced to the indoor Caribbean Carnival initiated by Claudia Jones in response to civil unrest and the need for communal celebration following racist attacks and widespread harassment and discrimination and to the development of a street parade led by Rhaune Laslett which offered the local community a means of expression and safety-valve release. Such Carnivalesque Leadership has meant that Notting Hill Carnival has grown into Europe's biggest street carnival offering safety-valve release to millions of people as well as a celebration of heritage and the history of productive subversive challenge. Notting Hill Carnival takes place over one bank holiday weekend in August in London, but it does not simply "end" at the break of day on the Tuesday when workers return to their normal routines and the streets are full of traffic. The impact is not temporary.

The opportunity for collective expression and communal belonging not only offers safety-valve release but also represents an opportunity for celebration and increased visibility. The discussion in Chapter 6 of how Pride grew out of a riotous response to police harassment and brutality reflects a Carnivalesque Leadership approach. The historical development of the Pride movement and its use of carnivalesque components in festive, carnival style shows the power of the carnivalesque to drive longer-term change. By maximising the potential of carnivalesque, Pride has not minimised its protest potential for affecting change. Instead, Pride, accentuated by the carnivalesque, shows how meeting the "very human need" for communal safety-valve release can be transformative.

A Carnivalesque Future for Leadership?

What might an understanding of the carnivalesque, with its millennia history of communal bonding and safety-valve release, its history of temporary subversion and challenge to hierarchy, offer to leaders in society and leaders in organisations today and in the future?

This book has suggested that, by strategically employing carnivalesque components, leaders can shore up their own power, through employing mechanisms for safety-valve release at strategic times. Moreover, leaders seeking transformation within an organisation or social group, might consider how the hierarchical structures (on which they metaphorically sit atop), might be subverted, temporarily, to affect change. This is not to blithely infer that a Carnivalesque Leadership approach can solve every leadership challenge, of course. Even the naivety and idealism of the exploratory approach adopted in this book has its limits.

Separated out, different carnivalesque components all have impact as considered in Chapter 2. When combined, carnivalesque components offer an intoxicating mix that increases the intensity of the safety-valve release and the potential for communal bonding. Therefore, a leader can look to benefit from strategically providing regular opportunities to facilitate different carnivalesque components at different times and/or a leader might plan for maximum effect through facilitating multiple components at the same time. This strategic awareness exposes the carnivalesque process which can be so normalised that it seems to be "just" naturally occurring. To a certain extent, of course, the argument that the carnivalesque drive is naturally occurring is valid and is justified. Once basic safety needs are met and when groups of humans start to bond and function as a group, the mechanisms for enabling this bond and group functioning form, in part, some of the genesis of carnivalesque. Having satisfied basic needs, we share food and drink, we laugh, we dance and we sing in groups. Chemical messengers released via these activities bring about changes within an individual which can lead to changes within group dynamics. In this naive and simplistic model, the release felt during such collective activities enables the dispersal of group tension and offers a refreshing and rejuvenating break from the norm. Commodified versions of carnivalesque components are highly marketable, and commodified carnivals are calendared events, often with a rich history of how temporary subversion and carnivalesque release has led to, and reflects, significant social change.

Carnivalesque components are well established as considered through the case studies outlined in this book. Carnivals, in and of themselves, are part of a global calendar with increasing global reach and are potentially increasingly commodified. The tracking of the next stage development of Mardi Gras-style carnivals as part of calendared world tourism is likely to offer further case studies of how commodified carnival can not only provide safety-valve release but also be a means for significant transformation. The homogenisation of a commodified carnival style within a Carnivalesque Leadership dynamic requires further consideration. The recognition that carnival experiences are increasingly formulaic and the acknowledgement of the potential for influence from commercial partners does not, however, simply nullify impact.

Recent global events have meant that carnivalesque collective opportunities were suddenly absent. Chapter 5 features a brief discussion of the impact of the global response to COVID-19 in terms of social isolation and changing work patterns. More generally, and as briefly considered in Chapter 2, changes in social and cultural patterns in many parts of the world have also brought about recognition of decreasing opportunities for communal gatherings. The importance of the collective aspects of the carnivalesque not only in terms of safety-valve release but also in generating a sense of belonging may be being brought to the fore. Might this imply that a strategic Carnivalesque Leadership approach is potentially more vital and potentially more impactful? Are we craving greater communal belonging, opportunities for safety-valve release and the licence for subversion because of the ways in which social interactions have been, and are being, transformed?

Carnivalesque components do not appeal to everyone, of course. Far from enabling safety-valve release, for some people, such social situations and communal activities do not offer a sense of subversive liberation and the benefits of chemical messenger release. In fact, quite the opposite reaction could be triggered. This does not render Carnivalesque Leadership redundant, but it does suggest that leaders looking to strategically employ the carnivalesque, need to be mindful. Here, the tailoring of carnivalesque components employed becomes a crucial leadership skill. A shift from "just" boozy get togethers to other forms of collective safety-valve release is well underway in the world of group working and socialising.

Carnivalesque Leadership is not new, but it has become normalised to the point of invisibility. As highlighted throughout this text, this is the start of an exploration of Carnivalesque Leadership and it is offered up for discussion. There is a great deal of additional work required to ascertain concrete causal links between these components and the effect on workers in relation to corporate carnivalesque or the effect on pupils experiencing the carnivalesque in schools. However, despite this academic need for quantifiable data, the effectiveness of the carnivalesque as a leadership strategy has been evident for centuries, and it has released pressure within and across social groups since the most ancient of civilisations. In exploring how the carnivalesque operates in different contexts under different leadership models over a considerable period of time, this book seeks to show how Carnivalesque Leadership has operated in the past and how it operates today and how it might be harnessed in the future.

As a starting point for discussion, this book aligns with Mikhail Bakhtin's statement that there "is neither a first word or a last word" (Bakhtin cited by Clark and Holquist 348). Bakhtin's vision for the dialogic is never-ending, and engagement with his work takes on new forms. Extrapolated and manipulated, the ideas on the carnivalesque applied in this book offer a new engagement by exploring some old ideas but it runs the risk of oversimplification. This book introduces a modern perspective on leadership which is held in dialogic tension with ancient traditions, medieval representation and multifaceted Bakhtinian philosophy. Bakhtin argues that

> there are great masses of forgotten meanings, but these will be recalled again at a given moment in the dialogue's later course when it will be given new life. For nothing is absolutely dead: every meaning will someday have its homecoming festival.
>
> (350)

This book is no homecoming festival for the meaning of Carnivalesque Leadership, but it does seek to open new dialogues exploring how the carnivalesque supports, subverts and transforms power dynamics and established hierarchies.

Work Cited

Clark, Katerina, and Michael Holquist. *Mikhail Bakhtin*. Harvard University Press, 1984.

Index